D1288958

Women Priests in the Catholic Church?

Haye van der Meer, SJ

Women Priests in the Catholic Church?
A Theological-Historical Investigation

Translated and with a
Foreword and Afterword by
ARLENE and LEONARD SWIDLER

Foreword by
CYNTHIA C. WEDEL

TEMPLE UNIVERSITY PRESS
Philadelphia

Temple University Press, Philadelphia 19122
© 1973 by Temple University. All rights reserved
Published 1973
Printed in the United States of America

First published as *Priestertum der Frau?* © 1969 by
Verlag Herder, K. G., Freiburg im Breisgau

International Standard Book Number: 0-87722-059-X
Library of Congress Catalog Card Number: 73-79480

Contents

Foreword

The ordination of women is a lively issue within many churches and a potentially explosive one in ecumenical circles. Most major Protestant churches have accepted the ordination of women or have the subject under serious consideration. These same churches are in ecumenical relationship with churches of the more Catholic tradition who do not as yet ordain women.

No church has taken this break with ancient tradition lightly. It has been arrived at through serious biblical and theological study and represents the conviction that it is the will of God for our time. A decision so made cannot easily be put aside, even for urgent ecumenical reasons. A way must be found to open discussion between the Protestant and Catholic traditions in which each will be willing to take the other's position seriously and to open its own to honest and searching study.

Anglican churches are in an especially difficult situation. The traditional ministry of Bishop, Priest, and Deacon has been an essential tenet of Anglican theology from the beginning, held firmly in spite of refusal by the Roman Catholic Church to acknowledge the validity of Anglican orders. Since Vatican II there seems real hope at last of mutual recognition of orders. But pressure for the ordination of women is building up within many branches of the Anglican Communion. While Anglican studies have stated that there are no biblical or theological reasons for denying ordination to women, most have counselled caution lest it hurt relationships with Roman Catholics.

There are groups within the Roman Catholic Church interested in the question, but there is little indication that it is being considered officially. The impression of most people outside the

Roman Church is that any move toward ordaining women—or even really thinking about it—is a very long way off.

This situation makes Father van der Meer's book extremely important, not only to Roman Catholics, but to everyone in the Ecumenical Movement. The basic thrust of the book is simple. He admits that the practice and teaching of the Church from the beginning have been clearly opposed to the ordination of women. However, he points out—with incredibly detailed documentation—that most of the opposition has been based on Jewish rabbinical tradition, misreading of St. Paul, totally discredited biological and psychological concepts, and simple ignoring of many contrary opinions by Popes and other Church leaders. Even in early times and among the Church Fathers, there was far less unanimity than is assumed. Many of the most quoted statements against women were made in debates attacking heretical groups and not at all in the context of discussions on the place of women.

Father van der Meer also discusses the arguments of certain theologians on the concept of the Church as the "Bride of Christ": arguments which could be used to prove that women are better qualified than men to be priests in the Church. Above all, he makes it clear that God created whole persons. Men and women are more than simply biological entities—they comprise body, mind, and spirit. As van der Meer says, "The inequality of the sexes manifests itself where persons do not yet deal with one another completely as persons."

The force of the book is to help any serious student, Catholic or Protestant, to realize that a totally closed or inflexible position cannot be justified and that there is ground for an open reexamination of this two-thousand-year-old tradition.

Cynthia C. Wedel

Translators' Foreword

At this point almost every major Christian church has made or commissioned an official study on the question of the ordination of women. The two outstanding exceptions are, of course, the Eastern Orthodox churches and the Roman Catholic Church. But within the latter, at least, there has been much talk over the past decade, beginning with the petition of the Swiss lawyer Gertrud Heinzelmann to the Preparatory Commission of the Second Vatican Council.[1] Most recently the 1971 International Synod of Catholic Bishops recommended that an international commission be established to study the situation of women in the Church, including the possibility of ordination.

But until the Catholic Church accepts an official report on the question, the work of Catholic scholars must assume the primacy, and there is general agreement that the work of Father van der Meer is the preeminent study. Dr. van der Meer's credentials are impressive. The research for the doctoral thesis which preceded the present book was done in the early sixties, before Dr. Heinzelmann's appeal to the council; the thesis was written under Professor Karl Rahner in Innsbruck. Since receiving his degree in 1962, Father van der Meer wrote a paper on the position of women in the Church for the Documentation Center of the Second Vatican Council [2] and has been serving as Rector of the coordinated training of all Jesuits in Holland.

This book, then, stands as the major Catholic contribution to the dialogue.

Within the past several years two other traditions have been reconsidering their positions on the question of women in orders: the various American Lutheran churches and the worldwide Episcopalian churches.

The Lutheran or Evangelical churches of all but one of the *Länder* in West Germany have ordained women for a good many years. Despite the objections of a small, conservative minority, the experience has been that both women pastors and their congregations are satisfied with the situation.[3] The whole question arose during the period of upheaval during and following World War II when the churches were forced to grapple with the essential problems of faith and church life. As in so many other fields, women took over positions and tasks when there were no men available.

Another problem facing the churches in Germany today may have similar results, according to Margaret Sittler Ermarth. At this time both the Lutheran (Evangelical) and Catholic churches are supported by the *Kirchensteuer,* or church tax. Germans may be exempted from the tax, but this requires a formal declaration of withdrawal, and as marriages, funerals, and such are still customarily performed within the churches, people are reluctant to dissociate themselves. But if the membership begins to decrease as a newer generation comes to adulthood, the churches will be faced with a greatly reduced income. And if the assumption—prevalent in so many other areas—that women can, or simply will, work for less money prevails in the churches, women may find themselves more welcome in the future.

Ordained Lutheran women in Germany find themselves operating under some limitations. In some cases women pastors are forced to resign upon marriage, this despite the fact that neither male pastors nor professionally-trained nonordained women are subject to a clause of this type in their employment contracts. Such stipulations are illegal as well. Ermarth sees this inconsistency explained by the inheritance of the Roman Catholic concept of the priesthood as having an "indelible character," but as the "character" would equally mark the male priest, it seems more likely that a version of the old idea of ritual uncleanness is operating.

Some German women ministers find themselves relegated to serving only women, children, the hospitalized, and the imprisoned, and only a few are involved in general parish work. On the other hand, in East Germany, where it is against church law for women to lead a congregation, there are more women pastors than anywhere else.

The authorized report, *The Ordination of Women,* issued by

the combined Lutheran churches in the United States in 1970 states that by 1968 Lutheran women had been ordained in Norway, Denmark (including Greenland), Czechoslovakia, Sweden, and France as well as Germany.[4] The situation in the Church of Sweden seems to be best known in America, partly because the Scandinavian churches have served as parent bodies to some of the American Lutheran churches and partly because the tension between the Church of Sweden and the Church of England received international attention.

Dr. Lukas Vischer of the World Council of Churches summarized the situation in his Initial Statement in the WCC's booklet *Concerning Ordination of Women:* [5] "The Church of England has intercommunion with the Church of Sweden. The fact that the Church of Sweden has retained the Apostolic Succession made this intercommunion possible. When the ordination of women was considered in Sweden, the Church of England asked itself whether the same close relations could be maintained in the future, and many Anglican theologians expressed their misgivings. Actually, however, the relations between the two Churches do not seem to have deteriorated." [6]

In this connection the work of Krister Stendahl is especially important. Now dean of Harvard Divinity School here in the United States, Stendahl wrote a study for the 1958 Church Assembly of the Church of Sweden; it was at this assembly that the proposal for the ordination of women was voted through. His study, with a preface by the author and an introduction by the editor, Professor John Reumann, has been published in this country in pamphlet form and is read and quoted widely.[7]

Stendahl's approach is basically hermeneutic; he admits that the whole question in the Church of Sweden was concerned with biblical evidence and not with tradition. As a biblical scholar, Stendahl presents his case that the problem is not to discover exactly what Paul meant in his strictures on women, but to decide what elements of the message are binding for all time. There is a difference, he says, between something "truly biblical" and "an attempt to play 'First-Century Bible Land.'"

The final chapter of Stendahl's study is called "Emancipation and Ordination." Here he points out that the question of any cultic role for women in the New Testament is never separated from the role of women in ordinary life, and this role—subordinate, of course—is seen as founded in the order of creation. It becomes extremely difficult then to assent to women's emancipation in civil life and to hold to subordination in the ecclesiastical area unless one makes the church the last bastion of the biblical view. Yet this too contains a contradiction, because it is in *Christ,* not in the world, that there is to be neither male nor female.

Stendahl writes, "If emancipation is right, then there is no valid 'biblical' reason not to ordain women. Ordination cannot be treated as a 'special' problem, since there is no indication that the New Testament sees it as such."

It is worth noting that the decision was an especially hot one in Sweden because the issue of church-state relations entered into it so strongly.[8] The Church of Sweden, being a state church, was subject to pressures from large numbers of people who were not regular and active members of the worshiping community. Secular feeling, as is usually the case in matters such as these, was far ahead of ecclesiastical attitudes on female equality. The question of the ordination of women had first been officially studied in 1919, and in 1950 the government's commission reported itself in favor of the change. There remained then passage by the Church Assembly in order for the legislation to be completed. The 1957 assembly reported it needed still more time, but the government, feeling there had been sufficient time already, called the next Church Assembly for the following year. This time the majority voted in favor of the ordination of women.

The extent to which the civil government might enter, even indirectly, into the United States situation is unclear. In March of 1970 the U.S. District Court in Georgia refused to hear a suit challenging the Salvation Army on grounds of sexual discrimination, although the Equal Employment Opportunity Commission supported the plaintiff's contention, on grounds that Title VII of the Civil Rights Act of 1964 did not apply to religious organizations.[9] On the other hand, universities, denominational as well as state or private, are being forced to prove lack of discrimination in employment, and Jewish Orthodox rabbis have expressed great fears that the Equal Rights Amendment might mean the end of tax exemptions for sexually segregated synagogues and religious schools.

The contemporary Lutheran thinking on the subject is best summarized in the booklet *The Ordination of Women,* prepared by Raymond Tiemeyer. The problem was researched by a committee working through the Lutheran Council in the U.S.A.—a group including the American Lutheran Church, the Lutheran Church in America, the Lutheran Church Missouri Synod, and the Synod of Evangelical Lutheran Churches. The resultant study papers were then presented to an Inter-Lutheran Consultation on the Ordination of Women meeting in Dubuque, Iowa, in September of 1969. At this consultation, consisting of fifteen males and one female participant named by the various church presidents, the studies were reviewed. This report was then presented to the annual meeting of the Lutheran Council in February 1970, and findings were then distributed to the congregations by the presidents in the abridged and popularized form of this fifty-eight-page booklet.

The complete papers by the scholarly committee have never been published, and the brief summaries of course do not suggest any new insights. But other interesting facts emerge. Tiemeyer states, for example, that although there was strong difference of opinion on the ordination question, all the committee agreed that certain arguments could not be taken seriously: the incapability of woman, the masculinity of God, the fact that all the apostles were male.

The understanding of ministry became important. Tiemeyer notes that "at the inter-Lutheran consultation in Dubuque, . . . those who said headship was basically a divinely given rulership power thought it would be violated if a woman were ordained. Those who said headship was basically leadership service (diakonia), thought a woman in the ranks would not destroy the order." [10]

Statistical results of a survey included showed that the clergy were considerably more resistant to the idea of a female clergy than were the laity. In the Wisconsin Synod, for example, 39 percent of the laity approved ordaining, but 0 percent of the clergy did. Statistics also indicated that lay men are more open to equality than lay women: 79 percent of lay men and 71 percent of lay women favored an equal voice for women; 65 percent of lay men and 51 percent of lay women favored the ordination of women. [11]

A three-page "Statement of Findings" is attached as an appendix to the booklet. The overall tone and discussion stresses that an examination of the biblical material and theological arguments has shown "the case both against and for the ordination of women inconclusive." Nor are sociological and psychological

considerations or the "ecumenical argument" found decisively
on one side of the question. This coincides with the findings of
Dr. van der Meer in this volume. The Lutheran statement, reflecting as it does the meeting of four different constituencies,
continues: "It follows that a variety of practices at any given
time remains possible amid common confession."

Since the time of this report the Lutheran Church in America
and the American Lutheran Church have both ordained women;
one LCA woman is serving as a pastor in a New Jersey congregation. In 1972 the convention of the nongeographic "English"
district of the Lutheran Church Missouri Synod, traditionally less
conservative than the rest of that church, called for ordaining
women by a vote of 168 to 104. The whole Lutheran Church
Missouri Synod, however, is in the midst of a conservative-mod-
erate struggle, and the question of the ordination of women will
doubtless hinge on the outcome of that battle.

To some extent there has been less recent scholarly material
on our subject coming from the Episcopal point of view than
from the Lutheran and the Roman Catholic. Part of the reason
is that the subject has been treated seriously by a number of
scholars and a number of committees over a good many years;
although this has also been true of the Lutheran churches in
Europe, the American Lutheran groups act independently of
their European counterparts, whereas the Episcopal churches
work more in concert, and British scholarship has been considered valid for the American scene as well.

Already in 1862 the ordination of women became a live issue
when the Bishop of London revived the ancient Order of Deaconesses. Other bishops did or did not follow suit as they were
inclined, until the procedure was recommended to the worldwide Anglican communion at the 1920 Lambeth Conference. The
1930 Lambeth Conference again took up the issue and stated
that deaconesses are ordained, but in a special way; they are
sui generis. But all was still not satisfactorily clarified, and thus
another commission was appointed by the archbishop of Canterbury and York to investigate women in the ministry. The commission made its report in 1935; it could not agree on whether or
not women were capable of receiving priestly orders and hence
rested on the ancient tradition that restricted the priesthood to
males. In the years 1942–43 still another committee established

by the archbishops to study the question of women in the church failed to provide a final decision. During the Second World War the bishop of Hong Kong ordained a deaconess to the priesthood because of the sudden critical shortage of priests; his action, however, was repudiated by the rest of the church, and the woman priest was returned to the status of deaconess. After the war the standing committee of the Hong Kong diocese asked the general synod of the Chinese Anglican Church to establish for twenty years the experiment of ordaining some deaconesses to the priesthood; the matter was referred to the Lambeth Conference, which returned a negative response in 1948. The Lambeth Conference of 1958, also under pressure to deal with the issue, concluded: "The Committee has considered, in the light of present circumstances, the Resolutions on the Order of Deaconesses (numbered 67–70) of Lambeth Conference, 1930. The Committee has nothing to add by way of further recommendation." [12]

In the same period a number of Anglicans published personal studies of varying depth and breadth concerning the problem of the ordination of women. An early work by Canon C. C. Raven, *Women and Holy Orders* (London, 1928), favored ordination. Two later favorable though brief books are Canon R. W. Howard's *Should Women Be Priests?* (Oxford, 1949) and Edith Picton-Turberville's *Should Women Be Priests and Ministers?* (London: Society for the Equal Ministry of Men and Women in the Church, 1953). Kathleen Bliss's *The Service and Status of Women in the Churches* (London, 1952) provides massive documentation of the involvement of women in the Christian churches throughout the world in recent times, including the practices of the various churches concerning ordaining women.

The year 1958 saw the appearance of a more extensive study of the issue by an Anglican. *The Ordination of Women to the Priesthood* (London, 1958) by New Testament scholar Margaret E. Thrall is a careful study of the biblical evidence, but also of the theological issues involved in the question of the ordination of women. It is a sober, scholarly work which very precisely analyzes each of the pertinent portions of the Old and New Testaments, the theological issues flowing from them, and the credal and liturgical heritage of the Anglican church; in no case does she find a sustained objection to the ordination of women. Yet the author casts her earlier, straightforward conclusions in

favor of the ordination of women into a subjunctive mood at
the end when she states: "No doubt a great deal more theological discussion would be necessary before the question could be
regarded as conclusively settled one way or the other."

In 1962 the Central Advisory Council for the Ministry prepared
a report entitled *Gender and Ministry* for the Church Assembly;
it asked that the theological basis of the Anglican tradition on
the ordination of women be reexamined, and called for still
another commission. That commission met and issued another
inconclusive report in 1966, to be followed by the *Report of the
Lambeth Conference on Women in Orders* (1968), which ad-
vised the Anglican churches to refer the matter to the about-to-
be-formed Anglican Consultative Council.[13] That council met in
Kenya in March of 1971 and recommended that each member
church deal with the issue itself, allowing the ordination of
women by an individual bishop "with the approval of his
province."[14]

In the meantime a Joint Commission of Ordained and Licensed
Ministries of the American Protestant Episcopal Church made
its affirmative recommendation to the General Convention in
October 1970. The House of Clerical and Lay Deputies gave the
recommendation a majority approval (87 to 61), but the measure
was defeated by the clergy in a call that the vote be taken by
orders. However, at the same convention a resolution was
passed to ordain women deacons in the same manner as men
deacons, thereby making them regular clergy (no longer *sui
generis*). Then at the fall 1971 meeting of the House of Bishops,
upon the initiative of Bishop C. Kilmer Meyers, still another
committee was called for to make "an in-depth study of the
ordination of women as priests and bishops."

The reaction to this move was immediate and strong: an
Episcopal Women's Caucus was formed on a national basis in
October; "their first action was to urge the Presiding Bishop *not*
to form yet another committee to study the ordination of women
to the priesthood, but to act. . . . Further, the EWC informed
the Presiding Bishop that its members would not serve on any
committee and would urge other women not to serve. Hence,
there is now no new committee, but rather a small group of
bishops is to compile previous findings and report to the 1972
meeting of the House of Bishops."[15]

However, there is still a good deal of very strong feeling against the ordination of women in the Protestant Episcopal Church, and as the possibility of a move in this direction becomes less remote the opposition has become more vocal. An article which is considered by involved Episcopalians to be a good summary of the arguments against priesting women appeared in the July 1972 issue of *The Episcopalian.* "Why I Am Against the Ordination of Women," by Canon Albert J. duBois, is especially interesting from an ecumenical perspective because all of the author's reasons are discussed—some at great length—in Dr. van der Meer's book. DuBois's essay makes it very clear that a number of churches are approaching the same problem from the same direction, each being somewhat fearful of making significant changes lest it outpace the others, and each failing to profit by the theological and scriptural thought of the others.

Ecumenism is, as a matter of fact, one of duBois's chief concerns. As a participant in the COCU (Consultation on Church Union) discussions, the Episcopalians have felt a certain pressure to reconsider their position on the ordination of women to bring it into line with that of the majority of the other COCU participants. Canon duBois argues against making a change for the sake of a comparatively small federation and thus destroying the possibility of a later and larger union of the Episcopal, Orthodox, and Roman Catholic churches, among others.

The ecumenical argument for ordination is particularly inappropriate, according to duBois, because the Protestant concept of the ministry and the Catholic concept of the priesthood are quite different: the ministry is basically lay and pastorally oriented; the priesthood eucharistically oriented and sacramental. (That the distinction tends to be blurred today is borne out by duBois's own statement later on that "we find our Lord and the primitive Church restricting the ministry to males," when of course he is referring to the priesthood.)

The Tiemeyer study mentioned earlier noted that there was a clear relationship between the concept of ministry and the openness to the ordination of women, and the Lutheran study had concluded its Statement of Findings: "We urge, therefore, that appropriate commissions of the participating churches share in further joint study of broader topics of the 'ministry,' 'laity,' and 'church' as a context in which such specific questions must be addressed, and invite representatives of the churches to join with us in exploring fully these areas." Stendahl, too, had noted that the Church of Sweden used the term women priests, and wondered how much of the hostility had been generated simply by that term,[16] and van der Meer states that the case of the Church of Sweden needs to be considered more seriously by Roman Catholics than must the practice of some of the free churches.

All of duBois's other points as well are considered relevant to the discussion and analyzed—and disputed—by the present book. They include, briefly, the argument from the usage of the primitive church; the protective function of the male which is "symbolized in the office of the priest as the one who guards the temple and offers sacrifice"; the male priest reflecting the creative activity of God the Father; the argument from the dependence of the married woman upon her husband; the supposition that women cannot speak to us for God (though van der Meer finds that the argument that women cannot speak for us to God is more usual); the priest as *Alter Christus;* the relationship between the priest and his flock as analogous to the relationship of the Father and the Son; the testimony of the Fathers; the fact that Mary was not a priest (though van der Meer would take issue with the statement that nothing resembling a sacerdotal office was attributed to her even in "notoriously extravagant" popular piety, and presumably would dispute the view that she was not present at the Descent of the Spirit on Pentecost); and the fact that Jesus chose only males as apostles.

Nevertheless, as the flood of responses to Canon duBois's article indicates, granting women equal leadership possibilities in the church is being taken seriously by a growing number of concerned Episcopalians. The question of the ordination of women priests will come up again for a decision in England in 1973, and already the Anglican churches in Wales, West Africa, and Burma have voted to ordain women priests. Perhaps more unexpected was the 1 November 1972 vote of the American House of Bishops, 74 to 61 in favor of women priests, particularly in view of the contrary efforts led by Bishop C. Kilmer Meyers in the House of Bishops just a year before. The General Assembly of the American Episcopal Church, of course, still must decide on the question in its triennial meeting in the fall of 1973, but with the House of Bishops already on record in favor of women priests, the theological buttresses opposing women priests have been weakened. In the meantime, however, two women have already been ordained to the priesthood. The breakthrough came in the same place it occurred once before, during World War II, though in abortive fashion—namely, in Hong Kong.

Since the movement for the emancipation of women is a Western phenomenon of the past 150 years, there has been relatively little reflection on the question of the ordination of women priests within Eastern Christianity. However, the essays of the two Orthodox contributors to the booklet *Concerning the Ordination of Women* published by the World Council of Churches in 1964, which can be taken as rather typical of Orthodox Christianity's traditionalist stance on the subject, are worth a brief review. Professor Nicolae Chitescu of the Theological Institute of Bucharest stated clearly: "Women cannot receive the sacrament of ordination in the Orthodox Church. The ordination of women is prohibited both by Scripture (1 Cor. 14: 34) and by the subsequent rulings of the Church." One of the sources of the prohibition is the blood taboo:

Then there is the period when women are "impure," stressed in the Old Testament (see Leviticus 12 and 15: 19 sq.), during which according to certain canons women were not permitted to receive baptism. During this period women could not carry out priestly duties. There is a special canon prohibiting women-priests, based on this point of view. It is the second canon of Denis of Alexandria (cf. *Synt. At.*, IV, 7). The sixth and seventh canons of Timothy of Alexandria express the same point of view (*Synt. At.*, vol. IV, pp. 333–36). The forty-fourth canon of the local Synod of Laodicea forbade women to approach the altar in churches. . . . In the Orthodox Church of Roumania old women are also employed especially to prepare the "artos" bread needed for Holy Communion, and to keep the church clean—excepting the altar.

The second essay, by the Reverend Georges Khodre (now Bishop of Beirut, Lebanon), lists the inferiority and subordination of women as reasons for not ordaining women:

Is not the submission of the wife to her husband "as to the Lord" an acceptance of that hierarchical order as a divine order, in which the wife regards her husband as the mediator of God's splendour? The idea is somewhat similar to monastic obedience. As the superior is the representative of God, by obeying him one obeys God. So that if women are not called to be mediators in the natural order, they should not assume

the role of mediator in the supernatural order either through
the priesthood. . . . Woman is the sign of the religious life,
because womanhood means sacrifice and self-surrender.

All of the arguments presented by both these churchmen are
considered in detail in the present volume.

In its form as a dissertation in 1962, the present work by
Father van der Meer was the first serious favorable discussion of
the ordination of women in the Catholic Church. But it was soon
followed in the activist field by the 1963 resolutions of the Conference of St. Joan's International Alliance, which included:

St. Joan's International Alliance welcomes the setting up by
His Holiness Pope John XXIII of a commission for the revision
of Canon Law. Encouraged by the words of His Holiness in
Pacem in Terris,[17] the Alliance expresses the hope that special
consideration will be given those Canons which refer
to women.
    St. Joan's International Alliance re-affirms its loyalty and
filial devotion and expresses its conviction that should the
Church in her wisdom and in her good time decide to extend
to women the dignity of the priesthood, women would be
willing and eager to respond.[18]

The request for the ordination of Catholic women priests has
subsequently been ever more pressingly urged by the Alliance.
    During the Second Vatican Council, Archbishop Paul Hallinan
of Atlanta, Georgia, made what was considered a strong statement on the role of women:

In proclaiming the equality of man and woman the Church
must act as well as speak by fraternal testimony not only in
abstract doctrine. . . . We must not continue to perpetuate
the secondary place accorded to women in the Church of the
20th century. We must not continue to be late-comers in the
social, political and economic development that has today
reached climactic conditions. . . . But the Church has been
slow in denouncing the degradation of women in slavery,
and in claiming for them the right of suffrage and
economic equality. (Fourth Session)

There were, however, no women participants in the council,
though at the final session four "auditors" were allowed in the
gallery; the world-famous Catholic economist Barbara Ward was

not allowed to address the council but had to have her paper read by a man. Nevertheless, in the course of the council several significant statements emerged:

There is, therefore, in Christ and in the Church no inequality on the basis of race or nationality, social condition or sex because "there is neither Jew nor Greek; there is neither slave nor freeman; there is neither male nor female, for you are all one in Christ Jesus" (*De Ecclesiam* No. 32).

With respect to the fundamental rights of the person, every type of discrimination, whether social or cultural, whether based on sex, race, color, social condition, language or religion, is to be overcome as contrary to God's intent (*Gaudium et Spes* No. 29).

Two recent studies authorized and presented to the American Catholic hierarchy (the National Conference of Catholic Bishops) deal briefly with the ordination of women. These are at the moment the nearest approach to an official study.

The first of these deals only with the Permanent Diaconate, a recent reintroduction in the Roman Catholic Church which is intended as an office for older, often married, men who wish to devote themselves, either professionally or in their free time, to service in the church but do not intend to study for the priesthood. Since the topic of a permanent diaconate was first mentioned there have been women who requested that it not be limited to men, arguing that there were clearly women deacons in the early church.[19]

A booklet *Permanent Deacons in the United States, Guidelines on their Formation and Ministry,* by the Bishops' Committee on the Permanent Diaconate, published by the United States Catholic Conference (1971), included mention of the question in its epilogue. After discussing possible changes in the present age requirement (thirty-five) and the stipulation that a man once ordained to the diaconate may not marry or remarry, the report continues:

The third critical question concerns the ordination of women as deacons. Many women, lay and religious, have offered to serve in the ordained ministry and question the justice of being excluded. Among deacon candidates themselves and leaders of training programs, there is growing conviction that women would strengthen the diaconal ministry immeasurably.

The Bishops' Committee has spent many hours of discussion

on all three of these questions, listening to people who sincerely seek a change in church law in order that the gospel message and the charity of Christ might be communicated more effectively. After the widely circulated February 1971 report of the Catholic Theological Society of America had offered strong arguments in favor of the ordination of women, the Bishops' Committee discussed the question with individuals and groups who expressed reactions for or against. The committee of bishops has continued to pursue all three questions by listening to what people in the apostolate are saying and by carrying that message to churches in other countries and the Holy See.[20]

The National Conference of Catholic Bishops also commissioned a massive, many-leveled study of the priestly ministry, one portion of which was a theological study by a number of outstanding American Catholic theologians under the chairmanship of Carl Armbruster, S.J. This study has not yet been published, but in the spring of 1971 a progress report on it was made public.[21] The report stated that there were no biblical or theological grounds for opposing the priestly ordination of women.

There have been other important and scholarly works on the woman question within Catholicism, and many of them have dealt with the ordination of women. However, none of these has limited itself to this question or considered it in such depth as does Dr. van der Meer's book. The work of José Idigoras, SJ, *La femme dans l'ordre sacré* (Lima, Peru, 1963) is positive in its evaluation of the problem, but it is only a few score pages long in mimeographed form (summary in *Informations Catholiques Internationales*, November 15, 1963). The likewise positively oriented book by Sister V. E. Hannon, *The Question of Women and Priesthood* (London, 1967), is somewhat longer than Father Idigoras's work, but not nearly as extensive in its treatment of the matter as the Van der Meer book. Dr. Mary Daly's *The Church and the Second Sex* (New York, 1968), Sister Mary Lawrence (Margaret) McKenna's *Women of the Church* (New York, 1967), Father Charles R. Meyer's article "Ordained Women in the Early Church," *Chicago Studies*, vol. 4, no. 3 (Fall, 1965), pp. 285–309, Sister Albertus Magnus McGrath's *What a Modern Catholic Thinks about Women* (Chicago, 1972), and the work of Joan Morris dealing with the important roles achieved by women in the medieval church (*The Lady Was a Bishop*, New

York and London, 1973) have all been important in directing the present impetus toward a reevaluation of the role of women in Catholicism. Yet none has come to grips with the ordination problem as has Dr. van der Meer.

Perhaps the most significant other Catholic work in the area is another German-language thesis. In 1970 Dr. Ida Raming successfully submitted her lengthy doctoral dissertation, "Zum Ausschluss der Frau vom Amt in der Kirche. Eine kritische Untersuchung von Kanon 968, § 1 des Codex Iuris Canonici" ("The exclusion of woman from office in the church. A critical investigation of Canon 968 § 1 of the Codex Iuris Canonici"), to the Catholic theology faculty of the University of Münster, Germany. Dr. Raming's work is an analysis of the sources of the legal exclusion of women from Holy Orders in the Catholic Church. It traces the sources of Canon 968 § 1, "Only the baptized male (*vir*) can validly receive Holy Orders," back to the great codification of church law by Gratian in the twelfth century, and beyond him to his sources: the Bible, the Fathers, and earlier conciliar decisions. A number of things become clear in this analysis: a large part of Gratian's work in this area was based on earlier forged documents (the pseudo-isidorian decretals), on documents that were erroneously thought to be conciliar decrees (Statuta Ecclesiae Antiqua), and serious misreadings or misunderstandings of other documents; at the base of Gratian's work in this area was his conviction of the decided metaphysical and moral inferiority of women and their consequent "status subjectionis." Dr. Raming further analyzes the developments from Gratian's time forward.

The work of Dr. Raming is an important scholarly complement to the present work of Dr. van der Meer, for next to the theological objections to the ordination of women the arguments from tradition and canon law are most important. Pope Paul VI already began to strengthen this secondary bulwark in his *Motu proprio* of September 1972, in which he excluded women from Holy Orders on the grounds that it was a venerable tradition to insist that, "only the baptized male can validly receive Holy Orders."

Two other recent events concerning the question of the ordination of Catholic women priests are of significance. In the fall of 1971 the National Conference of Catholic Bishops appointed an episcopal committee, under the chairmanship of Archbishop Leo

Byrne of Saint Paul, Minnesota, to investigate the rights of women in the church and society; to date the committee has been gathering information. Secondly, the International Synod of Bishops meeting in Rome in the fall of 1971 provided a broad platform for the discussion of the disabilities women suffer in the Catholic Church (the two themes for the synod were the priesthood and justice). Between October 2nd and 22nd there were seventeen speeches concerning women. Cardinal George Flahiff of Winnipeg dismissed the arguments traditionally used to bar women from the priesthood as invalid, calling them "sociological, not doctrinal or scriptural reasons." He continued:

> Texts of Vatican II . . . made categorical statements against
> all discrimination against women in the church. But . . .
> many excellent Catholic women in particular, and other persons
> as well, find that no notable effort has been made to implement
> this teaching. . . . The bishops of Canada invited highly
> qualified representatives of Canadian Catholic women . . .
> to discuss the question. . . . In a General Assembly . . . the
> Episcopal Conference of Canada almost unanimously adopted
> the recommendation which in the name of the same conference
> I hereby submit to this synod: That a representative of the
> Canadian Catholic Conference urge the forthcoming Synod
> of Bishops to recommend to the Holy Father the immediate
> establishment of a mixed commission (that is, composed of
> bishops, priests, laymen and laywomen, religious men and
> religious women) to study in depth the question of the
> ministries of women in the Church.[22]

Archbishop Leo Byrne, spokesman for the U.S. bishops at the same synod, applauded contemporary woman's sense of equality with man as "wholesome and Christian, liberation in the best sense," and seconded Cardinal Flahiff's request for an international commission. He further urged every episcopal conference to undertake a study of its culture, church law, and practice, to eliminate discrimination against women.[23]

During the last week of October 1971 the 210 bishops of the synod met in twelve language groups to discuss the main issues of world justice. Nine of the twelve reports demanded action with regard to women's rights. The French group, chaired by Cardinal Suenens, asked for the immediate placement of women in parish and diocesan councils, Roman congregations and commissions, and also proposed that a representative committee be formed by the synod to prepare a theme for the next synod—i.e., the role of women in the church (participation in ministry, juridical status).

In the end the synod did pass a resolution to recommend the establishment of an investigatory committee concerning the status of women in the church, which was to report to the next meeting of the synod (later determined to be held in 1974), but after the bishops left Rome and before the resolutions were put in absolutely final form to be delivered to the Pope, the text was changed to make the committee responsible to the Pope rather than the synod. To date there is no indication that Rome has begun to establish the committee.

The Pope's September 1972 *Motu proprio* on the restructuring of minor clerical orders (which specifically barred women from officially receiving the "ministries" of lector and acolyte) was shown not to be significant when Archbishop Anthony Jordan of Edmonton, Canada, noted that "the two documents of September 14, . . . while maintaining that sacred orders are conferred only on men, have no relation at all to the recent movement in the church to have women admitted to the ministry of the church. . . . The study which produced the two documents was undertaken years ago, before the latest Synod of Bishops." This judgment was corroborated by a later Vatican clarification; the National Catholic News Service story on it read in part:

Stung by protests from women, especially champions of women's rights, the Vatican has pleaded innocent to charges it demoted women in its recent rulings on minor orders. . . . The Vatican's clarification, however, said it would be "inopportune to anticipate or prejudice what might subsequently be established at the end of the study on women's participation in the church's community life." This was the first public indication that the Vatican had accepted the request of several participants in the 1971 World Synod of Bishops for a serious theological study of the possibility of ordaining women.[24]

In late 1972, however, the American Catholic Bishops' Committee on Pastoral Research and Practice, chaired by Bishop John R. Quinn of Oklahoma City, issued a very brief (four page) report entitled "Theological Reflections on the Ordination of Women." It briefly rehearsed seven traditional arguments against the ordination of women, devoting a paragraph to each. It concluded: "For the present, however, we can see from theology only a continuation of the established discipline [that is, excluding women from ordination]. Considering the strength of that discipline and the numerous uncertainties detailed in this paper, the needed study on this question is now just beginning. As is evident, every one of the points listed in this report calls for a major study." Since Father van der Meer's book painstakingly analyzes—and finally rejects—all of the arguments in this short report, we are certain that the translation of his book into English will be of immense assistance in this forthcoming study.

American Catholic women, however, have already begun to enter theological seminaries. The first was Mary B. Lynch, who entered the Catholic Seminary, Indianapolis, Indiana, in 1971; since then several other Catholic seminaries have indicated that they are open to accepting women. In those Protestant churches which do ordain women there has been a pattern: the seminaries were first opened to women, and then, only after there was a group of theologically trained women, was the question of the ordination of women officially decided in the affirmative.

On the ecumenical level there has long been a keen interest in the question of the status of women in the church and particularly the ordination of women, since some churches ordain women and some do not, thereby providing at least a possible obstacle to church unity. At the Third Assembly of the World Council of Churches in New Delhi, 1961, the Department on Faith and Order was requested to establish a study in conjunction with the Department on Cooperation of Men and Women in Church, Family, and Society, on the theological, biblical, and ecclesiological issues involved in the ordination of women. This they did in the form of the booklet *Concerning the Ordination of Women* (Geneva, 1964), which consists of an introduction summing up the issues, a statement by a small consultation on the subject held at the WCC headquarters in Geneva, two papers on the scriptural evidence, and three personal comments from the Anglican tradition and two Orthodox traditions. All of the Protestant contributions were favorable, the Anglican was ambiguous, and the Orthodox was strongly negative toward the notion of the ordination of women.

In September 1970 the WCC sponsored a broader Consultation on the Ordination of Women, at Cartigny, Switzerland; it produced a number of mimeographed reports which included the statement that

the right ecumenical attitude is surely *not* for one church to refrain from change because another church has not moved, but to declare that discrimination cannot be permitted in any part, and attempt to persuade towards the truth those parts which still practise and indeed institutionalise discrimination. Within confessions, a Church may be called to lead her sister Churches into a fuller understanding of women's ministry and a greater readiness to explore and manifest this ministry.

On the American scene doubtless the most important ecumenical project is the Consultation on Church Union (COCU), an effort begun in 1962 to unite into one church nine American Protestant churches, ranging from the Protestant Episcopal Church to churches from the Calvinist tradition. The Plan of Union now before the participating churches has taken a clear stand in favor of the ordination of, and equal authority for, women. How many of the nine churches participating in the consultation, or others, will actually join together to form the "Church of Christ Uniting" remains to be seen. Nevertheless, the pertinent portions of the present Plan of Union are worth quoting since they have been agreed to by the representatives of the nine churches to the consultation:

The structures of the church shall provide for inclusiveness of all its members, and for their full participation and representation in every aspect of the church's fellowship and ministry . . . embracing the unity of all persons, regardless of race, age, sex, wealth, or culture (chapter 2, no. 17).

The ministry of the laity is one ministry within the structures of the world and of the church. No differences of vocation, situation, age, or sex shall obscure this essential participation in Christ's ministry (chapter 7, no. 18).

In ordination, the united church recognizes that the call to the individual man or woman is of God, prays that the one to be ordained will continue to receive the gifts of God, believes that God gives grace appropriate to the office, accepts and authorizes this ministry in and for the church (chapter 7, no. 32).

In every area of the new structure, in both lay and ordained leadership the united church shall assure all races, various age groups and both sexes the right of full participation. To assure such wholeness, the church will: . . . (2) enlist women for all offices of the ordained and lay ministry and provide for full participation by women in all policy-making groups (chapter 8, nos. 14, 16).

Each parish and each governing body beyond the parish shall elect a committee on equity that shall include a fair representation of minority groups, men, women, and young people, whose duty it shall be to assure implementation of these principles, to review the performance of the church, and to report regularly to the body which elected it with recommendations for any needed corrective action (chapter 8, no. 19).

One section of the officially established bilateral consultation between the Roman Catholic and Reformed family churches in America devoted several years study to the status of women in their churches. Their final lengthy report included the following strong recommendations:

2. That seminary education in all the Churches be opened to qualified women; that qualified women be admitted to ordination; that in those Churches where the ordination of women presents theological difficulties and no theological study of the matter has been made, a theological committee be established immediately to investigate the problem and make recommendations. . . .

3. That the North American Area Council, World Alliance of Reformed Churches and the Bishops' Committee on Ecumenical and Interreligious Affairs establish and fund an Ecumenical Commission on Women, inviting other Churches involved in bilateral consultations with the Roman Catholic Church to join them on an equal basis in responsibility and funding for this commission and sharing the fruits of its labors; that the members of this commission be predominantly women from all the sponsoring Churches who are actively engaged in the lives of their Churches and also positively concerned for women's dignity, freedom, and rights; that the purpose of this commission be to facilitate the fulfillment of the first two recommendations and to safeguard and extend the gains made.[25]

Save for the fact that some individual Catholic seminaries have since accepted women students, these recommendations have not been acted upon.

In the late 1960s the women's liberation movement burgeoned into a mass movement in the United States and overflowed into other countries. It very quickly began to be reflected in the churches and in religious publications, resulting in a flood of books, special issues of magazines, and individual articles on women in the church. The most comprehensive monitoring of publishing in this field is carried out by the Philadelphia Task Force on Women and Religion, in a newsletter entitled *Genesis III* (P.O. Box 20043, Philadelphia, Pa. 19139). Another ecumenical group active in the field is the Ecumenical Task Force on Women and Religion of the National Organization for Women (P.O. Box 836, Berkeley, Calif. 94701), which also puts out a newsletter. The Boston Theological Institute (a consortium of six theological seminaries and universities) has given birth to a Women's Institute: there are nearly two hundred women postgraduate theological students in the BTI institutions and women on all the theological faculties. The largest professional organization of religious scholars in America is the American Academy of Religion; in 1971 a section on women's studies in theology and religion was formed within it, and in 1972 it began to sponsor papers on the subject at the annual conferences.

The range of concern of these and other ecumenical groups usually extends to all aspects of the involvement of women in religion, but many of them center their focus on problems around ordination of women.

Within this ecumenical and social context the need for a scholarly investigation of the ordination of women from a Roman Catholic viewpoint is clear. We hope Dr. van der Meer's work will make a major contribution to both Catholic and ecumenical thinking.

Arlene and Leonard Swidler

Women Priests in the Catholic Church?

Preface

The text of this book—originally a dissertation at the University of Innsbruck in Austria—was completed in the summer of 1962. The author regrets very much that he is not in a position to completely rework it at the present time. Since 1962 much has happened, much has been published, and in a number of aspects theological thinking has progressed further, not only in the area of our topic, but in others as well. Unfortunately these advances could not be incorporated into either the German or English printed editions of the typescript manuscript, which was constantly being requested from the Innsbruck archives. Nevertheless the author ventures to publish the old text, being encouraged to do so by many who have read it; only with this encouragement does he do so, for he is aware of the many things that are missing. He can only hope that his collection of material and his reflections can nevertheless be a help to others in the theological analysis of the problem of the priesthood of women.

Haye van der Meer, SJ

Amsterdam, 1973

PUBLISHER'S NOTE: The seventeen-page bibliography in the original German edition of this book has been omitted here. It was felt that the review of the English-language literature in the Translators' Foreword was thorough and more up-to-date, and that the French- and German-language publications forming the bulk of the bibliography would be of lesser interest, and largely inaccessible, to the readers of this edition.

I   Introduction

Writers of manuals on dogmatic theology do not spend much time on the thesis "Subjectum ordinationis est solus mas"—only a male is a subject for ordination. The reader gets the impression that they really think that the matter is not only quite clear but has long since been conclusively and neatly proved by theologians. It is noteworthy that not only the manuals written many years ago now being reissued but even the newly written works proceed as though no real new investigations on this point were necessary. In reading, for example, Joseph A. Wahl's dissertation *The Exclusion of Woman from Holy Orders*,[1] or the article by H. Rondet, "Éléments pour une théologie de la femme," [2] or a few excerpts from G. Philips's article, "La femme dans l'Église," [3] one notices that these authors at bottom do nothing but (1) quote a few Scriptural passages—1 Cor. 11, 3–16; 1 Cor. 14, 33–36; 1 Tim. 2, 11–15, and what the *Haustafeln,* or household rules, say about the subjection of woman; (2) quote a few passages from the Fathers and several ancient synods and other documents like the *Didascalia,* the *Constitutiones Apostolorum,* and the *Statuta Ecclesiae Antiquae;* (3) quote the *ratio theologica* from Thomas Aquinas.[4]

There are of course several attempts at a more profound analysis, as for example E. Krebs's article "Vom Priestertum der Frau," [5] or the article by A. M. Henry, "Le mystère de l'homme et de la femme," [6] or R. Laurentin's investigations in the second part of his book *Marie, l'Église et le Sacerdoce,*[7] or F. X. Arnold's treatment in his book *Woman and Man;* [8] but these authors too, it seems to me, treat the matter too facilely.

Other contributions on this theme are limited to the purely historical area, relating, for example, to the question of whether the deaconesses of the first eleven centuries received a truly sacramental ordination; or they may refer merely to various ecclesiastical statements pertaining to woman.[9]

But it seems to be really necessary that the question of priestly ordination for women be reconsidered completely afresh. The first reason for this is clearly the dialogue with our fellow Christians of the Reformation. The Catholic side can no longer ignore the fact that various major Protestant groups such as the Danish, Norwegian, and Swedish Lutheran churches have admitted women to the ordained ministry.[10] And the largest of the Dutch Calvinist denominations, the Nederlandse Hervormde Kerk, has recognized female pastors as complete equals since 1958 (even if only as exceptions and with the dispensation of the synod in each case).

We are thus no longer concerned merely with a step taken by the smaller churches or by the distinctly spiritualizing sects, but with movements that are almost high church in nature. In general it is in the high church movements (Anglican,[11] Orthodox,[12] Old Catholic [13]) that there is the least inclination to admit woman to orders.[14] But it is wrong to accept this too easily as a reason for not having to engage in the question oneself. It is, of course, possible to take the view that the high church groups have preserved a better sense of the sacraments than have our other separated brethren. But one should really ask oneself whether in this case the high church groups have not mistaken two different problems—the idea that the community is the final source of ecclesiastical authority, and the question of the possibility of the admission of women into the apostolic succession. To accept the second is not to affirm the first. In any case it has still never been demonstrated that the priesthood of women is the same thing as the rejection of apostolic succession or that it even implies this. Many advocates of priesthood for women have of course thought along these lines,[15] but the two ideas are nevertheless distinct.

There are now, at least in the Scandinavian churches, women on whom the bishops have imposed hands and upon whom the Mass vestments have been conferred.[16] That means that now, even among Christians who make the same efforts as we do to deal with the full traditions of their churches—and not merely among groups like the Quakers, the Salvation Army, the Congregationalists, and other such churches and groups in which the community is considered the unrestricted bearer of all authority [17]—the opinion prevails that the female priestly office does not contradict the essence of Christianity. The Catholic dogmatic theologian, then, should not pass over the problem but must come to terms with it afresh. Otherwise there will arise a breach in the dialogue with his Christian brethren.

From the Catholic viewpoint too, we can no longer hold that the usual thesis presents no problem. Even independent of these developments within Protestantism the simple fact that women can now enter many professions and, what is more important, assume offices which until a short time ago were closed to them can have consequences in the religious area. The question of whether they can now also be priests follows naturally, as—to mention only one example—it actually did for Edith Stein.[18]

And a contemporary dogmatic theologian can no longer be satisfied with the methods of theological demonstration which are still employed by very many writing on this problem. The mere citation of a few passages, even if they are chosen from among many, brings us, I feel, nowhere. The texts must be analyzed with care, and the conditions of the times which gave rise to these statements or formed their background should be borne in mind. When, for example, an Epiphanius of Salamis reacts vigorously against the women priests who officiate in a number of heretical communities, these texts cannot simply be accepted without further attention as a valid "argument from the Fathers," for a further reading makes clear that Epiphanius feels there is a necessary close connection between the female priesthood and the adoration (*cultus latriae*) of Mary. The authors citing him make no mention of this! But this circumstance makes his repudiation a time-conditioned factor.

The task which this book takes upon itself is to scrutinize carefully all the proofs which dogmatic theologians offer on this thesis. It will not be asserted that these usual proofs have no value. But question marks will be placed alongside the various points, and from time to time I shall point out arguments which are defective in their demonstration, ambiguities, unexplained leaps in the development of an idea, places where a writer has jumped to the desired conclusion too quickly.

This book will therefore not make a judgment on the correctness of the thesis itself, and still less on the correctness of the Church's practice, but merely on the finality of theological speculation up until the present, or rather on its integrity and adequacy. I shall not go into the question of whether ecclesiastical practice has been correct, for in an earlier age it possibly was. On the other hand I shall also not go into the question of whether the practice of the Church could perhaps be altered, to say nothing of whether it must be. Likewise I shall not investigate whether in this reference a genuine *intuition* illuminates the Church, stating something about its essence or about the essence of its hierarchical office, which is quite possible in and of itself, even if the theological basis is incomplete. I shall suspend the question of whether the contemporary closing of office to woman is a *de facto* practical measure (as, for example, the contemporary stipulation on communion *sub una specie* or the earlier stipulations that one could not be reconciled with the Church more than once), or whether it belongs to the essence of office by "divine law." I shall thus not consider whether a better theological understanding might be possible and shall myself make no attempt at this.

I am not attempting to prove either that a woman can be consecrated as a priest now or that she never can be, for a theological response to this question would exceed the limits of this book. Such a study would have to include (1) a penetrating investigation of the essence of the sacrament of orders and of the episcopal office; (2) the same for the Church and for Mary; (3) the same for the correct use of Scripture and the Fathers in theology; (4) the entire metaphysics, psychology, and sociology of man and of woman.

In reference to these four points, I cannot go along with Karl Barth when he says (speaking of the tasks of man and of woman in general) that he is determined to avoid all phenomenology and typology of the sexes because he believes we have no right to attribute specific differences to the sexes as such if we are asking about God's commandment. Specific differences, even if we think we have some knowledge concerning them, cannot be presumed, says Barth; otherwise we would be asserting that we already know the content of the divine commandment, about which ethics can hope only to raise rather limited questions.[19] As this subject would lead us much too far from our task, however, we must leave it unsettled.

These four points will come up for discussion again and again, but not all—or, in fact, any one of them—will be elaborated exhaustively. Our method will be this: as individual arguments presented by dogmatic theologians are considered, material from these four points will occasionally be presented in order to show that the arguments need at least expansion and sometimes even serious correction. The real purpose of this work will thereby be achieved: proof will be furnished that the problem is still far from settled, that it needs more investigation—in other words, that Catholic dogmatic theologians may not hold that according to the present position of theology it is already (or still) established on a scholarly basis that "office" should, by divine law, remain closed to women. Perhaps it is indeed forbidden to women by divine law; but up until now there still has not been a satisfactory scholarly presentation of the thesis. Writers have comfortably referred to passages from Scripture and the Fathers without feeling any obligation to think the question through for themselves and to examine the passages critically; and even where rethinking has been attempted, the work has not been sufficiently deep and critical. I shall merely present these errors.

This work will thus be more a synopsis of all that would have to be investigated and taken into consideration for the proof of the thesis than a proper demonstration pro or con.

The customary proofs from Scripture, the Fathers, the magisterium, and speculative theology will be discussed.

II   Holy Scripture

Because a really adequate biblical theology of woman and office would extend far beyond the limits of this work, this book makes no attempt to investigate all the pertinent texts. This chapter will present merely a critical investigation of the relatively few texts which the dogmatic theologians offer as proof for their own thesis; it is not itself a demonstration proper.

1. Jesus and the Apostles Chose Only Men

Several Fathers as well as later dogmatic theologians point to the fact that Jesus and Peter selected only men for the apostolic office. Thus, for example, the *Didascalia* states:

> It is therefore neither fitting nor necessary that women teach, especially concerning the name of Christ and the redemption of his passion. For you are not established for this, to teach, women and especially widows, but to pray and implore the Lord God, for the Lord God Jesus Christ our teacher sent us twelve to teach the people and the tribes; although there were with us the disciples Mary Magdalen and Mary the daughter of James and the other Mary, he did not send them out to teach the people with us. For if it had been necessary that women teach, our Master would have ordered these to teach with us.[1]

In Epiphanius of Salamis we find the same idea:

> If women were authorized by God to be priests or to administer an office in the Church then actually Mary herself would have had to hold a priestly office in the Church. . . . But he did not so will. Not even baptism is entrusted to her, for in that case Christ could better have been baptized by her than by John.[2]

10

Ambrosiaster writes:

The Montanists firmly hold with baseless arrogance that
deaconesses should also be ordained, although they know that
the apostles chose seven males as deacons. Was it that
there were no suitable women to be found, when we read
that holy women accompanied the twelve apostles? [3]

From among dogmatic theologians, we quote from Diekamp-
Hoffmann:

Christ handed on to no woman . . . the power of conferring
sacraments.[4]

We can only ask how the Church knows that a woman can
baptize validly, to say nothing of conferring the sacrament of
matrimony on her spouse. Reasoning similar to the above is found
in such writers as Pohle-Gummersbach.[5] Even Karl Rahner refers
to the "will of Christ" and "apostolic practice." [6] Edith Stein says,
"Christ transmitted the priesthood to his apostles but not to the
women who ministered to him. For this reason I believe the
exclusion of women from the priesthood is not something conditioned by the times." [7]

Jesus wished to have witnesses to himself (Acts 1, 8), and Peter
also wished to choose a witness to the resurrection to replace
Judas (Acts 1, 24), and both, it is true, chose only males. Both
passages are concerned with the special office of the twelve;
"witness" and "apostle" are here synonymous in Luke's usage.[8]
The proof thus might seem complete.

But in fact it is not. First it must be demonstrated that Jesus
and Peter and the primitive Palestinian church in general chose
only males as witnesses precisely because divine law decreed
only males could be apostles, and not simply because it was more
appropriate to the concrete situation of time and place. Such a
proof would not be simple. On the other hand, to prove that the
choice was made only because it suited the concrete situation is
also difficult. We know little of the times in which Jesus lived.
The later rabbinic precepts do permit certain deductions about
earlier times, but their coercive power was not always the same
in Jesus' day as in later rabbinic orthodoxy. Nevertheless in what
follows we will have to draw on many passages of the rabbinic
Halaka [religious law], for these passages in general do certainly prove that in the Jewish world of Jesus' day it was simply

impossible for a woman to play a leading role in the area of religious office.

According to rabbinic opinion a woman could "neither read aloud nor even speak, neither expound nor teach," in the Jewish worship service.[9] In the synagogues women sat behind gratings in special places. "The woman should bear no witness, teach no children, say no table prayer." [10] Indeed, she was not even permitted to learn the Torah! "He who teaches his daughter the Torah teaches her licentiousness." [11] Because this last passage is disputed, we would like to clarify this point with a longer quotation from Kosmala.

The Mishna establishes that the lustral water which a woman suspected of adultery should drink according to Numbers 5 takes effect not immediately but only after one, two, or even three years, if the woman has any merit at all. From this Ben Azzai concludes that one must teach his daughter the Torah so that, in case she must drink the lustral water, she will know that merit postpones the effect of the water. For a more precise understanding of this opinion it must be noted that Ben Azzai, as we know from his other utterances, judged more broadmindedly than did his contemporaries. He often advocated a view completely contrary to traditional interpretation and attitudes. Moreover, he was not an ordained rabbi, but merely a wisdom scholar. Although held in high regard, personally, he nevertheless had no independent teaching office. Although he probably took part in halachic discussions, he nevertheless did not speak with the same authority as, for example, Rabbi Eliezer. The latter responded, "Whoever teaches his daughter Torah teaches her wantonness." For if she were instructed in the Torah she would also know the means to use to delay the effect of the lustral water and thus postpone her conviction. Her transgression would then remain concealed for a longer time. In this way the knowledge of the Torah could seduce her into taking sin lightly. To utilize knowledge of the Torah for one's own purpose was insolent; to make use of it for sinful conduct would be much more insolent. From this debate we gather that Ben Azzai's pronouncement was an attack on an old custom become law. This attack was repulsed. The dictum of Rabbi Eliezer, who could say of himself that he never taught anything that he had not heard from his teachers, persisted in the time which followed. Later rabbis only added on a little word so that the dictum could not be misunderstood to say that teaching the Torah is of itself an introduction to a wanton life:

"To teach a daughter Torah is as if one taught her wantonness." The Gemara [later rabbinical commentaries on the earlier rabbinical writings of the Mishna] does not take up Ben Azzai's proposition at all.

Despite the direction in Deut. 31, 12, and despite the pattern set by Ezra (Neh. 8, 2 f.), there was, according to ancient rabbinical tradition, no obligation at all for fathers to instruct their daughters, or have them instructed, in the Torah, nor for women and daughters to take instruction in the Torah. The regulation was based on Deut. 11, 19, which says: "And teach them [the words of the Torah] to your sons"; the rabbinical explanation adds: "but not your daughters." That the Jewish religion is a "man's religion" there is not the slightest doubt.[12]

This detailed citation—more could be added, such as "The words of the Torah may be burned, but they should not be handed over to women"[13]—may serve to prove that Billerbeck is probably not correct in saying that there is no unanimity on the question of whether women are to be instructed in the Torah.[14] With Kosmala one must respond:

With his citation of the Talmud [these words are intended for another author, but are just as valid for Billerbeck] he makes us believe that opinions have been actually and in principle divided. But in reality only once on a special occasion and in a special context was a contrary voice heard, and this was swamped on the same day in the broad stream of legalistic tradition! The Torah remained a masculine affair.[15]

One must thus simply respond to Ambrosiaster: of course "there were no suitable women to be found"; no woman knew the law. How would she be able to interpret it? How could the daughters of Philip, although themselves prophetesses (Acts 21, 9), interpret the passages from Isaiah like their father (Acts 8, 32 ff.)?

And apart from this (for the women supposedly did ultimately take part in the worship services in order to listen and to learn the commandments from the Targum [vernacular translation] reading[16]) how could the women be apostles, that is, witnesses, when the witness of a woman, as we saw above, was not valid? "And Sara [falsely] denied it: I did not laugh (Gen. 18, 15). From this passage it was taught that women are unfit to bear witness."[17] One of the nine punishments for woman as a result of the sin in paradise is that she is not a valid witness.[18] In this

respect she is likened to the slave.[19] There were but few exceptions to this.[20] On the whole, words of a woman were not
counted as reliable:

Manoah spoke to the angel: Until now I have heard it from
the woman (that a son should be born to me) and women are
not daughters of instruction (instruction does not come from
them), and one cannot rely on their word; but now let your
word come out of your mouth.[21]

Note the universal meaning of "women"; it is not a question of
just one unreliable woman.

If this was the case in Judaism, it follows that Jesus and the
apostles could not add women to the apostolic college as witnesses of the resurrection: their witness would never be taken
seriously at that time. The oldest tradition, as seen in Pauline
thought in 1 Cor. 15, 3 ff., failed to mention women among the
witnesses to the resurrection, perhaps for this very reason.

The position of woman in the social and religious life of Jesus'
day will be investigated later. For the moment it is enough to
confirm that this very simple explanation for not proposing
women as witness-apostles is an obvious one. New and very
serious reasons must be presented before we can say that women
were excluded because Jesus and the primitive church made such
a decision and that they intended it as a permanent principle. On
the contrary, it is much more likely that Jesus and the apostles
never concerned themselves with the idea that the social-religious
position of woman might one day be different. For it is clear that
our problem is not one of the religious status of woman, but of
her official status in the religious community. Office is a social
function (see chapter 5).

Joseph A. Wahl adds to this that Jesus was speaking only to
males when he said, "Do this in commemoration of me." With
these words Jesus constituted the twelve apostles priests, and he
ordained them and the other priests to offer his body and his
blood, as the second canon of the twenty-second session of the
Council of Trent says.[22] And only men were present at the Last
Supper.[23]

But, it may be asked, do the words "do this" signify only the
consecration explicitly and exclusively? Or do they also mean
the celebration of his death, the anamnesis, the entire Last Supper, including the eating and drinking of his body and blood?

If the latter is the case, how do we know, if it is stressed so strongly that only men were present, that women too may receive communion?

According to Matt. 28, 16–18, Jesus said only to the eleven (and thus only to males): Baptize. If that is so strongly stressed, as in Wahl's work,[24] how do we know that women can baptize validly?

2. *The Texts from 1 Cor. 11*

The first Pauline text which is brought up again and again in this connection is 1 Cor. 11, 3–16. In itself this passage offers more difficulty than aid to the dogmatic theologians who attempt to offer scriptural arguments that women are incapable of being priests. For Paul appears to presume that it is perfectly normal for a woman to prophesy. He adds of course that she puts her head to shame if she prophesies with her head uncovered, and he therefore says "let her be covered"; but in this passage he does not forbid her to speak. On the contrary! Saying *how* a woman ought to do something seems to place value on the fact *that* she does it.

Immediately of course the contradiction of 1 Cor. 14, 34 comes to mind: "Let women be silent," and in the same passage, v. 35: "For it is a shame for women to speak in assembly."

There have been many attempts to solve this problem. The contradiction has misled many into explaining this second passage away as unauthentic; especially because the position of verses 34 and 35 in the fourteenth chapter is not always the same in the manuscripts. These verses, according to some, were a gloss, taken from 1 Tim. 2.[25] But the text is now considered authentic by the great majority of exegetes.

Commentators like Allo seem to be entirely off the track when they claim that in 14, 34, Paul forbids the prophesying which in 11, 5, he mentioned only as hitherto exercised improperly. According to their view, he reserved his decision on this point for later, and then, in chapter 14, came to a negative judgment.[26] Lietzmann held this view; but Kümmel rejects such an interpretation in the new edition.[27] Ambrosiaster also expounds in this direction. He simply skips over the word "prophesying" in chapter 11 and says of 14, 34:

Now he states what he had avoided above, for earlier he commanded (only) that women be veiled in the church; now he indicates that they should be silent and reticent.[28]

In 11, 5, Paul does not call the prophesying of women an actual erroneous development; he merely commands women to pray and prophesy in an appropriate manner, not like the men but according to feminine decorum: πρέπον ἐστίν, "Is it fitting?" (v. 13). He wishes her to cover her head.

Likewise very improbable is Cornely's interpretation that "prophesying" is here identical with reciting "Amen" to the prayers and prophecies of the men, and it is this that the women should do with heads covered.[29]

Many commentators, Church Fathers as well as later exegetes, both Catholic and Protestant, have been of the opinion that the words "in assembly" in chapter 14 can resolve the contradiction. Prophesying by women could be permitted in home worship or in group gatherings, but not in the public gatherings of the congregation. Women could thus prophesy "privately" at home, but not "publicly" in the church. So, for example, thought Origen,[30] Jerome,[31] Theodore of Mopsuestia,[32] Primasius Afer,[33] Ambrose,[34] Peter Lombard [35] and many others, as well as Thomas Aquinas [36] and almost everyone after him.[37] From among the Protestants we can mention Bachmann as an example.[38]

There are, however, many objections to this interpretation. First of all 1 Cor. 11 is not concerned with assemblies of small groups but with the entire congregation. This is clear from the context. Verse 2 begins with "I praise," which is repeated in the passage on the eucharist in verses 17 and 22. The repetition makes clear that in the passage on women Paul is already speaking of the congregational assembly; although he cannot approve their eucharistic customs, he does praise the Corinthians for observing his "traditions" (v. 2); what these are, however, remains obscure.[39] He adds to this only that women should be veiled when they prophesy. Even verse 16 suggests our interpretation; in conclusion and as a sort of *argumentum ad hominem* Paul says, "Neither we nor the other assemblies of God have such usage." This wording obviously admits of only one interpretation: it treats a matter which has something to do with congregational worship.[40] It would also be difficult to understand why Paul would wish to command a woman to put on a veil in her own home and in the exercise of household prayer.[41] Several commentators succeed in contradicting themselves when they apply the expression "on account of the angels" in verse 10 to the bishop or priest present, as, for example, do Peter Lombard [42] and Thomas Aquinas.[43]

The presence of the bishop or priest does indeed at least indicate a public quality even if one does not go so far as to say that such a presence itself makes the gathering public. Strange to say, even Irenaeus (unlike Origen) states that in his letter to the Corinthians Paul acknowledges there are men and women who prophesy in the church:

It is truly unfortunate, for those who make themselves into pseudoprophets rob the church of the prophetic charism. . . . It is to be understood that such people did not accept the Apostle Paul. For in his letter to the Corinthians he spoke carefully of prophetic gifts and mentioned men and women prophesying in the church.[44]

And finally the word "prophesy" itself has the meaning "to speak in the congregation and for the congregation." "Prophecy is always in public and in the congregation," says H. Greeven.[45] Even in chapter 14 of 1 Cor. that is clear enough. "He that speaks in tongues builds himself up, but he that prophesies builds up the assembly" (v. 4); cf. verses 5, 24, 29–32. According to Paul, too, prophecy is a charism which ought to build up the congregation: [46] 1 Cor. 12, 28 (cf. Eph. 2, 20). How could he say that if prophecy were not open to the congregation?

We must conclude that 1 Cor. 11, 5 is concerned with congregational discipline, not with household life nor with private prayer gatherings in the home. Allo,[47] Lietzmann,[48] and Tischleder,[49] to mention only a few authors, agree in this. It is a question of the manner and way in which men *and* women should pray and prophesy in public congregational assembly.

This conclusion is important because it follows that women were permitted to prophesy publicly in the Corinthian church with Paul's approbation. A distinction between "public" and "private" is untenable. The contradiction between this passage and 1 Cor. 14 thus remains.

A further attempt at glossing is the distinction between "to testify" and "to instruct." Women, according to this approach, would be permitted to testify but not to teach. This idea has recently been proposed by J. Daniélou, among others.[50]

Many attempts at explaining that contradiction [that is, the contradiction between 1 Cor. 11, 5 and 14, 24] have been made. For my part, it seems to me that the matter concerns two different activities. . . . The woman is not known to have the role of instructor. . . . But the role of the prophet in the assembly is not primarily to teach but to give testimony. It is essentially one of praying. . . . If teaching is thus forbidden to women, it does not appear that they should be forbidden to pray in a loud voice in the assembly.

This distinction, in any case, does no violence to the text of 1 Cor. 11; thus for these present paragraphs we will let it stand; later we will investigate whether it really fits the text of 1 Cor. 14 or not.

The text of 1 Cor. 11 therefore is really a source of difficulties for dogmatic theologians, not an aid. Only the assertions on the primacy of man over woman could be of any use to them. Now a contemporary theologian, Dr. Else Kähler, in her book *Die Frau in den paulinischen Briefen, unter besonderer Berücksichtigung des Begriffes der Unterordnung* ("Woman in the Pauline epistles, with special consideration of the concept of subordination"), has demonstrated in detail that Paul is not trying to teach a simple subjection of woman but rather a reciprocal orientation of man and woman.[51] But for the purpose of the present book it does not seem useful either to accept her demonstration uncritically (several points in fact are questioned by other exegetes) or to discuss it in greater detail (that would overstep the framework of my book). Nevertheless, E. Kähler cannot avoid recognizing, in the last analysis, a certain subordination as inherent in Paul's thought, not of course in 1 Cor. 11, but in Eph. 5 and 1 Tim. 2 (although she denies that the last passage is Pauline). She does not find a subordination in the sense of sheer obedience—a purely passive "orders are orders" mentality—but as an active personal decision in favor of obedience to the order willed by God.[52] Charlotte von Kirschbaum also formulated this in the same way: "To subordinate oneself means to occupy a place within a determined order as the partner over whom another is foreordered; it means to acknowledge the other in his position and with him become a part in this order and thus preserve the order."[53] So too Karl Barth says that Charlotte von Kirschbaum is following the same line he himself took.[54] Even E. Kähler must admit frankly that in 1 Tim. 2 teaching is in any case forbidden to woman: the duty of silence and subjection there are not valid merely (as in 1 Cor. 14, which we shall discuss later) for a special occasion, but in principle.[55] However, where she apparently deplores the slant of the pastoral letter ("the primitive

Christian proclamation is overlaid by a new layer of thoughts and formulations, so that it is in danger of losing part of its power") [56] we cannot approve uncritically. It seems better to us that we concern ourselves with the question of what Paul's ideas of woman mean *for us*. E. Kähler observes that "the voices of serious scholars who, on the bases of history and textual criticism, banish certain assertions of the pastoral letters 'to the periphery of the canon' are multiplying. It does not occur to anyone to reject all the pastoral letters as a result or to deny them a hearing for their other witness. . . . But where their assertions are not Christocentric but indicative of a bourgeois morality, strongly stamped by a given situation, we must reserve for ourselves an independent attitude." [57] Obviously I do not agree if she means by that an independent attitude *opposed* to the Scripture. But I can certainly agree if she means a differentiation between those things which are strongly stamped by a given situation and those which refer to the real, deeper intentions of Scripture which are of more basic significance than a few directions for the concrete order of the community.

Let us, therefore, let the discussions on the subordination of woman in 1 Cor. 11 rest, for the moment, and even the analyses of the question whether and to what extent woman is an image and glory of God and whether she can represent God, which according to Allo [58] is the kernel of Pauline thought. That will be discussed in the fifth chapter. It occurs to me that the argumentations which serve to show that Paul grants woman everything that we grant her will always be artificial. But anyone who has taken note of how much the views of the exegetes on Paul's position on woman diverge [59] comes to the conviction that, from this quarter at least, no definitive answer is now to be expected.

It is also not the task of this book to seek a final solution for the question of what exactly Paul asserted and thought about woman—held without reflection and unconsciously handed down as the authentic material of faith—but rather whether the texts which the theologians cite without analyses are themselves conclusive. Later we shall see that supertemporal decrees should not too quickly be read into what appear to be statements of principles. My only task here is to eliminate such things which in my opinion are incorrectly read into Paul. Something does then remain before the theologians, but it is the question of whether there is sufficient reason here to exclude woman from office for all time. I shall do away only with the misunderstanding that Paul has settled that. For he does not say this in 1 Cor. 11, nor in 1 Cor. 14, and in 1 Tim. 2 the author says it in a very fixed context. Whether it is nevertheless contained implicitly in the Pauline theology of woman, insofar as his theology states a *jus divinum,* does not belong to the theme of this work.

3. *The Texts from 1 Cor. 14*

Theologians have felt absolutely no need to analyze the text of 1 Cor. 14, 34–35; indeed it says only too clearly, "As in all the churches of the saints, women are to remain quiet at meetings since they have no permission to speak; they must keep in the background as the Law itself lays it down." Without further ado some cite this passage as the ultimate and decisive word on the problem. F. Solá for example says:

If a woman is never permitted by virtue of divine law (for St. Paul is acting as an apostle in Christ's name) even to ask a question in the congregational assembly for her own instruction . . . , then it can even less be permitted that she offer the sacrifice, which presupposes leadership, teaching, and so on.[60]

The Fathers of the Church and the ancient ecclesiastical writers like Origen, Ambrosiaster, Epiphanius, Tertullian, the Didascalia, Chrysostom, Jerome, and Peter Lombard cite this passage as the final word; [61] even at the present time J. A. Wahl and many others do the same.[62] The argument runs, "We no longer have the task of investigating whether a woman may speak or not; Paul in 1 Cor. 14 already forbade it for all times. We can at most still investigate why he did that" (this is the general line the arguments often take).

Unfortunately in this interpretation it seems too easy to be led astray by the wording of the individual passage without looking at the context of the entire chapter. And the conviction that 1 Tim. was likewise written by Paul himself is apt to lead to the explaining of the passage from 1 Cor. 14 in the light of 1 Tim. 2, 12. Actually, however, it would be better (if only because the authorship of the letter to Timothy is doubtful in Catholic circles) [63] to interpret 1 Cor. 14, 34 by itself and to see 1 Tim. 2, 12 as a later application—whether by Paul's secretary or by someone else does not matter—of the text of Corinthians. Of course there is the inclination to believe that Paul, treating the same material later on, has expressed more clearly in 1 Tim. what he really wished to say in 1 Cor. 14. But it is always better to look first at what he has actually said in 1 Cor. 14. Then later one can still turn to 1 Tim. to see whether it says the same thing, though more clearly, or something different.

The main concern of chapter 14 is that everything should happen in such a way as to build up the congregation πάντα πρὸς οἰχοδομὴν γινέσθω (v. 26; cf. 3, 4, 5, 12, 17); and for this it is necessary that "everything be done with propriety and order" (v. 40), "since God is not a God of disorder but of peace" (v. 33); that is, God is not to be found where irregularity and disorder are present.

When it is said in this context that the women should be silent (*taceant in ecclesia*)—just as it is said that those speaking in tongues should be silent in the assembly (*taceat in ecclesia*) if there is no interpreter present (v. 28), and that one person should be silent (*taceat*) if another is given a sudden revelation (v. 30)—then this commandment is certainly meant for other times and circumstances only if in these other circumstances it is also true that the speaking of women works against the "edification of the congregation"; it can be said with certitude to be Paul's wish that women of all times and places should be silent in the congregation only if it is established that the speaking of women at all times and places occurs in an improper manner. If the text of 1 Cor. 14 is to prove this thesis of the theologians, it must first be demonstrated that the speaking of women of itself deters the "edification of the congregation," that of itself it cannot take place "in order," and with "propriety."

The dominant concern in 1 Cor. 14 is not that of charisms in worship, but rather that of order in the service.[64] The commandment of silence for women stands in the same context as verses 26–33: one person may have a song of praise, another a piece of teaching, another a revelation. Not more than two, or at most three, should speak in tongues, and of course one at a time. The rule of silence for women thus should not be given any further, broader meaning either. Indeed both passages (the one cited above and the one on women) conclude with the same thoughts: "God is not a God of disorder," (v. 33), and "everything should be done with . . . order" (v. 40). And the same "subjection" is recommended for the prophets (ὑποτάσσεσθαι, v. 32) as for women (ὑποτάσσεσθαι, v. 34).

It must of course be admitted that vv. 34 f. *seem* to extend further than merely the protection of "edification" and "order." For Paul does argue in a rather general and abstract way. Women should subject themselves—not merely because they talk in a disorderly manner, but because the law speaks of it generally (Gen. 3, 16) and because it is in general indecorous for a woman to speak in a congregational assembly. However, as I shall later set forth, it is dangerous to depend on the Pauline *arguments* when trying to interpret his statements correctly.

Woman is not prevented from participating in the utterance of prophetic inspiration (what else could be possible in the light of Acts 2, 17?); she is commanded to submit herself to the order in the congregation. The meaning of verse 34 is that she must subject herself to an order, namely, the order of worship. What is not meant (at least not in this passage) is that she must subject herself to her husband, and still less that the female sex as such must subordinate itself to the male. "If the rules for propriety in 1 Cor. 11 were given for the woman active in worship, then the directives in 1 Cor. 14 are concerned with the woman who participates in worship in a passive manner, passive in the sense of nonprophesying." [65]

This explanation depends, apart from the context, also in part on the meaning of the word λαλεῖν in verse 34. If it means "to speak prophetically," then there would be another contradiction to chapter 11, and women would be completely prohibited from speaking. But that is not so certain. Investigation into the precise meanings of the words λαλεῖν and λέγειν and their relation to προφητεύειν has not yet been made, according to Else Kähler.[66] The pertinent articles in Kittel's *Theologisches Wörterbuch* also offer nothing decisive. Only one thing is certain: according to 1 Cor. 13, 11, and 1 Tim. 5, 13, λαλεῖν *can* in any case also mean speaking which is not Spirit-filled. If it is thus confirmed that Paul in 1 Cor. 11 does not forbid Spirit-filled speech to woman, indeed even supposes it is normal, assuming that she does it with feminine decorum, then a healthy exegesis commands us to understand λαλεῖν in our passage of 1 Cor. 14 as "the word used without the impulse of the Spirit." [67]

This interpretation in corroborated by verse 35: Paul forbids women to interrupt in order to ask about the meaning of a prophecy they did not understand. As no speaking in tongues is permitted without a translator (v. 28), as even a prophet must be silent if a revelation is imparted to another present (v. 30), so the woman must be silent if she wishes to speak in order to ask for *her own instruction.* For that does not contribute to the edification of the *congregation.* She may not take part in the subsequent detailed discussion of the prophetic declarations. Why? Here one can only say: because *de facto* it did not happen in a decorous manner, or because the women were too ignorant.

This same interpretation—that Paul does not intend to forbid all speech in the assembly to women—is also followed by Delling,[68] Kümmel,[69] Hick,[70] Tischleder,[71] H. Greeven,[72] Leenhardt,[73] each in his own manner and with his own reasons.

A few, such as Karl Barth,[74] Rondet,[75] and Refoulé,[76] have been of the opinion that the words "That which I write to you is a commandment of the Lord" (1 Cor. 14, 37) refer especially to the precepts relative to women. But this is very improbable; they refer to the entire pericope of verses 26–40, whose theme is order in the community. The section on woman is indeed somewhat of a parenthesis (this comes through much more clearly in the manuscripts which place it only after verse 40), or only one link in the entire chain of precepts.[77]

We may thus now say in summary that even this passage in the fourteenth chapter of the first letter to the Corinthians is not at all clear in forbidding women to speak in the congregation completely for all time. And the passage says nothing on instruction by women.

4. The Texts from 1 Tim. 2

The text which is clearest and also most useful for dogmatic theologians is undoubtedly 1 Tim. 2, 12. For this passage really says, "I permit no woman to teach." The syllogism then proceeds: but teaching is of the essence of the priesthood, therefore . . . ! It is also true that the authors who make a thorough study of this matter ultimately build their proof only on 1 Tim. 2. Hick, for example, concedes fully that no proof is to be found in 1 Cor. 14, but only in 1 Tim. 2.[78] And Daniélou, if one looks carefully, appeals only to 1 Tim. 2.[79]

I have already conjectured that 1 Tim. 2 does not express the same ideas as 1 Cor. 14, but rather presents a heightened further development.[80] In any case, teaching is here forbidden to women. In 1 Cor. the woman is seen as an independent person who may correctly take part in worship even in an active way, but who must also be able to be silent: most important, she should ask her husband at home about anything she has not understood. In 1 Tim. 2, on the other hand, the woman is seen solely as a learner; she is the object of instruction, which comes through the man. Keeping silence is not, as in 1 Cor. 14, only for special occasions, but a principle.[81]

Thus, although the other texts, as we have seen, are of no great significance for the thesis of the dogmatic theologians, this one does remain relevant. Are the theologians then correct in considering the problem settled once for all?

The immediate context suggests another idea. The verses immediately preceding, from which the thought proceeds to verse 12 without any break, says: "Similarly, I direct that women are to wear suitable clothes and to be dressed quietly and modestly, without braided hair or gold or jewelry or expensive clothes; their adornment is to do the sort of good works that are proper for women who profess to be religious. During instruction, a woman should be quiet and respectful" (vv. 9–11). Women thus should not pray adorned with gold and jewels or in expensive clothes! And the question then arises why this issue ought not be considered settled once for all. But where is a canon in the Code of Canon Law which enjoins *that* for our times? Of course popes and bishops urge simplicity and humility, but according to the text of the first letter to Timothy they ought to demand something more than this, perhaps in the spirit of Tertullian.[82] It would be most interesting to discover why later times have quietly let verse 9 gradually fall out of use and have held verse 12 in high honor. Does Paul not speak just as categorically in verse 9 as in verse 12?

If the dogmatic theologian now answers that the interpretation obviously proceeds from the very nature of the matter, then he is more than ever caught in a theological cul-de-sac. For in saying this, he implicitly admits that the real proof for his thesis is not the biblical text but proper knowledge of the nature of the matter. And his opponent can justifiably ask whence the theologian has obtained this knowledge, why he does not present the necessary new analysis, and also how he still dares to assert so loudly that the problem has been dispatched by Paul once for all.

For in this case he has himself dispatched it, and indeed—this much one must grant him—he can even produce a nice Pauline text to illustrate and supplement his explanation.

Several authors also concede this more or less, for example, Yves Congar, who says: "Be silent! One cannot say everything with these words of the Apostle." [83] This view is also found among Anglicans; M. E. Thrall, for example, alleges: "In the debate on the ministry of laywomen, the convocation of Canterbury was told, and, for the most part, apparently agreed, that the evidence of the Pauline passages in the New Testament was in itself inconclusive." [84]

Obviously the issue of the Church's right to ascribe various qualifications to the scriptural texts in reference to their binding character falls outside this discussion. Nor will this work raise the question of whether or not the *Church* can say that (a) a woman can never become a priest and (b) such an understanding should be deduced from 1 Tim. 2, 12. But the *theologians* have made the matter too easy for themselves when they hold that the question can be settled with the mere citation of this passage.

The pastoral epistles give very detailed directions, which flow from certain events that have actually occurred. The author was not thinking of us in writing the lines. And—it must be soberly acknowledged—the thinking of today's Church in many areas mentioned in the pastoral letters is very nuanced indeed. A few examples (besides verse 9) may suffice.

On the statement on what we today call an impediment to ordination—having married twice (3, 2)—the Church says that a consecration that has been imparted anyway would be valid. But the consecration of a woman would be invalid (and this because of 2, 12)! How do we conduct ourselves toward widows? Where are priests today still publicly reprimanded (5, 20)? Of course, the answer comes, that made sense at the time. But here we are once again in a blind alley. And what bishop would still write, "All slaves 'under the yoke' must have unqualified respect for their masters" (6, 1)? Nor do we keep in mind his other words: "Tell the slaves that they are to be obedient to their masters and always do what they want without any argument" (Tit. 2, 9).

No exegesis of the pastoral letters should lose sight of this conditioned, time-limited situation of the pertinent texts.

5. *Divine Law or Church Law in Scripture?*

To put it more precisely, dogmatic theologians have not yet got around to working out exhaustively the principles by which they qualify a few texts as "indispensable divine law" and others as mutable "church law." If that is true for many other scriptural proofs presented by theologians, it is especially true of the problem of the priesthood for women. Of course, even here it must be said that ultimately the Church decides upon these through the mouth of the magisterium. But the question is how the Church came to this perception. It must of course have had its reasons, more or less conscious and reflective. And it is precisely the task of theology to discover and to explain those reasons.

It might be asked, for example, on what basis F. Solá is really convinced that 1 Cor. 14 is concerned with a "divine law." Perhaps it is, but how and by what reasoning does he know? Why, for instance, does he not say that a woman should wear a veil at worship "by divine law"? Why does he not say on the basis of Romans 12, 4–8, and 1 Cor. 12, 4–30, that the gifts of the Spirit are distributed "by divine law" among various persons? He may of course maintain all that; but it is more than mere curiosity that makes me hope and expect that he as a theologian will make his reasons evident.

It appears, as will be shown in chapter 4, that on this matter there is no statement of the magisterium which is actually binding for our time. But whether or not this is true, there certainly does not now exist any adequate theological reflection pertinent to our problem. That, in any case, is what the present book is attempting to show.

Protestants too have been perplexed by the problem of whether a given text from Scripture asserts an "ecclasiastical law" or a "divine law." It would take us too far afield to go into that in detail. In Sweden, where the problem of female office bearers has called forth such great discussion, it has of course been treated specifically. Because these discussions are very instructive, I shall take a closer look at the detailed and important article by F. R. Refoulé, O.P.[85]

The Lutheran bishop J. Cullberg expressed it this way: Scripture gives witness to what God has wrought with man in and through Christ. These works of God are valid for all times, but they are accomplished in a certain moment of history, in a social, political, and religious situation which then existed but no longer does. It is not the mission of the Church to lead Christians back to the time of the Bible. But there follows the difficulty of stripping off these time-bound forms and at the same time taking care not thereby to adopt new time-bound interpretations as criteria.[86]

B. Gärtner points out that Paul himself joins to his precepts a substructure of principle: from the argumentation of the apostle, which is universally valid and thus not time-bound, it follows that he by no means considers the matter a concrete principle of order. There would thus already be a principle for the distinction of whether a certain text should be viewed as "ecclesiastical law" or "divine law," namely, the kind of reasoning used.[87] Such Swedish protagonists for the female priesthood as E. Sjoberg and K. Stendahl [88] also concede this. But they add that the question is still whether Paul was right. That seems to me, however, to be a questionable way to put the issue. It would be better to ask whether *we* are right in understanding Paul as saying that these regulations are just as valid for all time as for then. Stendahl himself makes another distinction between what is done out of principle and what is valid for all time. Thus, although Jesus deliberately preached only for the Jews and not for the Gentiles, that was not intended for all time. But this, in my opinion, gets us no further. Much, however, can be said about Paul's argumentation. In the following section we have used especially H. von Campenhausen's *Die Begründung kirchlicher Entscheidungen beim Apostel Paulus* ("The basis of ecclesiastical decisions for the apostle Paul"),[89] although we do not follow the author on all points.

First of all, Paul's argumentation is noteworthy. It breathes a rabbinic spirit, a rabbinic use of Scripture; it is, in my opinion, often inadequate and here and there not even feasible.

To stay with the passage under discussion: in 1 Cor. 11, 7–10, Paul's attempted basis for the custom suddenly takes no more notice of verse 3. Why does he suddenly abandon the idea? Merely in order to advance additional reasons? Why does he not complete the idea of verse 3? Verse 7 is quite remarkable in other respects. Paul appeals to Gen. 1, 27 (LXX): "God created man ($\tau \grave{o} \nu \ \ddot{a} \nu \theta \rho \omega \pi o \nu$) in the image of himself, in the image of God he created him," and to Gen. 5, 1 (LXX): "On the day God created Adam he made him in the likeness of God." But in doing this he makes the ἄνθρωπος simply equivalent to the male, and he takes "Adam" as the individual, as the man with the name Adam—although both times this ἄνθρωπος is more precisely characterized as "man and woman." Such an argument is not very feasible. And who among us would still say that a woman is not "the image of God"? There are passages in the writings of Pius XII in which he calls woman the image of God. Nor does the reasoning in verses 13 and 14—the appeal to custom and nature—provide any illumination. Who today can build his ideas on this? In many places it has been a long time since women have had to cover their heads in church. And how many Negro women simply cannot wear their hair long! The "teaching of nature" operating in those regions where women cannot wear their hair long really teaches us that Paul was limited by time and place.

Von Campenhausen says:

The rationale for this demand [of the veil] did not particularly please him. . . . The argumentative force of this combination [verses 3–10] probably did not satisfy him. So he appealed in a new attack to the natural feeling of decorum in his congregation [v. 13]. Here as so often the customary is declared the natural by Paul. . . . But when Paul heard the objections which were also raised against this argument, he broke the discussion off: It is not the custom with us. Driven into a tight spot, he then reveals the real motive, which was certainly the most strongly determining factor for him: The veiling of women at the liturgy is now the prevailing Christian custom, and it would result in a bad image if his Corinthians would be the single congregation to disregard it.[90]

The reasoning in 1 Cor. 14, 34 f. is also noteworthy: (a) "as in all the churches of the saints," (b) it is indecorous for a woman to speak in the assembly, (c) the appeal to the law. The first we have just seen in the quotation from von Campenhausen; the second is decidedly rabbinic and, moreover, known to the Greeks and Romans; [91] for the third, usually Gen. 3, 16 or Gen. 18, 12 is quoted. But in those texts speaking is not forbidden to women. Nor is Gen. 3, 16, a law (in the sense of "precept"), but an existing fact; the man lords it over his wife, and that is experienced by her as a punishment. If Gen. 3, 16, presented a basis on which to forbid women's (public) speaking, then the extremely conservative Dutch Calvinists would also have been correct in declaring on the basis of Gen. 3, 16, that the modern methods of painless childbirth are not permitted and in forbidding on the basis of Gen. 3, 17–19, any injection against disease (even among cattle)! It is better to see this as part of the rabbinic custom which designated even traditional customs as "Torah"—as Billerbeck has shown.[92] In this case Paul is appealing to something equally unenlightening: namely, the rabbinic mode of thought.

The same thing is true of the reasoning for 1 Tim. 2, 12–14. There the author of the letter to Timothy suddenly cites, onesidedly, the second report of creation. The contemporary exegete would say: Be careful, Holy Scripture in the text of Gen. 1, 27, and Gen. 5, 1, gives a theological correction to the one-sidedness of the Jahwist in the second chapter. In Gen. 1, 27, the man is no longer represented as the firstborn, from whom woman originates, being nothing but his bones; there man and woman stand on the same level, there both are also immediately the image of God.

Even stranger is the question of guilt in reference to original sin. The biblical report states quite clearly the shared guilt of Adam and Eve, while 1 Tim. 2, 14, has apparently attributed the sole guilt to the woman. Here the author of Timothy thinks in a totally rabbinic manner,[93] and in fact in a manner which we cannot accept, which Paul himself abandoned in Romans 5, and which—this is important—was also intentionally omitted by the Council of Trent.[94] If the reasoning of 1 Tim. 2, 14, were sound, one would have to deny the priesthood to males on the basis of Romans 5 and Trent. For Adam was also seduced. Sin came into the world through him! Paul's own assertion in Romans 5, which says that death came into the world through the sin of one person (Adam) is so much the more striking because there is not only in rabbinic literature but even in the Old Testament itself a tendency to ascribe the blame to the woman: Sirach 25, 24 (Vulgate 25, 33): "Sin began with a woman, and thanks to her we all must die." Paul is thus, in Romans 5, led in the other direction, and the Church has followed him. It seems therefore quite justifiable not to lay too much importance on the passage from Timothy. The author is attempting to prove something, and seizes, so to speak, on second-class material for his argumentation.

Secondly, Paul argues just as much on principle in those prescripts which we designate *ivs ecclesiasticum*. This is seen, for example, in his reasoning on the prohibition against two broth-ers' going before a non-Christian judge when they have a legal battle (1 Cor. 6) or in the prohibition of social contact with fallen brethren (1 Cor. 5). Both examples will be discussed in detail below.

We must conclude that we shall not get much further by reference to Paul's argumentation. Practical decisions and trans-actions, which in concrete situations are necessary for the sake of good order or brotherly love, or for pastoral reasons, but which in other situations may very well be decided in another way, even for the sake of good order, are supported by Paul with apparently quite basic arguments as if he were deciding some-thing connected with the inalterable essence of Christianity.

Von Campenhausen expresses it this way:

> The argumentation of almost every one of our examples rests on an emphatic and appealing salient, key idea which immediately accounts for and supports the demand arising from it. . . . Everything that Paul desires, requires, and recommends by way of definite order and lawful regulation in the congregation is to be understood as a necessary expression, as a development and protection, of that which is directly connected with the essentially new state of being, with the reality of the Church and the Christian situation of each individual Christian.[95]

This would mean that the style of argumentation can scarcely be a decisive principle in determining whether a certain scrip-tural passage contains "divine law" or "ecclesiastical law."

A further criterion was raised on the Swedish side: "divine law" refers to that which is bound together inseparably with the basic message of Christianity: i.e., justification through faith. Scripture, if it is taken formally, is no life norm. The teaching of *sola scriptura* (the formal principle of the Reformed faith) does not stand merely *alongside* the teaching of *sola fide* (the material principle of the Reformed faith). The message of Scripture and its binding precepts are not to be sought in the individual verses, but only in the basic message. The Bible is not a collection of individual precepts.[96]

As this view is not novel, one further quotation is sufficient to elucidate the idea. K. H. Steck said in his inaugural lecture (Uni-versity of Frankfurt on the Main, 1954):

One should also apply the critical method to the Bible for the sake of the fundamental revelation that was delivered. Applying the critical method to the Bible therefore means dealing with the letter which ultimately is shaped by the expectation and promise of the spirit, not in a mechanical obedience to the letter, which of course leads to death, i.e., to a non-understanding, but rather in an obedience which permits the Spirit of God to be and to become the master of the letter.[97]

Except for the incompleteness in the presentation of the actual fundamental message of Christianity, this view is not as "liberal" as it appears to be. To try to read many precepts, rules, and such into the Scriptures actually makes the gospel into a law again. In the light of the letters to the Romans and Galatians, that could not possibly have been Paul's intention. Then the mentality of "Do not handle, do not taste, do not touch" (Col. 2, 21) would return, as if that could save us; whereas all is decreed only by love (cf. Rom. 14; 1 Cor. 8; 1 Cor. 10).[98]

Barth, too, once spoke along these lines, although he is otherwise against the admission of women to office; in a discussion in Amsterdam (1948) he declared: "Without doubt, service in the church is also imposed on women. That can be denied in principle only with the aid of a legalist interpretation of Paul." [99]

If this is correct, it is also the task of dogmatic theologians to demonstrate how the prohibition of a female priesthood fits with the fundamental message of Christianity, or—let us avoid any echo of the "teaching of salvation by faith alone"—with the essence of the Church. Single texts cannot decide such a thing. To do otherwise would be to act like a person saying: Paul thinks that it is better "to eat no meat, to drink no wine" (Rom. 14, 21a). In this case it is obvious that the text is wrenched out of context, for the verse continues, "if your brother is offended at it" (Rom. 14, 21b).

Swedish theologians suggest still another possible criterion. Only those instructions to which a promise is linked are binding for all times.[100] It is not, however, completely clear how one should operate with this principle, which is also rejected by Lutherans with good arguments.[101]

Refoulé himself says to all this that one must not seek one universal principle to determine whether precepts of the New Testament are valid for all time or not. Rather, the burden of proof lies upon the other side: in each case the individual text should be investigated, and only when it is perfectly clear that something was intended only for certain circumstances may it now be set aside; otherwise it should be obeyed. And the fact that a precept may not be linked essentially with salvation does not alter its validity. Obedience to God should be unconditional.[102] This last statement is certainly true; the question is only whether God does command something, and especially how we can know that he has commanded it!

6. *Quaedam capitula*

There is another important consideration concerning the conclusiveness of the Pauline text. With the same force of argumentation as is used in discussing the theses on women priests, texts from Paul (as well as from old synods and also from the Fathers —this last is important because writers consider the correctness of their own interpretation of Pauline texts confirmed by these later sources) can be used to furnish proof that:

(a) One should have no contact with brethren who have fallen from the faith. The text (1 Cor. 5, 9–13) offers no special difficulties, although one might ask himself whether the word συνεσθίειν (to associate with) in 5, 11 is to be understood eucharistically. In that case the prohibition would still be valid. The only other occurrences of the word in the New Testament are in Luke 15, 2; Acts 11, 3; Acts 10, 41, and Gal. 2, 12. Of these passages only in Acts 10, 41, and even here in a manner to some extent forced, does it refer to a Eucharistic meal: in all other texts it means simply "to eat together" in the usual sense. H. von Campenhausen believes that in forbidding this Paul was not thinking of occasional contacts in worldly business, but of the life of the congregation.[103] That may well be. But Paul forbids not only the Eucharistic rite, which according to 1 Cor. 11, 23 ff., took place after the congregational meal, but even this meal itself. And later tradition interpreted the text even more strictly.

Ambrosiaster, for example, says: "He teaches not only the illicitness of the Eucharistic meal, but of the common meal altogether." [104] Cyprian says, "One should not speak with heretics." [105] The Statutes of the Ancient Church say: "Let him who will have communicated or prayed with one who is excommunicated be excommunicated, whether he be cleric or lay." [106] Leclercq notes on this: "It is clear that the two terms *communicare* and *orare* are not synonyms. The first concerns ordinary life." [107] The same prohibition is found in Toledo I (400) [108] and in Tours

(461).[109] And the severe medieval practice of "shunning the ex-communicated" is well-known.

It is interesting that Ambrosiaster and the Statutes of the Ancient Church are among the chief witnesses customarily summoned by dogmatic theologians to prove their thesis. Yet the latter hold that the precept of avoiding the fallen brethren is valid only as "ecclesiastical law"—for association with an apostate would constitute a danger to one's own faith. But then they should also have to prove that a woman priest would be an analogous danger.

(b) It could likewise be proved that in case of a civil lawsuit with a brother one may not go to a Gentile judge (1 Cor. 6, 1–11). This passage does not refer exclusively to what now falls within the competence of ecclesiastical jurisdiction, for Paul speaks precisely of ἐλαχίστων (v. 2) and of βιωτκά (v. 3, 4). Lukas Vischer, who has made an in-depth study of this passage, speaks of "little everyday matters, things of ordinary life, property transactions, etc." [110]

This prohibition was also taken very seriously in the first centuries. There is an abundance of passages on this matter incomparably richer than that which the dogmatic theologians can pull together for their thesis on woman. Vischer has collected the passages; it is not necessary to quote them all here—besides, it would be simply impossible.[111] Even the chief witnesses of the dogmatic theologians—Ambrosiaster, the Didascalia, Origen, Augustine—put in an appearance. Only Epiphanius is missing. We will cite only one passage, that from Cyprian. Under the heading "Several chapters on the religious order of our community" (Quaedam capitula ad religiosam sectae nostrae disciplinam pertinentia) there appear (we mention those which are relevant in our context): [112]

Chap. 44: do not go to a Gentile judge
Chap. 46: woman should be silent
Chap. 48: ask no interest on money
Chap. 72: believing slaves should serve their earthly masters still more industriously
Chap. 78: one should not speak with heretics.

All these "chapters" have been forgotten in the course of time—except the one on women. Can it be excessive then to expect an extremely tightly-reasoned demonstration for this exception?

Vischer brought up no synods. Nevertheless there are many

which could be cited: the Statutes of the Ancient Church,[113] the Irish synods under Patrick,[114] the Council of Seville of Pseudo-Isidor,[115] etc.

(c) Doubtless one could search through the old literature in reference to many other precepts of Paul with the same result, perhaps on the prohibition against wearing gold and pearls at Mass (1 Tim. 3, 2), which was taken quite seriously by, for example, Epiphanius. He is fully as convinced and articulate on this point as he is on the question of the priesthood for women.[116]

All these regulations were considered valid for several centuries in just as principled a way as the exclusion of woman from office. The proofs are just as correct in a formally and technically theological way as those on the priesthood for woman. Nevertheless these prohibitions are shrunken to marginal phenomena in ecclesiastical life or are considered "dispensable ecclesiastical law." The single difference between these proofs and those for our question is that there are texts on our problem which extend even up to the present. But do a few centuries more determine so much? The thesis of the "Creation of mankind from the dust of the earth," the literal creation of Eve from the rib, etc., can also be illustrated with texts from many centuries. That the sinner can be reconciled only once was also taught for six or seven centuries.

7. *The Same Subject?*

There arises from this another completely different question. Within the framework of this book it can merely be asked, and not answered. But it seems clear to me that it must be raised. It is this: may it without closer analysis be simply assumed that all these texts which even up to the present century make assertions about woman are treating the same subject as we when we speak of woman? To put it another way: does not perhaps every syllogistic proof that a woman cannot be a priest, as soon as this proof is adduced with the help of texts from Paul, from old synods, and from the Fathers, contain four terms? Could not an opponent justly again place the proof in question by making the distinction: for "the woman of that day" I concede; for "the woman of today" I demand proof? In other words is it already demonstrated that the old assertions communicate something concerning the inalterable essence of woman and not merely concerning her sociologically conditioned place or the time-conditioned appraisal of woman? That the latter has basically changed in recent times demands no separate demonstration. And in the course of this work I shall cite many judgments on woman from earlier times which seem to me to be no longer obvious at all.

Theology, in this case moral theology, has suffered once before by not recognizing such a change at the proper time—on the question of interest. After the economic function of money and its temporally conditioned place had already shifted, moral theology still remained inflexible in its prohibition of any charging of interest by appealing to scriptural texts and other newer and older documents. It was not seen that these texts did indeed use the same words—money, capital, and so on—but actually alluded to something quite different. The very danger that something similar could occur in our problem would obligate us to investigate the texts in a much wider context.

Another development in theology also suggests the need for greater caution. We refer to the newer views on natural law. To what extent is the natural law catalogable? Certainly many such individual material norms can be derived from transcendental deduction—but does that include the role of woman? Relevant to this problem are the early contributions of F. Böckle in *Fragen der Theologie heute* (*Questions of Theology Today*) and several articles by Karl Rahner in *Orientierung*.[117] The understanding of natural law seems to vary. Has only the insight into what natural law signifies changed, while man (the source of the material statements of natural law) himself has remained the same? Or has man changed along with his insight? Much more remains unclarified: What is the connection between nature and history? Did significant changes, such as we indicated above in reference to money, occur in man as well? Is, for example, the customary solution to the problem of polygamy in the Old Testament—a dispensation permitted by God—correct, or was man really different then?

One must at least agree with Karl Rahner:

The higher a being, the more significant its act . . . for it and its essence, and the more the act becomes the perfection of being. And if then this being is nevertheless historical and temporal, so much the more does it experience itself only through the history it undergoes; only in a historically real fulfillment does it measure off the boundaries of its potentialities which would otherwise remain concealed from itself. . . . [One] must

. . . reckon with the possibility that . . . even the image of one's own being in one's own reflective recognition might be so disturbed [by the demonic], that the person, and even the Christian, does not perceive from his own essence and natural law that which he must really perceive. Or can it not be said that Christianity has not a few times failed in practice to derive from human nature human affirmations which it should have derived? Friedrich Spee, in any case, has admitted that freely. Proceeding from there, an attempt could be made to write a history of the concept of natural law in Christianity.[118]

Because there is much still to be clarified in this respect, one may not immediately assert that woman too has now become a different subject. One should also reckon with the possibility that our time likewise is not right on target in the judgment of what woman is (and what man is). Perhaps we too exaggerate when we believe that certain things which are now permitted to women (and to men) are not against nature—an occasion for further investigations.

8. *The Subjection of Woman*

So there arises once again the question of the Pauline assertions concerning the subjection of woman to her husband or to man in general. There is no doubt that Paul wishes to see woman subject to her spouse. There is no purpose in twisting his words on the subordination of woman so that ultimately an equality appears.[119] The equality should not be sought in institutional things; it comes from the *agape*, through which the man makes himself the servant of the woman.[120] Else Kähler in her detailed investigations of the concept ὑποτάσσεσθαι brings in the necessary corrections, but ultimately—after the elimination of the implication of passive obedience and after the explanation that we are concerned with a mutual subordination because Christ, although Lord, is at the same time also the servant—there does remain the subordination by a voluntary decision under God's plan of salvation and order and in that framework under the husband.[121] Schlier's commentary on Ephesians contains the same view [122] and, indeed, still more pointedly than Kähler, who cannot entirely accept his ideas.

Many think that with the headship, with the superior position of man, there comes simultaneously the exclusion of woman from office—for example, St. Thomas.[123] The question is whether that is so certain. For (a) is this a matter of the subjection of the married woman or of the subjection of woman in general? And if it concerns woman in general, would that be relevant to our thesis? Indeed subjects can become even bishops over their princes and president! [124] And (b) is that valid for all times and circumstances?

Ephesians 5—which is the chief evidence for the subjection of woman—is concerned with the relationship of husband and wife, as Schlier says: "ἴδιος often indicates the possessive likewise, v. 28 states: 'τὰς ἑαυτῶν γυναῖκας.'" [125]

And further: "This passage concerns not man and woman as classes, as it is sometimes interpreted, but rather the individual man and the individual woman in the situation of their marriage." [126]

But we may not quote Schlier in this regard as witness, for he is of the opinion that this is valid merely for Ephesians 5. According to him, 1 Cor. 11, 3 ff. teaches a universal subjection of woman:

The man is according to Ephesians 5 the head of his wife. That follows naturally from the evidence which Paul mentions in 1 Cor. 11, 3 ff. in reference to man and woman in general. The man is (born) "through" the woman, the woman is (taken) "out of" the man. The one signifies the historical relationship, the other the real essence. . . . This apostolic opinion that such a ranking of man and woman is founded in creation and their marital ranking is based in the mystery of creation is of course contested, and it is argued that it could change with the current image of man of that time and area. What can change in accordance with the current spirit and understanding of the time is merely the form of the appearance of mankind, and even that only by a comparatively slight further development.[127]

According to Schlier, then, both the above questions should be answered in the affirmative: the subjection of woman to man is valid for man and woman as a class, and it is valid for all time. Thomas and with him almost all authors proceed from the same presuppositions.

Several questions yet remain open, however. First of all it still does not seem to me to be very clear that this contains any implications for the priesthood of women, as already amplified above. Later on, in chapters III and V, I shall go more closely into the question of how far one can say with a few Fathers and

Thomas that in certain circumstances (for example, through monastic vows) woman loses the "defect" of womanhood and is made equal to man. And I shall there raise the question of whether one can perhaps say that just as a slave in ancient church law became a freeman through the fact of ordination, so too woman through an eventual ordination would also no longer remain "in the state of subjection." Secondly there are already serious Catholic writers who believe it can be asserted that this condition of woman was only time-bound and is now outmoded. So, for example, V. Heylen writes: "It is true that he [Paul] occasionally demands from the woman submission before the man, but these are prescriptions inspired by the circumstances and the customs of the moment." [128]

And thirdly we are not entirely convinced that Paul in 1 Cor. 11 is suddenly considering man and woman as a class. Does not the question of man and woman as unmarried lie outside his field of vision? [129] Kähler argues for 1 Cor. 11 that Paul meant here an actual subjection of woman, and her arguments are worth noting.[130] One might consider what consequences that would have! It would mean that woman could not be a leader even in the secular area. Schlier would base his interpretation on creation.

With this we arrive at the second presupposition. For if it also be true (and this is not conceded) that Paul in 1 Cor. 11 wishes to subordinate women as a group, is what he said still valid for women of our time? Schlier believes the question must be answered in the affirmative. But will he then wish to exclude woman from secular office? He must say with Thomas and Aristotle: "When a woman attains command, a corruption of urbanity occurs" (corruptio urbanitas est quando ad mulierem dominium pervenit).[131]

We thus confront the question of whether Paul's views on the subordination of woman are valid for all times. Schlier believes that they are because they are founded in the mystery of creation. We have already spoken of the questionability of Pauline argumentation: he bases something which is time-bound in the order of creation. Equally moot is the question to what extent one can discover in Scripture in general a supertemporal *jus divinum*, as well as the question to what extent there is an unalterable feminine nature or to what extent each age can have a total picture of it. All these questions return here. We must look still farther.

9. Surmounted and Canonized Rabbinism

One cannot avoid concurring in great part with the authors who attribute to Paul a rabbinic interpretation of woman.[132] E. Kähler has, it is true, rectified much, but one certainly cannot deny the matter completely. (At most it could be added that these concepts were not exclusively rabbinic and that other, Hellenic influences also had an effect on Paul.) It seems important to me to investigate in which passages Paul speaks rabbinically. And it will be in the spirit of the Constitution on Revelation of Vatican II to say that here and there Paul is rabbinic and he speaks differently than in other places. If we find other understandings of woman in other passages in Scripture in general, or even in Paul himself, may we not then think that, in those texts which are less illuminating for us, he is perhaps speaking more directly from his rabbinically influenced situation?

Rondet says:

Paul accents more than is just the submission of the woman to her husband. Elsewhere to justify the silencing of woman in the church he recalls that Eve was not created first and that it was she who let herself be seduced. These ideas seem to bear the mark of the spirit of the Old Testament, and one is right to correct them by the other statements of the Apostle.[133]

Perhaps it is not actually Paul who needs correcting but rather our understanding of his texts. Perhaps it is merely necessary to realize that he is speaking of woman in a rabbinic manner only in the places where he *should* accommodate himself to the existing custom.

First I shall substantiate my assertion that Paul thinks of woman rabbinically. Then I shall show whether and when he himself has gone beyond this understanding.

At the beginning of this chapter the rabbinic background of the statement "Let the women be silent in the congregation" was shown. In the synagogue a woman could neither read aloud nor speak, expound, or teach. Indeed, she could not even study the Torah. She should and could bear no witness; her words were not considered trustworthy.[134] Besides, a woman's voice was accounted shameful (obscene),[135] and could thus not be tolerated in public. Behind 1 Cor. 14, 35 (to ask the man for instruction at home) stands the same precept from the rabbinic tradition.[136] The reasoning in 1 Cor. 11 and 1 Tim. 2 (the story of creation)

and 1 Tim. 2 (the Fall and seduction of woman) are likewise the rabbinic demonstration for the second-class status of
woman.[137] Eve should cover her head (cf. the veil of 1 Cor. 11),
because she must mourn on account of her sin.[138] Delling has
referred to the attempts of later Judaism to reinterpret everything in the Old Testament which gave evidence of the cultic
activity of woman. There are two reports in the Old Testament
of women "doing service" at the entrance of the tabernacle; in the
one passage the Septuagint alters it to "fasted," in the other it
simply struck it out. (Ex. 38, 8; Sm. 2, 22).[139] We have already
seen how knowledge of the Torah, which in Deut. 31, 12 and
Neh. 8, 2 f. is demanded of the woman, is described by the
rabbis as an occasion of debauchery for her; Oepke demonstrates
that later Judaism brought more retrogression than progress in
reference to woman. At the time of Jesus especially the situation
of woman was quite bad.[140] Flavius Josephus expressed the ideas
of his time correctly when he said: "The woman is in every respect less than the man." [141] Thus, if we seek the background of
Pauline thought on the position of woman, we find it here.

The following statement of Kosmala is also important:

As an example to weaken the basically negative attitude of
the rabbis toward women, Beruria, the wife of Rabbi Meir, is
continually named. But she has not been the ideal of the Jewish
wife to the rabbis. In later times a shameful story was told
of her to annihilate her moral reputation completely.

The story is, as far as Kosmala knows, nowhere translated. He
gives the translation and adds:

The story is not very probable and apparently invented only
ad hoc. That it was told, however, shows that a woman of
Beruria's cast has no place in rabbinic thought. She is in every
respect the exception which proves the rule.[142]

The great women of the Old Testament are often referred to:
Rachab the whore, Judith, Esther, and so on. But were they
really women? Or were they praised merely because, although
women, they nevertheless did men's work? For Judith this is
certainly clear. And Scripture itself praises the mother of the
seven Maccabee brothers because she "reinforced her womanly
argument with manly courage" (Macc. 7, 21).

Up to now no one has alluded (says Kosmala) to the fact that
all favorable expressions of opinion—that one should for example

esteem, love, honor, and not grieve his wife [143]—refer exclusively
to the married woman, not simply to woman. Of course the married woman shares the generally negative evaluation of woman,
in the religious sphere especially, for the married woman also
shares the natural station of her unmarried sisters. Nevertheless,
the married woman has a special position in contrast to the
single woman. For she is no longer merely a female human, but
the legitimate wife of an Israelite man. She actually makes the
man a full citizen in the Jewish religious community. She is the
mother of his children, she is "his house." She occupies this position even if she is not a good wife. But if she is a good wife, the
Haggadah bestows unstinting praise on her: she is her husband's
riches, his crown, his jewels, etc. The good wife—this we must
note—receives her honors only with express relation to her spouse
and lord. Of herself the woman is nothing. The statement that
the woman enriches the man as a jewel cannot be reversed.[144]

That seems to me to be the background of the Pauline assertions in 1 Cor. 11: "A man should certainly not cover his head,
since he is the image of God and reflects God's glory; but woman
is the reflection of man's glory. . . . Man was not created for
the sake of woman, but woman was created for the sake of
man." Also one must immediately think of Ephesians 5: "The husband is the head of the wife, as Christ is the head of the
Church." Paul could speak in this way from his own background:
the woman was in truth the *house* of the man.[145] The expression
"head of the woman" is more easily understood in this context.
Head of the woman then means head of the house or of the
family. The point can be further developed. For the rabbis the
concept "woman" included at the same time the children born of
her and those to be born; the woman was in herself the essence
of the family. That may have been the case in that time, for
there were scarcely any unmarried women, and the married
women had no other goal than just to be good mothers to the
family.

But one wonders whether all this really describes the nature of
woman, as Schlier feels. Is our time so unchristian in thinking that
a woman (yes, even a married woman) is more than merely a
mother? May one not think that Paul in 1 Cor. 11 and Eph. 5
spoke only of one limited, though obviously true, aspect of
woman, namely of her role as member of the family? It is not the
intention of this work to question the position of the husband as

head of the family and thus also as head of the wife *insofar* as she is precisely a member of the family community. But is not the woman more, outside marriage and even within it? If that is true, the Pauline assertions in 1 Cor. 11 and Eph. 5 would be no point of departure for a total theology of woman, but at most only for a theology of woman insofar as she is a member of the family.

Did Paul not know that a woman is more than that? Or did he correct himself in other passages, namely, those where he did not speak in a concrete manner? To discover that, we must first listen to still another rabbinic statement in reference to woman.

The Jew was (and is) obligated to say daily three prescribed benedictions. The Jew should praise God that he has not made him (a) a Gentile (b) a woman (c) an ignoramus.[146] The basis of this is the following: (a) according to Is. 40, 17 all Gentiles are as nothing before God; (b) no commandments are enjoined on the woman (in the newer prayer books the woman should say in the second passage "that you have created me according to your pleasure"); (c) the ignoramus has no fear of sin.[147] The ignoramus, however, can become knowledgeable through the study of the Torah. Therefore Rabbi Akiba (who came from the family of an Am-ha-arez—an unknowing, or ignoramus) recommends saying "that you have not made me a slave." To this another rabbi responds that the mention of the slave is not necessary, for in reference to the religious rank the slave stands precisely on the same level as the woman. The answer was given him: "The slave (is differentiated nevertheless from the woman for he) is more to be despised." The Gentile, the woman and the slave thus are of lesser religious value; they do not stand in the same divine community as man, and this of course is a result of their station, not merely of their concrete conduct. Only the free Israelite man is, by virtue of his being a son of Abraham (by virtue of his circumcision), participant in this convenantal community.[148]

Now Gal. 3, 28 f. is clearer to us: "There are no more distinctions between Jew and Greek, slave and free, male and female, but all of you are *one* in Christ Jesus. Merely by belonging to Christ you are the posterity of Abraham, the heirs he was promised."

Galatians 3 treats of the relapse into the belief that being a son of Abraham and fulfilling the law are still necessary or mandatory for salvation. Paul here issues a reprimand and in conclusion expresses the new belief in a statement which obviously has its origin in the old, familiar Jewish formula.

Obviously this passage is not directly relevant to our discussion of woman in office, for it concerns salvation and not salvation-service; and it is (as Schlier says in his commentary on Galatians) founded on the fact of baptism, while office proceeds from its own mission.[149] But Gal. 3, 28 does show us how very true it is that Paul himself in principle—in other illuminating passages—transcends the rabbinic assertions on women. This passage from Gal. 3 shows us how unjustified it is to appeal to 1 Cor. 11 and Eph. 5 for a theology of the sexes.

Certainly Oepke is correct in emphasizing that the removal of the distinction (in Gal. 3) should be understood in the light of the new era,[150] and that it therefore does not press for practical consequences of a revolutionary sort. The same is true of von Allmen, where he says: "One does Paul an injustice when one believes it possible to infer from Gal. 3, 28, a notion of political and social egalitarianism of the sexes. That text is an eschatological statement." [151]

But how the text could have no consequences at all for this world is not comprehensible to me. Certainly Christianity has not explicitly wished revolution (slaves, women), but the utterances of Oepke and von Allmen breathe, in my opinion, a too eschatological mentality. The new era, much as it is still also to come, nevertheless is already begun!

Therefore we may conclude some things in Paul certainly point to an apparent canonization of rabbinism. But the question is: What precisely does he canonize? Not the interpretation that the woman is a member of the convenantal people only through the medium of her husband. Thus he rejects the fundamental rabbinic principle relating to woman. But he has no intention of changing what at that time could be changed only with disruption of good order. Perhaps he never saw that such a social change ought to come. What he says is that the distinction between man and woman no longer has significance in Christ; we would say that from a "religious" perspective it no longer has significance. The alteration of the social structure does not lie within his field of vision; the world had already settled that. Rather, one gets the impression that Paul reacted against those who too freely misused the changes of meaning in religion (cf. 1 Cor.).

Already in the gospel it is clear that Christianity rejects the system of the rabbinic concept of woman in its entirety. It is not necessary here to point out the various aspects: polygamy, the bill of divorce, etc.[152] But even in Paul it can be seen particularly in those places where he is not speaking in exhortation, and thus does not need to be concerned with the existing circumstances but stands in the center of the Christian message of salvation, as in Gal. 3, 28. But it is not only in the letter to the Galatians. He recognizes prophesying women; that too is rabbinism transcended. He also recognizes in 1 Cor. 7 the woman who can abandon her husband, which is an almost impossible idea for a rabbi.[153] And the relegation of the woman to the household sphere, which we read in 1 Tim. 2, is transcended by the frequent mention of feminine activity in the congregation. In Rom. 16, 3, Prisca is given the same title as Timothy in verse 21: fellow worker! Rom. 16 mentions nine women among twenty-nine persons. Daniélou notes of this:

> The terms which he [Paul] employs are important to note. He names [Rom. 16] first of all Phoebe, our sister, who is a servant (διάκονος) of the church of Cenchreae. She has been a support (προστάτις) for me and for many. Greet Prisca and Aquila who are my coworkers (συνεργούς) in Christ Jesus. . . . Greet Mary who has worked (ἐκοπίασεν) hard for us. . . . Greet Tryphoena, Tryphosa and Persis who have worked (κοπιᾶν) in the Lord. In the epistle to the Philippians it is a question of Evodia and Syntyche who struggled along with me in the Gospel (ἐν τῷ εὐαγγελίῳ).[154]

All this is so, not because these women had entertained the male preachers as guests in their homes so well or something of that sort; and also not merely "because they have children," which according to 1 Tim. 2, 15 is the way for women to become blessed.

Leenhardt is right in saying:

> So much is certain, that we could not find such a large number of women who were connected with his apostolic office if he basically were as determined as he is described to be that the woman must be silent in the Church and that she is to be relegated to the circle of her household duties and family tasks.[155]

We may really infer from this that Paul himself in many places overcame his "rabbinism" in reference to woman except, perhaps, in the passages where he speaks of woman in household and in church life (in any case in 1 Tim. 2). Why is that, and is the distinction valid for us? May we say on the basis of the other passages that Paul himself knew better and that he only accommodated himself on account of the temporal circumstances?

Perhaps we may suggest the following hypothesis. The primitive congregation confronted the task of ordering the religious community. There were models; the Christian congregations formed themselves mostly in connection with Jewish and Jewish-proselytizing circles. But not only was a form of organization taken over with the models, but in some cases perhaps also the attitude on which this order was based. Tendencies toward innovation were certainly there, and Paul himself had not forbidden such things as the prophesying of women. But the development of a radically new social and sexual teaching and practice (slaves!) did not occur then.[156]

To the question of whether this attitude toward women should be determinative for us, the answer in this case is clear. Paul's regulations are to a certain extent a regression to rabbinic Judaism, which is so much the more easily comprehensible because the primitive community wished no revolution, in any case not in the social area. And office is a social function in Christianity! On the matter of salvation the correct concept of woman was clearly comprehended. On the matter of salvation-service, thus in the external-juridical-sociological aspects, existing sociological structures were accommodated to, just as had been done in reference to the sociological phenomenon of slavery. How could it be otherwise? Moreover, was not the Second Coming of Christ in his glory near, and would not a new order begin then?

One would like to think that the new order is already in process; it comes through more and more in this age. The eschatological word (Oepke) of Gal. 3, 28, is already true. Should not then the sociological structure of the Church also be altered as soon as it is possible in the concrete situation? To those to whom this seems to be true, it would have to be incontestably shown that God has willed it otherwise, that is, it would have to be demonstrated either that today's secular development is a false development, or that the matter is different in the religious sphere than in the secular.

But the mere citation of scriptural passages, as we have seen in this chapter, does not further the argument significantly.

III   The Church Fathers

The texts from the Fathers are, without exception, quite uni-
vocal on the question of whether a woman *may* be a priest. A
woman may not be a priest. But on the question of whether she
can be ordained—that is, on the "validity"—there was no speculation. Among the Fathers the universal view prevailed that Paul
forbade it once for all time and that, moreover, according to the
Divine Will, woman should occupy an inferior role. She is already by her nature, but even more by the Fall, unfitted for a
leading role in the Church and in secular society. If it were permitted for a woman to baptize and to preach, then Jesus and the
apostles would certainly have sent women forth, for there were
so many good and holy women in their midst, and so forth. In
brief: the Fathers reject the idea that a woman is capable of
holding an office almost as if this were an atrocity.

Yet immediately several things must be added. The fullness of
texts is not as great as might be expected.[1] Montanism as well as
Priscillianism in Spain recognized women as priests. Despite this,
one finds, for example, in P. de Labriolle's book *Les sources de
l'histoire du Montanisme,*[2] in which various texts relating to
Montanism have been collected, only 9 out of 229 items which
explicitly go into the woman question. That could of course mean
that, even right after the death of the Montanist prophetesses
Maximilla and Priscilla, the problem was no longer a real one.
But from the statements of someone like Epiphanius of Salamis
(c. 375) one rather gets the opposite impression; [3] he is too vehement in his rejection for this. However, the Synod of Constantinople in 482, which still treated Montanism as an existing movement, apparently found other controversies far more important,
such as whether and how "the Montanists, who are called Phry-

gians," should be rebaptized if they convert to orthodoxy.[4] Thus it must not be assumed that just about all the Fathers spoke out against the priesthood of women. There are but relatively few passages on the subject, and these were mostly in commentaries on the letters of Paul or as a reaction against the heretics.

The texts which are cited again and again are the same for all authors: Epiphanius, the *Didascalia,* Tertullian, Ambrosiaster—occasionally Irenaeus and Augustine.[5]

Because many of these texts occur in a very defined context which is not always taken into proper consideration, I shall sometimes have to be very detailed in my citations. The passages themselves are very clearly against a female priesthood—this neither can nor may be denied—but when cited in context they often lose their harshness.

1. The Decisive Texts

Epiphanius of Salamis is without doubt by far the most important witness. He makes a distinction between the Montanists and the Pepuzians or Quintillians or (Cata-)Phrygians. In reality, however, these are all the same heretics. Thus I cite the relevant texts without distinction.

He confirms that these heretics permit women "to be leaders and priests." [6] Speaking of the Montanist prophetesses Maximilla and Priscilla, he especially reproaches Maximilla for asserting that she was the last prophetess.[7] He tells of the Phrygians that they ascribed to Eve a special grace because she was the first to eat from the Tree of Knowledge; they call Miriam, the sister of Moses, a prophetess as a precedent for their own women clergy. The same is said of the daughters of the deacon Philip. Among these heretics women are bishops, presbyters, and so on. For, they say, there is no difference between man and woman, and on this point they cite Gal. 3, 28. Epiphanius however refutes them with the following texts: Gen. 3, 16; 1 Cor. 14, 34; 1 Cor. 11, 8; and 1 Tim. 2, 14.[8] Contrary to the heretics, who repudiate the gospel according to John and the Apocalypse, he demonstrates that the Apocalypse is certainly a part of Holy Scriptures, for an authentic prophesy can be found within it, namely, concerning Thyatira: "Nevertheless, I have a complaint to make: you are encouraging the woman Jezebel who claims to be a prophetess, and by her teaching she is luring my servants away" (Ap. 2, 20). This prophecy, Epiphanius says, refers to the prophetesses Maximilla and Priscilla, who later actually did appear.[9]

The locus classicus, however, comes from *Adversus Collyridianos*. After Epiphanius has written against the Antidicomarianites, who do not honor Mary sufficiently, he turns his attention to a group who show Mary divine honor. Who perpetrates this disorder? Who else but women! "For the female sex is easily seduced, weak, and without much understanding. The devil seems to vomit out this disorder through women." Among other things they offer bread "to the name of Mary." He begins his refutation like this: "We wish to apply masculine reasoning and destroy the folly of these women." Never from eternity forward has a woman occupied the priestly office. Not even Eve, who of course committed the transgression, attempted *this*, nor did her daughters. Then follows a long list of male priests from the Old Testament, "and nowhere did a woman serve as priest." Moving to the New Testament, he immediately starts out: If God had enjoined the priesthood or "the administration of any kind of office" in the Church on women, then Mary would have had to be a priest. "But He did not will it."

Even baptism was not entrusted to her; for in that case Christ could better have been baptized by her than by John. Then follows a long list of apostles and bishops: "And nowhere is a woman introduced among them." Philip of course had four daughters who were prophetesses, but they were not priests. Likewise Anna was not a priest, but a prophetess, for Joel 2 must be fulfilled. There are deaconesses in the church, though not to fulfill sacerdotal functions but for the sake of propriety in baptisms and so forth. Beyond this he cites 1 Cor. 14 and 1 Tim. 2. From where did this new myth, this "female folly" arise? Let us examine the words of Job and also say, "You speak like a foolish woman" (Job 2, 10). Then he proceeds on to his chief concern, the false worship of the mother of God. Which of the prophets has ever commanded that a human being be worshiped? To say nothing of the worship of a woman! God did not become human of the virgin Mary so that she might be worshiped, nor that many generations later women might be priests. Nor did God will that Mary herself be a priest; he did not enjoin her to baptize, nor to bless disciples, nor to rule on earth. And then he gives a list of women in the gospels, none of whom were priests. And the point of the entire exposition is that Mary should be held in honor; the Father, Son, and Holy Spirit should be worshiped. But no one should worship Mary. In conclusion a few more citations from Proverbs on the evil woman are produced and repeated: every heresy is an evil woman, but how much more these heresies of women! Eve should be honored but not imitated.[10]

Lafontaine [11] should be read on the justice of Epiphanius' statements on the Collyridians. Information can also be found there on the offerings of cakes to the feminine deity (Ishtar, Venus?) by all the Semitic peoples (cf. Jer. 7, 18; 44, 19). More details on the Philomarianites are also included. Lafontaine should also be consulted on the reliability of Epiphanius' statements on the question of whether the Montanists did or did not have female priests.[12]

More can be read in Epiphanius about Eve and woman in general: The devil, completely unable to direct thoughts of the male, who gets his strength from the knowledge of God, from the truth, turned to the woman—that is, to the ignorance of humanity. And he seduced those who were in ignorance. The ignorant, people without firm ideas—that is the feminine in humanity.[13]

John of Damascus, who is clearly dependent on Epiphanius, presents similar ideas.[14]

What can be said to all this? Certainly Epiphanius is a witness to the idea that there have never been women priests and that they were not thought desirable. We have seen that he did refer to what was according to him a universal principle: there have never been women priests, even Mary was not a priest, Paul has forbidden it; but his chief concern was to demonstrate how great an offense it is to worship Mary. The reader is left with the unavoidable impression that in his mind, "female priests in the Church" must inevitably lead to the adoration of a female deity, or vice versa. Thus his rejection of a female deity forced him also to repudiate women priests. But that, in our opinion, makes his witness rather weak, for it can immediately be objected: If it is a fact that these two questions are necessarily connected, then there must be no female priests. But if it is not so—and the burden of proof lies in this case upon those who believe that Epiphanius' ideas can be adduced as a basis for the repudiation of a female priesthood—then Epiphanius is eliminated from the chain of Patristic witnesses.

But the argumentation of the text from Epiphanius has the

same weakness we pointed out earlier in reference to Paul: Is he really speaking on the same subject as we are when we talk about woman? Has not woman, or at least her position, become something else? Yes, we too can now and again speak of the "weaker" sex, of its talkativeness, and so on. But we cannot say any longer in all seriousness, "The female sex is easily led astray, weak, and without much intelligence." Obviously Epiphanius was correct in excluding women, who at that time were "without much intelligence" (or whom he then judged to be so), from office. But we can no longer ascribe these characteristics to the sex as such. And who of us still seriously believes that Satan began with the woman with good reason because woman as such is frailer and the man has received his strength from the knowledge of God? (We will later see more texts in which woman's being an "image of God" and therefore also her knowledge of God are denied.) One dogmatic theologian of our time still agrees with Epiphanius in this respect, but what he says will appear to most other people as pure fantasy:

> The devil tempted Eve, not Adam, because she—although both possessed the gift of *integritas*—could fall more easily than the man; for she—prescinding from the more abundant grace which Adam doubtless was given—was more easily led astray and weaker in resistance.[15]

Is that true only of Eve? In that case it might be asked how Sagüés knew that. Or is it true for all women? That would be just as difficult to prove; in any case it must not be presumed, but must be demonstrated.

The feminine is not to our way of thinking the archetype of ignorance, of humanity without firmness of mind. Were that true, males might again pray the Jewish blessing which Paul rejected in Gal. 3, 28.

The *Didascalia* and *Apostolic Constitutions* are not especially friendly to women. These writings are concerned with, among other things, widows, who at that time filled some ecclesiastical functions. I am working here with the German translation of the Syriac *Didascalia* made by Achelis and Flemming.

> A widow should not concern herself with anything but praying for her benefactor and for the entire Church. And if she is asked anything by anyone, she should not respond immediately, unless it is a matter only of justice and faith in

God, and she should send those who would learn to the authorities. . . . But on the matter of the destruction of idols and the fact that there is but one God, on torment and peace, on the kingdom of Christ's name and on his Lordship, no widow and no layperson is obliged to speak. For inasmuch as they speak without knowledge of the teaching they bring calumny upon the Word. . . . If the heathens who are converted hear the Word of God, unless it is proclaimed to them in an orderly fashion as is proper for the building of eternal life, especially if it is taught to them by a woman how our Lord was clothed in a body and about the passion of Christ, they laugh and jest instead of praising the word of teaching, and each makes himself guilty of the great Judgment. It is thus not necessary or even urgently demanded that women be teachers, especially in reference to the name of Christ and the Redemption by his passion. For you women and especially you widows are not installed to teach but to pray and to entreat the Lord God. For he, God, the Lord, Jesus Christ, our Teacher, sent forth us twelve to teach the people and the heathens. There were women disciples with us: Mary Magdalen . . . ; nevertheless he did not send them with us to teach the people. For if it had been necessary that women teach, then our Teacher would have commanded them to instruct with us.[16]

Concerning woman, we advise her not to baptize or to be baptized by a woman, for that is a transgression of the commandment and very dangerous for her who baptizes and her who is baptized.

For if it were permitted to be baptized by a woman, then our Lord and Master would have been baptized by his mother Mary; but he was baptized by John. . . . Bring then no danger upon yourselves, brothers and sisters, by behaving as though you stand outside the law of the gospel.[17]

Prescriptions follow that a deaconess should assist at the baptism of a woman. And there are houses to which one cannot send a deacon and therefore sends a deaconess.[18]

Thus we see that even the apparently universal and principled assertions on women of the *Didascalia* and the *Apostolic Constitutions,* if they are quoted individually, do have a very definite context. Women should not give information on religion to the heathens: it is presupposed as obvious that they lack the knowledge. The prohibition of baptism is clearly merely for the sake of decency: the person to be baptized was completely naked.

And in the special material of the *Apostolic Constitutions* the Greek female deities emerge: thus here too, as in the writings of Epiphanius, the female priesthood is considered bound up with the veneration of female deities. Beyond this, as Achelis points out, the widows in their spiritual functions (teaching, baptizing, visiting the sick and sinners) were out for money [19] and thus in this way were in competition with the bishops. He believes that the deprecatory attitude of the author (who was himself a bishop) stems at least in part from that fact, as does the warning that they should merely remain at home and pray.[20] But Achelis does perhaps push too far when, without further proof, he adds: "The principle 'Let the woman be silent in the Church' held true almost nowhere in the Church. They exercised all rights which were reserved to the charismatics; they taught, baptized, celebrated the Eucharist, forgave sins. There were certainly many congregations which were ruled only by a woman or by women." [21]

In the case of Tertullian it is known that a distinction must be made according to the period from which the pertinent text comes. It is quite clear that in his Montanist period he was not as vigorous in excluding women from the area of charismata, although he never did completely lose his misogyny. For the dating of his works I am following Bardy in *DThC*.[22]

From his Catholic period:

And even the heretical women, how bold and indecorous they are! They dare to teach, to argue, to undertake exorcism, to promise healings, perhaps also even to baptize.[23]

De Baptismo. He amplifies:

That a poisonously swollen adder from the heretical party of Caius, who recently resided here, seduced very many through her teachings in which she rejected baptism. Completely according to her nature! For according to the law of nature the adders, vipers, and basilisks seek out the dry and waterless places. But we, the little fishes, in accordance with our Ichthus, Jesus Christ, are born in water and are saved only if we remain in water. Therefore that monster, who never had a proper right to teach, understood very well how to kill the little fishes by taking them out of the water.[24]

Speaking later in this same work about who has the right to dispense baptism, he says:

The highest priest, who is the bishop, has the right to impart it, and after him the priests and deacons, though not without the permission of the bishop. . . . In other cases even the laity have the right.

The laity however baptize only in emergencies, in which case it is also an obligation. Women alone are not permitted to baptize, even in emergencies:

The arrogance of women who presume to desire to teach will, let us hope, not also appropriate the right to baptize, lest perhaps a new beast similar to the earlier mentioned one should arise, so that, just as she abolished baptism, in similar fashion another woman would of herself confer it.

If women believe that they can refer to the *Acta Pauli et Theclae* (in which it is told how Thecla herself baptized), they are to be told that the document is forged. For how could it be believed that Paul permitted something like that:

How probable is it that he [Paul], who consistently denied women permission to learn, would have granted them the power to teach and to baptize? "They should be silent," he expressed himself, "and ask their husbands at home." [25]

From his semi-Montanist period we quote from "De Virginibus velandis." In what precedes he had spoken on the question of whether everything which is predicated of the word "woman" (*mulier*) is also true of "virgin" (*virgo*).

We wish to consider whether . . . the prescriptions on church discipline for the woman also hold for virgins. It is not permitted to the woman to speak in the church, nor to teach, to baptize, to present [the offering], nor to pretend to any kind of function reserved to man, to say nothing of the sacerdotal office [sacerdotalis officii sortem sibi vindicare]. We wish to inquire however whether something of the above may be permitted to virgins.

The answer is clear: of course not! Did she take the veil in order to play the most important role once again? None of these is proper for her.[26]

In *Adversus Marcionem,* he shows his Montanist tendencies. Speaking of the charismata, he says:

In precisely the same manner, when enjoining on women silence in the Church, that they speak not for the mere sake of learning (although that even they have the right of prophesying, he has already shown when he covers the woman that prophesies with a veil), he goes to the law for his sanction that woman should be under obedience. Now this law, let me say once for all, he ought to have made no other acquaintance with, than to destroy it.

And further on he invites Marcion to prove the authenticity of his teaching:

Prove to me that even a single woman from among his specially saintly women prophesized.[27]

In *De exhortatione castitatis* he approves of an idea which "was proclaimed by the holy prophetess Prisca." [28]

Thus Tertullian in his Catholic period rejected any cultic activity for women. But what was his understanding of this creature he thought necessary to repel on the basis of its sex? His misogyny is famous enough that we wish only to present one illustration. In *De cultu feminarum* he writes:

If there existed upon earth a faith in proportion to the reward that faith will receive in heaven, no one of you, my beloved sisters, from the time when you came to know the living God and recognized your own state, that is, the condition of being a woman, would have desired too attractive a garb, much less anything that seemed too ostentatious. I think, rather, that you would have dressed in mourning garments and even neglected your exterior, acting the part of mourning and repentant Eve in order to expiate more fully by all sorts of penitential garb that which woman derives from Eve—the ignominy, I mean, of original sin and the odium of being the cause of the fall of the human race. "In sorrow and anxiety, you will bring forth, O woman, and you are subject to your husband, and he is your master." Do you not believe that you are [each] an Eve?

The sentence of God on this sex of yours lives on even in our times and so it is necessary that the guilt should live on, also. You are the one who opened the door to the Devil, you are the one who first plucked the fruit of the forbidden tree, you are the first who deserted the divine law; you are the one who persuaded him whom the Devil was not strong enough to attack. All too easily you destroyed the image of God, man. Because of your desert, that is, death, even the Son of God had to die. And you still think of putting adornments over the skins of animals that cover you? [29]

How extreme his exaggeration is can be seen in his admonition to expiate for Original Sin (cf. Denz. Schönm. 2319 for a contrary opinion); Jesus died on account of her sin; and emergency baptism was forbidden a woman. For this reason he could not understand that a woman is a full member of the Church and can be an instrument of Christ in baptism. Thus he proceeded logically in holding that a woman might not "sacerdotalis officii sortem sibi vindicare." But whether that reflects the authentic tradition of doctrine is in itself the question.

In the text *Adversus Marcionem*, nothing of course can be concluded from the phrase "prophetandi ius," because this writing comes from his Montanist phase.[30]

The statements of Ambrosiaster leave nothing to be desired as far as clarity is concerned. From his commentaries on Paul, I cite a passage on 1 Cor. 11:

Although man and women are of the same essence, nevertheless the man, because he is the head of the woman, should be given priority, for he is greater because of his causal nature and his reason, not because of his essence. Thus the woman is inferior to man, for she is a part of him, because the man is the origin of woman; from that and on account of that the woman is subject to the man, in that she is under his command. . . . The man is created in the image of God, but not the woman. . . . Because sin began with her, she must wear this sign [the veil]; as she may not let her head remain uncovered in the church out of reverence for the bishop, so too she should have no power to speak; for the bishop assumes the place of Christ.[31]

He does not in any way recognize the prophetic role of woman, who must only pray silently to herself.

On 1 Cor. 14 he writes:

Now he states that which he [above] passed over, when he commanded that the women should veil themselves in the congregational assembly; now he shows that she should be silent and reticent. . . . For if the man is the image of God but the woman is not, she is on the basis of the law of nature subordinate to him. How much more must she be subordinate in the church on account of the reverence for him who is the ambassador of him who is also the head of the man: "For they are not allowed to speak, but must be silent, even the law says." What does the law say? "You should turn to your

husband, he will rule over you." This is a special law; because
of it Sarah called her husband Abraham "Lord," and because
of it they should be silent. . . . If she also is one flesh
[with the man], she should, moreover, be subordinate for
two reasons: first because she came from the man, and then
because through her sin came [into the world]. . . . For it is
shameful for women to speak in church. It is shameful
because it is contrary to discipline that in the house of God, who
has commanded that they be subordinate to their husbands,
they should presume to speak on the law.[32]

On 1 Tim. 2 he writes:

He placed man over the woman because he was created
first so that the woman is inferior [to him], because she was
created after and out of the man. He adds a second reason,
that the devil seduced not the man but the woman.[33]

On 1 Tim. 3, 11:

Because the apostle addressed women after the deacons,
the Cataphrygians seized the opportunity for error and hold
with baseless arrogance that deaconesses should also be
ordained, although they know that the apostles chose
seven males as deacons. Was it that there were no suitable
women to be found, when we read that holy women
accompanied the twelve apostles? But as the heretics appear
to base their reasoning on the words rather than on the
meaning of the law, the words of the apostle strive against
the meaning of the apostle; thus, although he commands that
woman shall be silent in the church, they on the contrary
claim for her an authority of ministry in the church.[34]

On Col. 3, 11:

Woman is the image of God only as she is redeemed,
not through Creation.[35]

Because Ambrosiaster obviously was familiar with the Montanist heresy with its women priests, it must be asked whether
in his battle with the heretics he did not with one sweep throw
away something good together with the false. More about this
later. In the chapter on Scripture we have already seen that his
interpretation of 1 Cor. 14 is false: Paul in 1 Cor. 11 is not
speaking about soundless prayer which women should perform
veiled in order to treat the authentic teaching on women's speaking later in 1 Cor. 14. And what Ambrosiaster says of 1 Tim. 3,

11—that it is a "vain presumption" to consecrate deaconesses—is certainly no witness to a "unanimous teaching of the Fathers," but merely a witness to his vast ignorance of what was happening in his own time. The popes permitted the consecration of deaconesses up into the eleventh century! Finally, Ambrosiaster's general attitude toward women makes no sense to us. It is understandable that he thought that a woman should not be a priest, for she was according to him not an "image of God" by nature but only subsequently by the Redemption. If it is going too far to say that woman has altered her state (like money, cf. chapter II), it is yet true that our insight into the essence of woman has altered. Should not the view of what a woman can become change at the same time? In any case a proof accomplished with the help of passages from Ambrosiaster has an ambivalence in the use of the word "woman."

The Irenaeus passage, which is quoted copiously,[36] is not especially significant. In statements on the heretic Mark, Irenaeus tells how these women were permitted to fulfill some kind of eucharistic procedure, and he disapproves in fairly indefinite general terms.

Augustine calls upon Epiphanius in his passage on the Pepuzians and Quintillians in *De haeresibus,* and then relates that these heretics have women priests.[37]

Praedestinatus likewise refers to Epiphanius and says the same, word for word, as Augustine.[38]

These last passages signify very little. Naturally they reject, along with the heresy, the heretics' custom of ordaining women. But here arises the question of the criterion which we must apply to see clearly where the Fathers, in their battle against the heretics, brought a matter of faith to the level of consciousness, and where they were merely conservative and more time-bound than the heretics. The latter possibility obviously is not an implicit reproach against these Fathers. It is completely legitimate to let the temporal circumstances be a factor in the battle against overhasty sectarians. But it is the task of later researchers to go into the question of what was time-bound and what was supratemporal.

These are the Patristic passages customarily cited by the dogmatic theologians to demonstrate their thesis that a woman cannot be a priest. A few more could be added:

Firmilian of Caesarea says in an anti-Montanist writing:

Here suddenly there arises a woman who fell into ecstasy
and pretended to be a prophetess and behaved as though she
were full of the Holy Ghost. . . . This spirit had also duped
one of the presbyters, by name of Rusticus, and still another
man, a deacon, so that they were involved along with this
woman. . . . But that woman had also been so bold as
frequently to do the following: amid an in no way contemptible
invocation she affected to sanctify the bread and celebrate the
Eucharist and offered the sacrifice to the Lord, [not] without
the mystery of the usual customary words; and she undertook
many baptisms with the use of the customary and proper
formula of questions, so that she seemed not to deviate
at all from the ecclesiastical rule.[39]

John Chrysostom, in his commentary on 1 Tim., Homily 9,
says, after an elucidation of the text, that in Paul's time the
women were in fact silent, but now there is much noise, more
than in the marketplace or in the baths. But Paul said not only
that the women should be silent on day-to-day affairs but also
on spiritual affairs. In order to cut off any possibility of speech,
he further said that they should not teach. Through their silence,
women show their subjection. "For somehow the [female] sex is
given to chatter; therefore he does not permit it to utter a single
word."

Then he speaks further on the subjection of woman. The male
sex is of higher honor, for the man was created first; once woman
did instruct man, and she brought everything to confusion; and
she brought him to disobedience. Therefore God made her subject, because she had misused her preeminence—or better, her
equal value. Thereupon he explained how Paul could say that
Eve was seduced, but not Adam. For the Old Testament states
that Eve said "The snake seduced me," but Adam said, "She
gave me to eat, and I did eat." Moreover Eve was deceived by
a lower being, Adam by a free being. And it is not written of
Adam that he saw that the fruit was good to eat. He was thus
not seized by sensual desire. Then he proceeds: the prohibition
on teaching is intended for *all* women, even now; "For the sex
(as such) is weak and frivolous." And Paul does not say that Eve
was seduced, but that the woman was seduced.[40]

Origen, in his Commentary on Isaias, allegorizes the washing
of the feet; he explains it as "instruction." Then he mentions the
widows who wash feet (1 Tim. 5, 19) and also quotes the Paul-

ine passage: The older women are to teach what is good and so train the young women to be chaste (Tit. 2, 3 f.). Then he says:

The widows have earned ecclesiastical honor for they wash the feet of the saints through the word of spiritual teaching—not, however, the feet of holy men, but of holy women. For it is not permitted that woman teach or rule over man. He desires that the women teach good by training young women, but not young men, to purity; for it is improper that a woman be the teacher of a man.[41]

Augustine says that although Eve was not yet created, God already spoke to Adam in the plural: "You should not eat." And that was correct, for the Lord's command was delivered to the woman through the man. "The apostle defended this order in the Church when he said: But if they desire to learn something, they should ask their husbands at home." [42]

2. No Accord on Woman

Earlier we raised the question of the criterion to be used to decide in which points the Fathers in their battle with the heretics had raised a matter of faith to the conscious level, and in which points they rejected material from the heretics that was useful of itself. In any case one thing is clear: there was not much accord either in the Patristic period itself or later on. The Fathers, for example, in their battle against the Montanists rejected several notions which we today hold as justified and which even in their own day had long existed legitimately elsewhere in the church. And that refers not only to certain customs concerning woman, but also to ideas on woman. Thus even on that there was no unanimity.

We must confront the various opinions with one another in a fairly explicit manner, in order to show that it can scarcely be said that there was a moral "unanimity" among the Fathers on the questions of what a woman is, what she may do in the Church, and what her essence is. And on some points on which a moral unanimity seemed to exist among the Fathers, their concepts were abandoned in later times.

Of course there was one point on which there has been unanimity through all times and in all places: a woman should not be a priest. But even if the problem and the evidence are limited to this, all the questions on "the same subject" and on the contrasting situations of woman in the secular and in the religious-official areas still return.

Here, however, we shall first discuss the diverging opinions on woman.

Origen does not wish women to speak "in the church"; they may speak elsewhere and even before a public which consists only of women (we quote here the translation of de Labriolle):

> Everyone speaks or would be able to speak, if he receives a revelation, except women who should remain silent in the church, the Apostle says. This is a prescription which is not obeyed by the followers of women, those who allow themselves to be instructed by Priscilla and Maximilla. . . . Let us respond to those objections which carry conviction. "Philip the evangelist," they say, "had four daughters and they prophesied." We are going to resolve the objection. . . . The daughters of Philip prophesied, but in no case did they speak in the church; we see nothing approaching it in the Acts of the Apostles. . . . A woman can have license to be a prophetess, but that can not give her permission to speak in the church. When the prophetess Miriam spoke [cf. Exodus 15, 20] she was at the head of a certain number of women.[43]

But Irenaeus says without qualification:

> In his letter to the Corinthians he spoke expressly of the prophetic charism, and he mentioned men and women who prophesied in the church.[44]

We have already seen in chapter II that Paul does not actually say that women should be silent especially in the *church*, at least not in 1 Cor. 11 and not in 1 Cor. 14, at most in 1 Tim. 2. Even Chrysostom still testifies that in Paul's time women spoke publicly: "There are men and women who spoke prophetically, for women too at that time had this charism, as the daughters of Philip, like others before and after them," as Joel (2, 28) and Peter (Acts 2, 17 f.) [45] have said.

Eusebius even used the fact that after the death of Maximilla the Montanists no longer had prophets and prophetesses as proof that they did not possess the Holy Spirit.[46]

Certainly those writers who asserted that women were not permitted to write books under their own name restricted too many of the rights of women in their battle against Montanism. From a debate between a Montanist and an Orthodox Christian we gather the following:

The Montanist defends female prophets with an appeal to the daughters of Philip and to 1 Cor. 11, 5. The Orthodox responds that he has nothing against prophetesses—Mary prophesied in the Magnificat: all generations shall call me blessed etc.—but they must not speak "in the congregational assembly," not "lord it over men so that they even write books under their own name": for they must not prophesy with uncovered head, and if they do perform such a forbidden act, they dishonor their head, i.e., the man. Mary could certainly have written books, but for that reason she did not do it. The Montanist: Is writing books then the same thing as prophesying with an uncovered head? The Orthodox: Yes! The Montanist: When Mary said, "All generations shall call me blessed, etc.," did she have her head covered? Orthodox: She had the evangelist as a veil, for the gospel was not signed with her name.[47]

We find the same ideas also in Didymus of Alexandria.[48]

On the prohibition of baptism by women there is in any case no accord in tradition. Tertullian, the *Didascalia,* and Epiphanius do of course mention it (see the texts above) and doubts on the validity of a baptism dispensed by a woman still appear to have existed in the eleventh century, for Pope Urban II had to speak on this expressly;[49] but on this point these writers were certainly no witnesses of an authentic tradition but were only vehement anti-Montanists.

The persuasive power of the tradition that Mary Magdalen was not commissioned to preach, which we have seen in Epiphanius and in the *Didascalia,* runs aground on another tradition —that Mary and Martha were apostles to Provence.[50] Whether or not this second tradition is historically tenable does not matter in this context, for it exists as a tradition and thus contradicts the first.

It is often emphasized by the Fathers that woman is subject to man and bound to silence in the congregation because she is not the "image of God," especially in connection with 1 Cor. 11.

Cyril of Alexandria: Woman is indeed created according to the image and likeness of God, but "only through the man, so that in a way she is distinguished a little [from him] in reference to nature."[51]

The excessively clear and almost harsh statements of Ambrosiaster on this we have already quoted above.

We find the same idea in Pseudo-Augustine:

How does it happen that, although man and woman are one flesh, the man is the image of God but the woman is not? In any case man and women are of one essence in spirit as in body, but in rank the man is higher, because the woman is from him, as the Apostle says: the head of the woman is the man. The fact that he was the original being, not his essence, gives the man a higher rank. For in a body there are more important and less important members, not according to nature, but according to class.[52]

Rabanus Maurus is already somewhat more nuanced:

The man is greater on the basis of his original being and his mind, not on the basis of his essence. Woman stands beneath man, for she is a part of him. The man, but not the woman, is created according to the image of God; on the other hand only the human mind, which clearly not only men but also women possess, is capable of perceiving and contemplating eternal ideas.

Nevertheless woman is not the image of God in "that part of the mind which is concerned with leadership in secular affairs." [53]

In the same spirit Peter Lombard writes:

The man is the head of the woman, just as the spirit rules the realm of the senses. For man is created according to the image of God, but not woman. In man understanding by nature rules much more than in woman. The woman is of course also created according to the image of God, but only in reference to the understanding, in which there exists no distinction between the sexes. The human being is as spirit the image of God; the man is so entirely; the woman, however, only insofar as she holds firmly to inalterable truth. For woman is a creature of the senses, because in her sensuality has precedence. It is a deplorable family situation where the woman rules over the man.[54]

In another passage he writes, "Woman is the type of the flesh, Adam is the type of understanding." [55]

That woman should not be called the "image of God," or is so only in her spirit, is, at least for us today, hardly believable as part of the traditional deposit of faith. In any case it is certainly a point which would have to be demonstrated, because it does not obviously proceed from 1 Cor. 11. Pius XII oftentimes said that woman is the image of God (cf. the papal addresses which are quoted in chapter IV).

But it is not only for us that woman is the image of God. On this point other Fathers too have spoken very differently than those just cited.

Basil in his homily on the martyr Julitta says:

Still she told the women surrounding her not to shudder weakly in the face of suffering for the faith, not to hide behind the frailty of their nature. "We are," she said, "of the same stuff as men. Like them, we are created according to the image of God. The female sex is made receptive to virtue by the Creator, just as the male is. How? Are we not related to men in all things? It was not merely flesh that was taken from him for the creation of woman, but also bone of his bone. For this reason we owe the Lord as much constancy, robust courage, and patience as do the men." [56]

Quite remarkable, and certainly not unanimously accepted in the church, is the comparison which we find in both Origen and Augustine: the higher portion of the soul is compared to the man, the lower part of the soul to the woman. Augustine expresses himself as follows:

Woman is, it is said, created as a helper [*adiutorium*] to man . . . while he rules, she obeys; he is guided by wisdom, she by the man. For the head of the man is Christ, and the head of the woman is the man. . . . Moreover it implies that the body occupies a subordinate position, which accounts not only for the fact that the soul governs the body, but also for the fact that the masculine reason subordinates to itself its ensouled part through whose help it commands the body. As an example of this, woman was created, who in the order of nature is subordinate to the man, so that there can also be observed in *one* person what appears even more clearly in two, that is, in man and woman: Just as the spirit [*mens interior*], like the masculine understanding, holds subject the appetites of the soul through which we command the members of the body, and justly imposes moderation on its helper, in the same way the man must guide the woman and not let her rule over the man; where that indeed happens, the household is miserable and perverse. [57]

In another passage he allegorizes the words from Gen. 2, "bone of bone and flesh of flesh" and explains them as the virtues of bravery and moderation. And these two virtues belong to the "lower part of the soul." [58]

Origen writes in the same vein:

As man and woman he created them; and that is "according to allegorical exegesis": our inner person consists of spirit and soul. The man is called spirit, the woman can be called soul. . . . These two parts beget as sons good thoughts and useful considerations through which they fulfill the earth. [59]

Who goes along with this today? He would have had to have read a more convincing proof ahead of time!

Or how must one understand the following: the woman is equal to the man in the spirit but subject to him in the body? Augustine says:

We see how in the soul [of people] there dwells a power which rules through judgment, and another which subjects itself in obedience; so too is woman according to the body created for the man. Although according to the spirit she possesses the same rational knowledge as the man, through her sex she is subject to him, as the impetus for practical matters subordinates itself to reason, in order to receive from it the capacity to act correctly. [60]

But even these are the most favorable references. In other passages one scarcely can avoid concluding that the man is simply identified with the spirit, and the woman with the flesh. Augustine in his Commentary on John 1, 13, "Not out of the urge of the flesh," states:

Flesh stands for woman, because she was made out of a rib. . . . The apostle has said: Who loves his woman loves himself; for no one hates his own flesh. Flesh thus stands for the wife, as sometimes also spirit for the husband. Why? Because the former rules, that latter is ruled; the former should govern, the latter serve. For where the flesh governs and the spirit serves, the house is upside down. What is worse than a house where the woman has governance over the man? But that house is proper where the man commands, the woman obeys. So also is that person rightly ordered where the spirit governs and the flesh serves. [61]

In the same way, Origen in one passage simply calls good acts masculine, and bad acts feminine:

What is seen with the eyes of the creator is masculine, and not feminine; for God does not vouchsafe to look upon what is feminine and of the flesh.[62]

This reflects an understanding of woman which makes it quite comprehensible how these Fathers in their time could not admit any female priests, but we are not bound to this latter conclusion unless we arrive at it on the basis of some other evidence.

Yet not all the Fathers thought this way. A few actually recognized that a woman can be even more gifted than her husband and that she then should guide him.

Gregory of Nazianzus wrote of his dead mother:

To my father the woman whom God had given him was not only a helpmate . . . , she was also a guide. . . . She believed it was best to accommodate herself to the law of marriage and thus to subordinate herself to her husband, yet she was not ashamed to offer herself as a teacher in religious questions . . . through remonstrance, instruction, intercession, discretion.[63]

Chrysostom: in 1 Cor. 7, 12 ff., where Paul proceeds from the idea that the believing woman can save the unbelieving man— and that means, says Chrysostom, "if she teaches and instructs" —he asks how that may be permitted, for the woman should not "teach." Does Paul here raise the woman "to the professorial chair"? Yes! For the woman should not teach because she was seduced, whereas the man was not seduced (in paradise). But the believing woman is not seduced, just because she is believing; and the unbelieving man is seduced. And therefore what is valid elsewhere for women is valid in this case for him: "He should learn." [64]

Jerome: "The man should love [his] woman, but the woman should fear [her] man. For love is fitting for the man, but fear for the woman." But it is also notable that there are many women who are better than their men. "Whether these [women] should govern or fear their men, I leave to the judgment of the reader." [65] If then Augustine, as we hear, calls out, "Sad and perverse home, where the man lets the woman govern," it is not at all to be understood as a firm conviction of the Fathers, but only as illustrative material for the real assertion, namely, that the spirit should govern in people.

When Augustine says that the woman could come to "knowledge of God" outside of paradise only on condition that the man be made her lord (which was her punishment), he is cer-

tainly alone. He asks whether Adam, who was *spiritualis* in spirit
but not in body, could indeed have believed the deceptions of
the snake. No, he could not, for he was "gifted with a spiritual
disposition." Perhaps this is why he was given the woman (a
variant text: the snake went to the woman), "who had a limited
understanding and perhaps as yet lived according to the dispositions of the flesh, not according to the dispositions of the spirit."
Is that the reason why the apostle does not recognize her as an
image of God? Not that she was not capable of an existence as
an image of God, for the apostle says that in grace we are neither
woman nor man; but perhaps because "she had not yet received
what occurs in the knowledge of God, and what she would receive only by and by through the leadership and guidance of the
man." [66]

In another passage he does see woman in paradise, and thus
without the governance of man, as capable of the knowledge of
God and thus also of an existence as an image of God:

Just women are not excluded from the grace of renewal and
restoration as the image of God—although in their female
bodies it takes a somewhat different form, for which reason it
is said that only the man is the image and glory of God—so
also had she in the original state of humanity (in which woman
was also a human) her reason and her understanding on the
basis of which she too is said to be created in the image of
God.[67]

We have already mentioned that there was no unanimity on
the deaconesses. Ambrosiaster rejected them (or at least their
ordination), as later, for example, also did the first Council of
Arausicanum.[68] But even the most eager fighter against women
in office, Epiphanius, permits deaconesses.

Other Fathers too recognize women "in apostolic service." Origen writing on Rom. 16, 1, says: "And this passage teaches with
apostolic authority that even women [can] stand in the service
of the church." [69]

Jerome comments on the same passage from Paul:

Likewise here the apostle shows that not [only] man may be
accepted or chosen, but also woman, for he sends the Romans
a letter through a woman. In this same letter he offers his
greetings to other women. So today too among the Orientals,
for example, deaconesses publicly assist persons of their own sex

in their baptism or stand in the service of the Word, for we perceive that women have taught in the household circle, like Priscilla whose husband was called Aquila.[70]

Rabanus Maurus quotes precisely the passage from Origen [71] that was reproduced above.

In the fourth chapter we shall see prohibitions from the old synods, for example, that women may not enter the sanctuary. In other places, however, it was expressly permitted.

Old canons forbid women to hand the holy vestments to the priests and to touch the holy vessels. The latter, at least, is now superseded (for citations see the next chapter).

A few Fathers forbid women to pray aloud and sing in the congregational assembly. Cyril of Jerusalem, for example, says that virgins should pray the psalms in silence or read in silence in their meetings; they should speak only with the lips so that nothing can be heard; "for I do not permit the woman to speak in the church." Other women should act likewise.[72]

Gregory of Nazianzus, in the eulogy on his mother, says, "It is to be added that her voice was never audible in sacred assemblies." [73]

The Council of Auxerre (578) likewise forbids choirs of virgins.[74]

But Gregory of Nyssa mentions virgins' choirs in liturgical celebrations without opposing them. They should merely stand separate from the men.[75]

Odo Casel sees the reason for the various prohibitions against women singing in church in the reaction against the heretics who granted too much to women.[76] And still later, in 1784, the Propaganda Fide forbade the leading of singing in the church by women.[77] The prohibition of women singing in the church was enjoined still more by Pius X on the grounds that women could not be admitted to real liturgical functions.[78] Pius XII, as is well known, again permitted it, though with the stipulation "outside the presbyterium or the altar rail." [79]

So it is evident that the Fathers did not consciously create inalterable concepts in their battle with the heretics—and that something like this could continue to operate for hundreds of years and could be altered again too.

It is not necessary to explain further that the Fathers said many things which no longer obligate us today. Just one more example will be presented, which is also extremely interesting because it shows at the same time an anti-Montanist exaggeration.

Eusebius of Caesarea quotes an ancient writer (Apollonius) who reproached the Montanists:

> Does all Scripture seem to you to prohibit a prophet from receiving gifts and money? When, therefore, I see that a prophetess has received gold and silver and expensive clothes, how shall I not reprove her? . . . For, although the Lord said: "Do not possess gold, nor silver, nor two coats," [prophetesses] in complete opposition have offended by possession of these forbidden things. . . . Does a prophet lend money at usury? [80]

Thus we must conclude: there was no unanimity on the position of woman, nor have we a clear criterion to distinguish where the Fathers have consciously formulated dogma in their argumentation with the heretics and where variable time-bound concepts have prevailed. But—and this must always be kept in mind—there was certainly a moral unanimity on the idea that no woman may be a priest. No one doubted that. Nevertheless we must inquire further. For we have already noted in many of the texts previously cited that the Fathers had almost a different subject before them than we have when we speak of woman.

3. The Other Subject of the Patristic Statements

Applicable perhaps for some of their contemporaries, but certainly not for us, are many statements on woman in general which show to what a great extent the Fathers thought in a time-conditioned way and thus how greatly their repudiation of the priesthood of woman arose from a remarkable—to say the least—conception of woman; thus we are justified in asking whether they were not actually speaking of a completely different subject.

An excellent example is Augustine, who very categorically and expressly asserts that woman was created only for the reproduction of the human race and that in all other matters a male can be more "congruently" helped by another male.

> But if it is asked why this help [woman] was created, it is probable that there is no other reason than for the generation of children, just as the earth is a help for the seed. . . . For if woman were not created as such a help for man, to produce children, for what other help would she be made? If also to till the earth, it must be answered that there was no laborious task

for which man needed her help, and if there were, a man would be a better helper. The same can be said of companionship if the man perhaps were bored with his solitude. For how much more fitting for common life and conversation would it be if two male friends rather than a man and woman lived together? But if they should live together so that the one commanded and the other obeyed, so that no contradictory decisions disturbed the peace of those living together, then—for the sake of this relationship—the order is not out of place according to which the one is created earlier, the other later, most especially if the later be created from the earlier, as occurred in the creation of woman. Could anyone say that God was able to create only a woman from man's rib, and not a man—had he so wished? Therefore, I cannot see how woman should be made a help to man except by childbearing.[81]

If that is true, men would also perform their priestly work better if they were supported only by one another. But who would have the courage to assert that Augustine was actually correct in this? When he says, "The same can be said of companionship if the man perhaps were bored with his solitude," he is certainly not speaking on the level of classic ecclesiastical teaching on the "secondary end of matrimony."

We find the same ideas in Thomas: according to him too woman was created only "as an aid to generation." [82] Here Augustine and Thomas are as rabbinic in their reference to women as the rabbis were only in their worst moments.

Ambrose too thought in a very "Old Testament" way about women when he wrote that a raped woman should remain in the power of the man if her father received money in compensation. Such an idea however was not at all universal: *raptus* soon became a ground for excommunication and later for even further punishments.[83]

Lactantius forbids women to participate in civil elections: "Plato even opened the city hall to women, and made war service, offices, and positions of command accessible to them. How great must the misfortune of a city have been in which the women take upon themselves the obligations of men." [84] He adds ironically, in another passage: If Plato allotted weapons and horses to women, then he should assign the wool and childbearing to the men.[85]

Chrysostom says in the same vein that because our life consists of two spheres, the public and the household, God has imparted to each sex its own—to the women the care of the household ($\tau \grave{\alpha} \ \pi o \lambda \iota \tau \iota \kappa \grave{\alpha} \ \kappa \alpha \grave{\iota} \ \iota \delta \iota \omega \tau \iota \kappa \grave{\alpha} \ \pi \rho \acute{\alpha} \gamma \mu \alpha \tau \alpha$), and to the men all concerns referring to the city and the agora, administration of justice, strategy. The woman cannot throw a spear or shoot an arrow, but she can sew and spin. She cannot vote in the city council, but can act in household affairs. She cannot order the affairs of the people. So God has neatly divided everything; no one is superfluous, no one can be proud as though he were capable of both roles. The more necessary and honorable God has given to the male, the slighter and less honorable to the female. Thus the man, because he is needed, will be the more diligent, and the woman through the inferiority of her service will not be rebellious toward her mate.[86]

It may now be said that Lactantius and Chrysostom are speaking here on a different subject from what we are talking of today. And, pity for Chrysostom, women have become rebellious, despite the neat regulations of God (were they really intended by God for all times?) and have wanted to become involved in the government of city and state. And the Church has not hindered them from it. In the contrary: since Pius XII, the Church has expressly pointed out to women their obligations in this respect (cf. Pius XII's addresses cited in the next chapter).

And Epiphanius' prescription for women, that when they receive guests, they must of course serve them with their own hands, but out of modesty should not show their face to the men, which instruction he borrows from the biblical passage "Sara laughed within the house" [87]—perhaps this instruction holds true for certain Muslim moralists, but certainly not for our women. Epiphanius' use of Scripture occurs in a remarkable context! He can of course adduce Gen. 18, 6–10 for his concept, but if we were fair, he would have to quote Luke 10, 38–42 as well. There it is said that Mary chose the better part!

"It is against the order of nature or of law for women to speak in an assembly of men," [88] says Jerome. Here he is really speaking about another natural order, or about other women.

And the opinion that a woman can bear no witness, or at most only in a very limited measure, seems to us to speak of another being.

Nevertheless Pseudo-Augustine says clearly (and Gratian accepted it in his collection of laws):

Woman certainly stands under the lordship of man and possesses no authority; she can neither teach nor be a witness, neither take an oath nor be a judge.[89]

The idea that a woman is inferior before the court can be found in still another place in the second part of the Corpus Juris Canonici of Gratian, where it is rather naïvely said that women could indeed be judges in the Old Testament (like Deborah) but not in the New Testament because the New Testament is more perfect than the old.[90] In the contemporary Code of Canon Law these ideas are already eradicated, as is the Augustinian opinion accepted in the Corpus Juris Canonici that a man is to be punished less for a false accusation than a woman.

In general it was held that whoever accuses someone falsely is subject to the same punishment as one guilty of the accusation; but this legal principle did not hold if the man accused a woman of something for which she must be stoned. For such a false accusation the punishment for a man was lighter:

Therefore it is sufficiently clear in what way the law wishes to subject women to men and see the wives almost as slaves.[91]

It can be seen to what extent also the Fathers almost without thinking handed on certain Old Testament and rabbinic concepts on woman without asking themselves whether these had perhaps been replaced by the basic Christian viewpoint. In addition, these pronounced rabbinic currents in the Fathers also corroborate our hypothesis at the end of the second chapter. This hypothesis is predicated on the fact that in the ancient Church there was much preaching in the rabbinic spirit (for it is scarcely credible that the Fathers themselves read the rabbinic writings, except perhaps Ambrosiaster, which would be in keeping with the hypothesis that he was a converted Jew). But if there was preaching in the rabbinic mentality, then it is also easy to explain how rabbinic social rules were taken over, certainly in reference to woman. And the concepts as well as the practice were continuously handed on since the time of the early Church.

One must not be offended by the Fathers, for it was probably in their time still a matter-of-fact and practical attitude, just as slavery could not and should not be done away with without prelude all at once. Grace does not make a leap—nor does nature.

But quotations must be used with care if something is to be proved for our times.

4. *The Fathers Themselves Progress Beyond Their Own Principles*

The Fathers often argue in a remarkable way. On this point they do not act differently from Paul. Thus the fact that Eve seduced Adam is adduced by very many Fathers as an argument for their thesis that a woman may not be a priest. We have already seen such a passage in Chrysostom. Theodore of Mopsuestia,[92] Theodoret of Cyrus,[93] John Damascene,[94] Oecumenius,[95] speak in the same spirit; we have also already heard Tertullian and Ambrosiaster on the subject; further passages might be presented from Jerome,[96] Primasius,[97] or Sedulius Scotus.[98]

Such argumentation is in my view quite extraordinary, but it could be thought nevertheless that something correct must lie in this direction; the underlying passage from 1 Tim. 2 is at least somewhat pertinent.

But then it is completely incomprehensible how the Fathers in other passages say expressly and baldly that the guilt of Eve and the female sex is completely canceled.

Ambrose says this in his Exposition of Luke 24, where he says women were the first to receive the report of the resurrection from the angel and were told to tell the news to the apostles:

As in the beginning the woman was the author of the guilt of the man, but the man was the executor of the Sin, so also she who tasted death earlier than the man now likewise was the first to see the resurrection; the first in the succession of guilt and in salvation. And in order that she not bear the reproach among men of an eternal guilt, she who had handed on to man the guilt also gave him grace; and the calamity of the ancient Fall she paralleled with the announcement of the resurrection. Death once entered through the mouth of a woman, life is restored through the mouth of a woman. But because the endurance necessary to proclaim the gospel was inadequate, because the female sex is too weak for effective action, the office of proclamation was given to men. For as through Jesus not only was the guilt of woman dissolved, but also grace was to be multiplied, so that she who once had deluded a single man now gives counsel to many, so also should the man who once trusted blindly again receive the bestowed office, in order that he who was too ready to believe for himself be ordained to proclaim for others.[99]

Origen had said that death was come into the world not through woman but through man; [100] but here we find the same result: the guilt is erased.

Gregory the Great too had the same idea. He says of the same gospel text:

See, the guilt of the human race is annihilated where it arises. For because in paradise the woman gave the man death to eat, the woman proclaims from the grave life to the men; and she who had spoken the words of the death-bringing serpent spoke the words of the one that brought her life. [And it is] as if the Lord said to the human race not with words but in deed: From that hand the drink of death was given to you, now take from it the cup of life.[101]

The same ideas we found in Haymo.[102]
Augustine speaks very clearly on this:

Women brought the message to men. And what is written? What have you heard? In their eyes this story seemed crazy (Luke 23, 11). O great human misfortune! When Eve spoke what the serpent said, it was heard quickly. When the woman lied, she was believed, and so we died; when women spoke the truth by which we live, they were not believed. If women were not to be believed, why did Adam believe the woman? If women are to be believed, why did the disciples not believe the holy women? Thus the good guidance of our Lord must be considered here. That is, the Lord Jesus Christ arranged matters in such a way that the female sex first proclaimed that he was risen. Because mankind fell through the female sex, it should also be renewed through her; because the Virgin bore Christ, the woman announced that he was risen. Through woman came death, through woman came life.[103]

Indeed it can even be said that Eve was an apostle; Hippolytus in Canticles writes (translated from the Slavonic):

Christ himself sent [Mary Magdalen], so that even women become the apostles of Christ and the deficiency of the first Eve's disobedience was made evident by this justifying obedience. O wondrous adviser, Eve becomes an apostle! Already recognizing the cunning of the serpent, henceforth the tree of knowledge did not seduce her, but having accepted the tree of promise, she partook of being judged worthy to be a part of Christ. . . . Now Eve is a helpmate to Adam. O beautiful helpmate through the gospel! Therefore too the women proclaimed the gospel [from here on the Armenian translation has a few differences; see below]. But the basic fact was this, that Eve's custom was to proclaim lies and not truth. What's this? For us the women proclaim the resurrection as the gospel. Then Christ appeared to them and said: Peace be with you. I have appeared to the women and have sent them to you as apostles.

The differences in the Armenian translation:

Therefore women too proclaimed the gospel to the disciples. Therefore, however, they believed them mistaken. . . . What kind of new thing is it for you, O women, to tell of the resurrection? But that they might not be judged mistaken again, but as speaking in truth, Christ appeared to them and said: Peace be with you. Wherewith he showed it as true: As I appeared to the women, sending them to you, I have desired to send them as apostles.[104]

Origen simply parallels the beginning of sin and the beginning of salvation:

As sin proceeded from a woman and then passed over to the man, so too the beginning of salvation took its starting point from women, so that other women as a result of abrogation of the frailty of their sex also imitated the life of those holy women who are especially clearly portrayed now in the gospel.[105]

Ambrose said:

Death once entered through the mouth of a woman, life is restored through the mouth of a woman. [See note 99.]

Cyril of Alexandria:

The woman, once a servant of death, is now released from her guilt, as she serves the voice of the holy angel and is the first to proclaim aloud the sublime and venerable mystery of the resurrection. Therefore the female sex succeeded in ending its disgrace and abolishing its ignominy.[106]

It must be said that the first understanding of Eve, as the one who was the first to sin and therefore could no longer teach, is thus now no longer valid. For Ambrose, who apparently sensed this, there remained nothing to say but that it is because women have not the necessary *constantia* that preaching is incumbent only on men. He had already said elsewhere in the commentary on Luke that "fickleness" rather than a "perversity of being" was responsible for the sin of the woman.[107] Well, the matter is certainly plain, but not exactly convincing.

Female weakness, stupidity, loquaciousness, instability are brought forward by many Fathers.

Chrysostom writing on 1 Cor. 14 says that Paul is treating the confusion which is brought about by women and cuts off their ill-timed chatter. Why has he reduced her to subjection? "Because woman is somehow weaker, more fickle and frivolous." [108] Damascene says exactly the same as Chrysostom,[109] as do Oecumenius [110] and Theophylactus.[111] For Cyril of Alexandria it is quite easy to explain why Mary Magdalen did not understand immediately that she was speaking with Jesus: "Somehow the woman [Mary Magdalen] or rather the female sex as a whole is slow in comprehension." [112] In other passages he says that women are uneducated and cannot easily understand difficult matters; much less can they grasp the miracles which surpass the spirit.[113]

Cassiodorus believes that Paul forbids women in 1 Cor. 14 to speak in church simply "on account of the infirmity of their sex." [114] Gregory the Great also considers woman something weak, even sickly. In reference to the passage from Job, "Man born of woman is short of life and full of woe" (Job 14, 1), he says:

In Holy Scripture [the word] "woman" stands either for the female sex (Gal. 4, 4) or for weakness, as it is said: A man's spite is preferable to a woman's kindness (Sir. 42, 14). For every man is called strong and clear of thought, but woman is looked upon as a weak or muddled spirit. . . . What then is designated in this passage by the word "woman" but weakness, when it says: Man born of woman? Just as when it is said even more clearly: What measure of strength can he bear in himself who is born from weakness? [115]

We have seen earlier a similar utterance from Epiphanius. Ambrose considers it proper that the man dominate the woman, else she would only fall, as she once fell in paradise.[116] Irenaeus held it proper that Miriam, Aaron's sister, was correctly punished more harshly than Aaron himself, although both had committed the same sin, for the sin of the woman was greater: nature as well as the law made the feminine subject to the masculine [117] (thus when she rose up against Moses it was more wicked than in the case of the man Aaron).

Not only stupidity, weakness, and so on are ascribed to women by Jerome, but even depravity. If women are included in religious questions, only "iniquity" results:

What do these wretched sin-laden hussies want! . . . Simon Magus founded a heretical sect with the support of the harlot Helena. Nicholas of Antioch, the contriver of everything filthy, directed women's groups. Marcion sent on to Rome before him a woman to infatuate the people for him. Apelles had Philomena as companion for his teaching. Montanus, the proclaimer of the spirit of impurity, first used Prisca and Maximilla, noble and rich women, to seduce many communities by gold, and then disgraced them with heresy. . . . Even now the mystery of sin takes effect. The two-timing sex trips everyone up.[118]

But on the matter of this weakness and iniquity of women there are also Patristic passages which undermine this kind of thinking.

Basil has the martyr Julitta say that women are not formed from the weak flesh of man but from the rib of man, that is from strong bone (see note 56). Augustine believes that woman is "bone of bone and flesh of flesh," and that these are virtues which belong to the lower part of the soul, but fortitude is nevertheless fortitude and not weakness (see note 58). And on John 4, 6 (Jesus, weary from his journey) he meditates:

What does "weary from his journey" mean but weariness in the flesh? Jesus was weak in flesh, but be you not weak; in his weakness you should be strong.

That was already figuratively presented in the creation of Eve. God should have taken flesh from Adam for the weak sex rather than bone. And why did God replace in Adam not a rib but flesh:

The woman, the church, was, so to speak, in the rib made strong; Adam was, so to speak, in the flesh, made weak; that is Christ and the Church; the weakness of Christ is our strength.[119]

Here Augustine has progressed beyond his own concepts of woman. Now suddenly the woman is the stronger, the rib is strong; and the man is weaker, flesh is weak. If he were logical, he could now say that the man is lacking a rib, that he is therefore weak, and that woman offers him precisely what he lacks: she is indeed his missing rib. She is thus the necessary complement of man, without which he is not entirely strong.

We have seen how in several passages, and especially in Gal. 3, 28, Paul breaks through his otherwise rabbinically tinged ideas on woman and considers woman as equal to man in Christ. This was true, as we saw, only for the reception of salvation, and not directly for salvific service. But in any case it was presumed that woman has access to God not merely through man. The Fathers obviously do not deny woman salvation in Christ, but they waver on whether that occurs through the man or unmediated. In other words, they do not always see the woman with unequivocal logic as of equal value in the religious area (we are not speaking here of the area of religious office). One is almost inclined to formulate the opinion of many Fathers in this way: as a baptized person the woman is of equal value to the man, but as woman she is not. Thomas later formulated that most clearly (naturally in philosophical terminology):

With reference to that wherein chiefly the essence of the image lies, that is, with reference to the spiritual nature, an image of God is found in woman as well as in man. . . . With reference to something of second rank the image of God does not exist in woman. For the man is the origin and goal of the woman, as God is the origin and goal of every creature.[120]

The Fathers did not pursue to their conclusion the ideas that on the one hand the entire woman is baptized and on the other hand the whole woman is woman, including the "rational mind, where there is no sex" (Lombard, see note 54). We say it explicitly: the Fathers did not think this through to its conclusion, for they already *knew* it. Indeed they even said expressly that if a woman believes, she becomes completely equal to man. They put it this way: "She has become a man." We would rather say that she is as woman of equal value to a man, for being a woman is not something that a woman should strip off in order to become a man in the end. But the Fathers did not mean this either.

To them being a woman implied some kind of blemish which woman loses if she believes. The following quotations from Ambrose and Jerome are very neat and clear in this respect. It seems to us that the significance of these texts can scarcely be overestimated.

Ambrose in his commentary on Luke refers to John 20, 14 (a reference to Mary Magdalen, who did not yet believe that Jesus was risen):

And finally you read thus: Jesus says to her: Woman. Whoever does not believe is a woman, and she is still addressed with her physical sexual designation; for the woman who believes is elevated to male completeness and to a measure of the stature of the fullness of Christ; then she no longer bears the worldly name of her physical sex, and is free from the frivolity of youth and the talkativeness of old age. Thus Jesus says, Woman, why do you weep? (Afterward Mary had expressed her belief.) Only after these words is she no longer woman but called Mary; for the general designation customary among the people is one thing, the special name of one who follows Christ is something else. And if she is also still not a witness of perfect faith, she is nevertheless sent as a messenger to the disciples. Nevertheless she is forbidden to touch Jesus because she had not yet comprehended, as Paul had, that in Jesus the fullness of divinity dwelled incarnate. . . . What does it mean: don't touch me? Do not lay hands on the greater, but go to my brothers, that is to the more perfect—for he who does the will of my Father who is in heaven, he is brother, sister and mother to me. Because the resurrection can be comprehended only by the more perfect, the prerogative of this faith is also reserved for those who already have a more established position. I therefore do not permit the women to teach in the congregational assembly; they should ask their husbands at home. She is therefore sent to husbands and receives mandatory tasks.[121]

Ambrose thus says immediately, after he explains that woman by faith "is elevated to male completeness," that she nevertheless may not proclaim salvation, for that is for "husbands." Here he stands again completely in the current of his age; nevertheless he knows that in the kingdom of God woman no longer stands below man, for what else can he mean with the words that she becomes a man? In this context he uses the words "man" and "woman" in their time-bound sense, that is, as though woman were something of lesser value, but in what he really intends to say he has already left this concept far behind.

Jerome in his Commentary on Ephesians 5 says:

But because in metaphorical language we have named men "soul" and women "body," so the soul should love the flesh, as Christ the Church, . . . especially because it knows that the flesh must be saved in the resurrection and will show forth God's salvation. The man has Christ as his head . . . and if he humbles himself for the salvation of the flesh and becomes one flesh with his wife, he thereby draws her up to the spirit.

As long as woman lives for birth and children, there persists between her and man the same difference as between body and soul; but if she wishes to serve Christ more than the world she will cease to be a woman and will be called "man," because we desire that all be elevated to perfect manhood.

It is commanded us that we should foster and care for our women, that is, that we should provide maintenance and such things. . . . If we express this in a metaphorical way, we must say that the soul should love, foster, and care for that flesh which will show forth God's salvation. . . . Souls care for their bodies, so that the transitory puts on immortality. We should thus both as men care for our women and as souls care for our bodies, so that our women are made into men and bodies into souls. And in no way should there be a differentiation of sexes: but as there is among the angels neither man nor woman, neither should there be among us, who will be like angels; already now we wish to begin to be that which is promised us for heaven.[122]

Jerome thus meant that the coming age, in which there would be no distinction of sexes, is already breaking through into this world in believing people who wish to serve Christ more than the world.

Of course a large number of questions raised here are still far from resolved. Will there really be neither men nor women in the coming age? Will sexuality really be completely without significance there? That is true, of course, at least for sexuality as a biophysical organ for reproduction. Jerome can certainly be believed that such will no longer exist in the eschaton. These texts give food for thought. But at the same time clarification of the questions has begun.

On the basis of her faith, woman is equal to man and stands behind him in nothing. These two texts from Ambrose and

Jerome say more than Gal. 3, 28, says explicitly and directly. Not only is the difference between man and woman in the religious area denied here, not only is it said as in Gal. 3 that both can participate in salvation, both are members of the people of the covenant; no, here more is said. Even if woman too can be participant in salvation, she can still be considered inferior (that is not excluded by Gal. 3). But in these two Fathers woman is elevated to the level of man: she loses her sex, it is said; i.e., she overcomes the inferior position of her sex. In other words, these Fathers have already surmised and said that woman is more than an embodiment of family, more than the mother of man's children, thus more than is cutomarily read into Eph. 5 and 1 Cor. 11. Jerome especially indicates this when he expressly says:

> As long as woman lives for birth and children, there persists between her and man the same difference as between body and soul; but if she wishes to serve Christ more than the world she will cease to be a woman and will be called "man."

A side remark: these words "as long as woman lives for birth and children" need not only be understood as a phase in the life of an individual woman! There are also collective changes.[123] The woman of today is no longer constantly pregnant during the most important years of her life, as was often the case in earlier times. And she no longer feels herself intended primarily for motherhood. But we cannot go farther into this.

There is of course no possible way to leap immediately from these two Patristic passages to the priesthood of woman. But these texts put those other texts on women which are always used in the argument against the priesthood of women in another light. In any case someone beginning to question carefully whether a woman can perhaps be a priest after all cannot immediately be stopped with a peremptory argument that the Fathers have always seen woman only as subject to man. The Fathers have of course often done that, but there are other opinions as well.

The same is true for Thomas. In chapter V we will hear a few negative statements from Thomas on women. But he too knew better! Motivated by the Pauline text "It is a shame for a woman to have her hair cut off" (1 Cor. 11, 6), Thomas objected: "On the contrary, it would seem to be proper for nuns to have their hair cut off." And he replies to this:

> Precisely because she takes the vows of the widowed state or virginity and thus betroths herself to Christ, she is raised to

the worth of man so that she is freed from subordination to the man [*liberatae a subjectione virorum*] and bound immediately to Christ.[124]

Through the bridal union of the holy nuns with Christ, says Thomas, they no longer have their relationship to Christ mediated only through man, as before, but rather they have an immediate relationship. Thus they are also no longer subordinate to men but participate in "manly dignity." One notices that Thomas speaks here not only of inner salvation but also outer; indeed he sees sociological realities. We will see in the fifth chapter how the "middle term" in the Thomistic argument against the priesthood of woman is precisely this "state of subjection." One might ask, if nuns are thus "liberated from subjection to men," what still blocks the way? But in the customary argument there are still many problems to be overcome. Nevertheless, several things seem to indicate that one can say that the woman becomes man, the bride becomes the bridegroom. As Jerome puts it:

If a man humbles himself for the salvation of the flesh and becomes one flesh with his wife, he thereby draws her up to the spirit.

But we will speak of Thomas, and of the Church as bride and simultaneously the priestly church, in chapter V.

5. Slaves

In concluding this chapter it may be useful to say a few things on the attitude of the Fathers toward slavery simply because several Fathers themselves considered the subjection of slaves and that of women to be on the same level. The attitude is also significant because it shows once again how the theologians changed their theology and exegesis as soon as the sociological structure changed. Earlier we saw something similar in reference to the question of lending money for interest. Here we will use the same example.

It is obviously impossible in the framework of this book to give even a superficial overview of the teaching of the Fathers on slavery.[125] I shall limit myself to a few ideas from Chrysostom and Augustine to show that it is no overstatement to draw a parallel to the question of the priesthood of woman. This will prove that from this perspective too it is necessary to place the opinions of the Fathers more precisely in their temporal context.

Chrysostom wishes to investigate how many kinds of slavery

sin has given rise to. For slavery came about only through sin.
The first is the slavery by which men rule over women. After sin
that was necessary. Before sin woman was equal in value (ὁμότιμος)
to man. Chrysostom demonstrates this from the texts of Genesis,
especially from the words "a helpmate who corresponds to him"
(Gen. 2, 18), which is not said of the animals. After sin however
it was said: He will rule over you. Thus God says: I have created
you equal, but you have not used your ruling position well; de-
scend to subjection. You have not borne freedom; accept slavery.
You were unable to rule; then become one of the ruled, acknowledge the man as lord. Then Chrysostom cites the famous Pauline
text and asks further: Why is woman subjugated, why may she
not teach? Once she taught Adam falsely, once she dominated.
And for that reason God removed her from the seat of teaching.
God has indeed moderated the slavery: Men, love your wives
(Eph. 5), but you women should not direct your attention so
much on that but rather on the fact that the nature of slavery
was brought about through sin.

The second kind of slavery is that of the slaves under their
master, the third that of underlings beneath the prince. The
second was brought about by the sin of the son of Noah, Cham.
On account of his sin his descendants are slaves (Gen. 9, 25–
27).[126]

In the following sermon Chrysostom says that a woman who
believes may instruct her husband, although Paul wishes it otherwise in his letters, where it is said that a woman may not teach.
In a mixed marriage, however, the roles are turned about:
there the wife instructs her husband. Thus it follows that the
slavery of a woman arises not from her nature but from sin.
Therefore it is true also of slaves (in the narrower sense): if
they believe, they are no longer slaves, but freed men of the lord.
In that case "slave" is from now on an empty word (ψιλὸν ὄνομα).
Therefore Paul too says (1 Cor. 7, 21): if you can be free, then
"rather remain so," which means "remain rather in slavery." So
even as it was a much greater miracle to protect the three youths
unharmed in the furnace than to quench the furnace fire, so too
is it a much greater miracle to attain freedom while slavery
endures.[127]

It is well known that there are two tendencies among the
Fathers in the explication of 1 Cor. 7, 21. The one says: if you
can become free, use this opportunity. The other: even in such a

case, rather be a better slave.[128] Chrysostom follows here the second explication, as he does in his homily on 1 Cor. 7, where he says that he knows well that other people interpret differently, but he himself rejects the first meaning.[129]

Thus Chrysostom too held that whoever believes is no longer a slave, just as we hear Ambrose say that whoever believes is no longer a woman. In these cases "slave" and "woman" are now only empty words. Chrysostom himself thought that the slave should remain a slave, that it is of no significance. Later times, however, have thought differently and believed that this "religious conquest" should have sociological consequences as well; they thought that it was necessary to equate the slaves with the free in the sociological realm too. Will a later generation also draw consequences for the sociological realm as well from the fact that "woman" is now only an empty word and that in Christ woman is equal to man?

For Augustine too this subjection derived only from sin:

Gifted with intelligence, created in the image of God, the human should rule only over irrational beings, not over humans, but over animals. . . . For one is right in accepting that slavery is a condition laid only upon the sinner. . . . Thus guilt, not nature, causes these names. . . . But of his nature, inasmuch as God originally created mankind, no one is the slave of another or of sin.[130]

Although it is prescribed for a Hebrew slave that he should serve six years and then be set free, lest Christian slaves impetuously demand the same from their masters, apostolic authority commands that slaves should be subject to their masters.[131]

Slavery is defended by natural law:

Penal servitude is ordained by that law which commands that the natural order be protected and forbids us to disturb it.[132]

In another passage:

That one human is the slave of another human is a result either of iniquity or of adversity: iniquity, as it was said, cursed be Cain, he shall be a slave to his brother; adversity, as happened to Joseph, namely, that he was sold by his brothers, a slave to a foreigner. . . . It is also the natural order among humans that the women serve the men and the children their parents; for there too it is right that the weaker intellect serve the stronger.[133]

This little may suffice. Both Fathers put the subjection of woman on the same level as that of the slave. Both are willed by God, even if not in the beginning, nevertheless as "penalty" for sin.

The existence of slavery is also supported with arguments from Scripture, especially Gen. 9, 25–27, just as the subjection of woman (and the rejection of a female priesthood) was supported with arguments from Scripture. This is the case not only with the Fathers. Until well into the eighteenth century there were still attempts to legitimize slavery with the aid of Scriptural passages! [134]

The Fathers of course consoled the slaves, fought for their liberation, urged the lords to better treatment (just as they said to husbands "Men, love your wives"), but they did not in any way see the human disgrace of slavery as such. They were aware that slavery as a matter of fact often led to degrading treatment, and that they deprecated. But they did not recognize slavery in itself as a scandal against natural law. On the contrary, Chrysostom and Augustine, for example, simply believed that Scripture commanded slaves to remain slaves. The judgment upon Cain was interpreted like that upon woman in Gen. 3, 16.

The Fathers, in imitation of Paul himself, attempted to give a religious sense to slavery by beautiful and rich speculations:

Every just slave is a free Christian, every master who is a sinner is a slave. Christ himself made himself into a slave in order to free us (1 Cor. 7, 21 ff.) etc.

But despite all this they remain conservative. They took pains to abolish hard treatment and other abuses, often even to move masters to set their slaves free—but slavery as such seemed to them an obvious fact not in contradiction to Christianity: they themselves had slaves.[135] In the circumstances of those times anything else was scarcely possible.

Nevertheless, theology gave up these ideas as soon as the sociological and economic situation had altered. The parallel to the question of the priesthood for women is quite evident.

It should not be thought that slavery was tolerated by the Church for only a short time because nothing else was possible, though the Church itself had already long before accepted a much better point of view. In that case the parallel to our problem would actually be much less rigorous. But that is not so. The better insight won out only gradually, and in fact much later than is customarily believed.[136]

In the New Testament, slavery is presumed and accepted, and thus nowhere made a problem or condemned as unjust. The possibility of its elimination, which would have meant a socioeconomic revolution, was not within the field of vision of the New Testament. Freedom was not claimed as a right, nor was the freeing of the slaves by the owners made a duty. In the ancient Church, freeing did become a Church concern, but a general principle did not arise from this. There was, moreover, no lack of theological justifications presenting slavery as a result of original sin which would endure until the end of the world.

The Middle Ages adhered to this understanding. Thomas expressed it clearly! [137] Of course, after Constantine the holding of Christian slaves and especially their sale to non-Christian peoples was often forbidden, and individual synods directed their attacks against the continuing dealing in humans. But on the other side even popes and ecclesiastical institutions like monasteries possessed their slaves.

Explorations and conquests created a new age of slavery. To mention only one example, Pope Nicholas V gave the Portuguese king the right:

to attack, to impress, to capture, and to subjugate kingdoms, dominions which are in the possession of Saracens, heathens, and unbelievers, and to make their inhabitants slaves at all times.[138]

There are just as many papal statements which forbid dealing in slaves, but an "accepted author" like Billuart could still write:

Slavery is not forbidden by any law: not by natural law, for the person has a right to use his body; not by divine law, as can be clearly seen from the Old Testament and the New Testament; and not by human law, which follows clearly from various statements on ecclesiastical and secular law. By the reordering of law any further slavery among Christians is forbidden, with the exception of America, where up to the present the Europeans have Africans as slaves.[139]

Here it must be feared that later generations will pass judgment on our theology exactly as we do on Billuart's theology of slavery. Of course that is not certain. But in reference to woman it is not sufficient to think: the Fathers and later theologians have spoken so clearly; what can we change? An over-careful, dogmatic theologian at the time of the abolition of slavery might have said the same thing. The Fathers and theologians were indeed clear enough on that question. Nevertheless the change came about.

Finally it must be noted that "slavery" was and remains an "impediment to ordination." But it was seen as a purely ecclesiastical law; an ordination performed despite this was still valid. But perhaps it is not going too far to say that the "impediment of slavery" is also "by divine law." For the Church always did assert that by the fact of ordination the slave was in fact free.[140] Priesthood and slavery just do not go together. So if a slave is ordained, then he becomes free.

Did not Ambrose say that woman already through her faith loses the blemish of womanhood and that, if she believes, she is by that fact a "man"? Would not ordination perhaps be able to free a woman just as much from the "blemish of womanhood" as it released slaves from their blemish?

This is of course no assertion, but merely a question on the level of parallel argumentation.

6. Afterword on Deaconesses

The problem of deaconesses does not, as such, belong to the scope of this work.[141] It is simply a fact that there were such things in the ancient Church and that they—and their successors, the abbesses of the canonesses' foundations (not those of monastic cloisters)—did much in the ecclesiastical and cultic area which is now forbidden to women. We will be speaking of this later. The real problem is whether they received an actual sacramental consecration—rather than merely a benediction—and whether this consecration also imparted to them the sacramental character as did that of the deacon. This problem is still not resolved. But it does not appear to be decisive for the question of a female priesthood.

It would certainly be interesting if it were established that the ancient Church had actually seen deaconesses as incumbents in a hierarchical office which was a major order, as members of the hierarchy. It would be a clear proof that the church had already overcome its low interpretation of woman. But it is not decisive.

For no matter how high the position of deaconesses can be fixed, the fact still remains that no one among the orthodox Catholics at that time had the remotest idea that a woman could be ordained a priest. And this book is concerned only with that.

Naturally we can amplify all the positive statements on woman we have gathered from old texts with what is known about deaconesses and ecclesiastical widows and virgins (the distinction is often very obscured in the sources). We have already done that in part. But as it is impossible to exhaust the subject within the framework of this book, and as a cross section suffices for my purpose here, I have avoided a detailed account of the texts on deaconesses, because that would have brought with it its own very specific problem. The few texts from Origen and the *Didascalia* which have been quoted speak about the activity of the deaconesses or widows. But they were quoted only insofar as deaconesses too are women, not insofar as they possessed any kind of ecclesiastical office.

In the next chapter we shall see that several prohibitions of popes and synods concerning women refer to deaconesses. Here it is important to note that although they present official statements on the status of woman in the cultic area, they cerainly do not remain uncontradicted. In other places deaconesses were officially admitted and much was permitted them: to read the epistle and the gospel, to lay on incense, to give communion, to wear a stole. Their ordination in the eleventh century was not merely similar to that of the deacon, but completely identical with it.[142]

According to K. H. Schäfer, up until the last century it was the custom in the cloisters of the female Carthusians for the abbesses to sing the gospel during Holy Mass on high feastdays. At their consecration the Carthusian nuns received stole and maniple. Now a nun sings only the epistle, but the stole indicates that the gospel was sung by her earlier. At the investment with the maniple the bishop says to the virgin: "Act manfully."[143]

Thus there is after all one circumstance in the question of deaconesses which is important for us. Because the interpretations were by no means unanimous (and they are still not, among historians), either on their official character or on their authority, it becomes even clearer that the citing of individual restrictions and condemnations of and by themselves say nothing on the question of whether *the* Fathers or *the* magisterium exclude woman from the priestly office. Careful investigations must study how

things were ordered, which abuse each prohibition was intended
to meet, which statements are isolated cases, which are contra-
dicted by other practices and other statements, what was permitted in the East but condemned in the West, and so on.

Nicea seems not to count deaconesses among actual clergy; [144]
Chalcedon on the other hand does.[145] Chalcedon and later synods
establish a minimum age for the ordination of deaconesses;
Arausicanum I [146] and the Synod of Epaon [147] forbid the ordination of deaconesses. Thus before the prohibition on ordination
is quoted as a witness that the Church desired no women in
office, there remains the task of investigating with care what
these synods intended by the prohibition, and whether other
synods held the office of deaconess so important that they protected it with practical measures against immature incumbents.
And in all this citation of restrictive measures it must never be
forgotten that popes permitted the ordination of deaconesses and
even performed such ordinations themselves up into the eleventh
century.[148]

To put it briefly: contemporary scholarship finds that nothing
decisive, either for or against the priesthood of women, can be
derived from the institution of deaconesses. Just one thing: that
we must be very careful in citing the various statements.

In conclusion, one more short comment on the chapter on the
Fathers. Nowhere in the entire Patristic literature on the priesthood of woman did we meet any deliberation that rejected the
priesthood of woman on *essential* grounds. We found only considerations such as these: apostles sent forth no women; Mary
did not baptize Jesus; Eve was seduced; woman did once teach
man—in paradise—and nothing but damnation came from that;
Paul forbade it; and so on. Only two reasons can refer to essential structures: the lower status of woman, and an apparently
assumed connection between a female priesthood and female
deities.

Now the first is far outdated by temporal conditions, and the
second we would rather see proved than assumed.

Thus, the yield from the Fathers is at this point only slightly
relevant theologically. Naturally, if the Fathers give a correct interpretation of Paul in this connection, their witness is certainly
relevant. But this does not advance theological reflection. And
that is what concerns us here. The Fathers have shown nothing

that would give us an indication that we should see essential structures in manhood and in office which would exclude the possession of office by a woman. And that seems significant to me. For in that case no connection with dogma is present, at least not in the concept of the Fathers. And that would leave room for a further development.

IV   The Teaching Office of the Church

After all the foregoing, the question naturally arises whether the Church may have expressed itself on our thesis through its magisterium. As a matter of fact, authors quote fairly many texts from ancient synods, popes, and so on. In this chapter we shall pursue these statements and investigate what they have to tell us.

It is amazing that there is no formal declaration of the *extraordinary* magisterium of the Church in reference to the question of the priesthood for women. There has of course always been an unchanging constant tradition and practice: the position of the male was always uncontested (and thereby the thesis too); but the heretical group which admitted women to office, the Montanists,[1] had at the time of the first ecumenical council still not become insignificant. For this reason it is noteworthy that the Fathers did not address the subject at all. The Fathers at the Synod of Constantinople, the canons of which are always quoted as canons of the ecumenical council, apparently found other aspects of Montanism more important—for example, the validity of Montanist baptism.

Luther of course called all women priests inasmuch as they are baptized,[2] but he did not desire actual women priests. In the exegesis of the first commandment he even designated women, because of their susceptibility to superstition and secret remedies, the priests of the evil spirit, who are not qualified for God's priesthood.[3] The Council of Trent thus reacted only to Luther's starting point for mentioning the priesthood for women—that is, to his thesis that all Christians are priests and thus the office-bearers are not distinguished in essence from the laity. Against this the council confirmed the existence and the divine origin of the hierarchy as differentiated from the laity.[4] (This is not the place to investigate exactly to what extent the council reproduced the precise meaning of Luther's assertions. That may be left aside here.) In any case the council's statement signifies nothing for the question of whether a woman can be *ordained* as a priest. The council determined only that the laity, and thus also women, cannot simply on the basis of the royal priesthood of believers preside at the anamnesis celebration of the congregation and make the Word of God present sacramentally and verbally—that is officiate as a hierarchical priest.

There is thus no formal statement of the extraordinary magisterium. And the authors who demonstrate the thesis of the "incapability" of woman for sacerdotal ordination have never appealed to any statement of that sort.

Obviously the case with individual synods and nondogmatic papal statements is different. The most detailed overview in recent times was given by Santiago Giner Sempere in the *Revista Española de derecho canónico*.[5] But he did not differentiate between forgeries and authentic sources.

As the first statement of the magisterium he quotes a prohibition of Pope Sixtus (c. 120), in which it is said that no one except males who stand in God's service may touch the holy vessels:

Only by hallowed men [males] consecrated to the Lord may they be touched. . . . For it is highly unbecoming that the holy vessels of the Lord . . . be touched by others than by men who stand in the service of the Lord and are consecrated to him.[6]

Sixtus does not explicitly exclude women, but obviously is thinking only of men. The text is a forgery.[7] It would thus be better to situate it in the later context of the Gallic opposition to deaconesses. Moreover, it possesses no conclusiveness in and of itself.

Giner Sempere next mentions Pope Soter, who speaks on women in reference to the same material. It had been thought this text was an immediate reaction to Montanist tendencies.[8] But apart from the fact that here again it is a matter of a later forgery[9] it would still be very questionable because Montanism began only in 172; the pontificate of Soter is usually given as 166–74. G. Bardy believes that Montanism was first known in Lyons in 177. The first pope who was acquainted with Montanism would have been Eleutherius, the immediate successor of Soter.[10]

Quasten says very decisively that Pope Soter did not write against the Montanists.[11]

According to the wording of the forgery, Soter wrote to the Italian bishops:

> That women consecrated to God or nuns touch the holy vessels or consecrated eucharistic linens and carry the incense around the altar has been reported to the Holy See. That this it full of every reprehension and vituperation is not doubted by any right-thinking person. For this reason we believe on the basis of the authority of the Holy See that you should put a stop to these actions entirely and as soon as possible: and so that this plague does not spread further through all provinces, we command that it be abolished with all haste.[12]

This text is taken up by Gratian in the first part of his decree.[13]

To interpret this text one must know precisely what is meant by the words "to touch the sacred vessels and consecrated linens." Does it refer to a touching during the liturgical celebration, thus to an active participation, perhaps by deaconesses, in the liturgical celebration? The words "to carry incense around the altar" seem to allude to this. In that case this forgery forbids something which elsewhere encountered much less opposition.[14] Or does it refer merely to the touching of the holy vessels outside of the sacred service? If so, then this prohibition has already long been outdated in the practice of the church.[15]

In the actual chronological sequence, the Council of Laodicea (between 343 and 381) stands first: in canon 44 it says, "It is not permitted women to enter the altar area." [16]

Even up to the present day this prohibition remains the most often quoted. We shall later see that it is not at all so isolated and apodictic; it is just that the other canons, as far as we know, are never quoted.

Then comes the Council of Saragossa, which was convened to oppose the Spanish Priscillians. In its first canon it had the following regulation:

> Let all faithful women of the Catholic Church be separated from men for reading and gatherings; and let them neither come together with those who read to others, nor for study, either teaching or learning. For the apostle ordered this.[17]

Hefele-Leclercq reads in this only that "all Christian women must keep away from 'gatherings,' *conventicula*." But Lafontaine translates:

Faithful women of the Church are instructed to take no part in the reunions of strange men; they are forbidden to come together with women who give lectures to instruct and educate themselves. That is proscribed by the apostle.[18]

According to him that would mean:

The council . . . lays blame on the public teaching given by women.[19]

That would be something more. But Giner Sempere is correct in saying that one still has no clear definition of the "incapacity" of women to receive priestly ordination.[20] The council had as its primary goal the condemnation of the Spanish Priscillians. And it is, if not completely certain, yet very probable, that these Priscillians recognized women as priests. We know from Sulpicius Severus that many women followed Priscillian,[21] and that they were ordained appears to follow from a canon of the Synod of Nîmes (394), which likewise was convened against the Priscillians:

In opposition to apostolic order and although it has been unknown until our time, certain people have suggested that women—in a place unknown to me—are seen performing priestly service; obviously church order does not permit this, because it is indecent; and such an illegal ordination should be annulled.[22]

Hefele-Leclercq[23] as well as Lafontaine[24] concludes from this canon that the Priscillians actually conferred ordination on women, and thus permitted women more than what the church otherwise gave to deaconesses. With this we have the first prohibition of the consecration of women in major orders.

For the period of about 418 to 422 we still have a prohibition, attributed to Pope Boniface I, rejecting the active participation of women in liturgical affairs. But here too we are dealing with a forgery.[25]

A further case of the same prohibition, in which, however, there is no doubt about authenticity, we find in Pope Gelasius, who wrote in the year 494:

As we have perceived with vexation, such a contempt of divine truths has occurred that even women, it is reported, serve at holy altars: and everything which is entrusted exclusively to the service of men is performed by the sex to which it does not belong.[26]

In the second half of the sixth century, the Collected Chapters by Martin, Bishop of Braga, repeat canon 44 of Laodicea: "Women are not permitted to enter the altar area." [27] But, more worthy of note, the Council of Tours II (567), after it first of all forbids the access of the laity in general to the altar, says:

For prayer and for the reception of the eucharist the holy of holies is accessible to the laity and women, as is the custom. [28]

Hefele-Leclercq explains the "praying" as private prayer outside the liturgical celebration. Thus it is definitely false to say, as does Giner Sempere:

In the year 567 the Council of Tours II issued regulations in canon 4 that segregate woman from the altar. [29]

There is certainly some regimentation, but this does not remove woman from the altar area. This regulation from Tours was moreover not universally valid. Besides the provision of Laodicea, which was often repeated by other synods, there can be found for example in the thirteenth disciplinary canon of the Council of Braga II (563) the following prohibition:

Only the clerics and not the laity return to the sanctuary of the altar to receive communion. [30]

The Second Council of Mâcon (585), however, says again in the fourth canon:

Every Sunday the faithful, men and women, must offer bread and wine at the altar. [31]

This is the same council at which, according to Gregory of Tours, a bishop appears to have said that a woman could not be designated as a human. For an estimate of this story—which was later often rejected—one can compare Hefele-Leclercq on the passage. It is not, in any case, possible to find a trace of this incident in the canons. And the interpretation of that bishop's expression is too disputed to be able to conclude from it that he or many others of that time had doubted that a woman is a human being. Perhaps—but we have no proof for this—it is an echo of the assertions of Pseudo-Augustine and of Ambrosiaster (cf. above in chapter III) that a woman is not "an image of God." It appears that Jungmann does not know the canons which permit access to the altar area: he mentions merely the prohibition. But he shows that where offertory processions occur today, no distinction is made regarding women.[32] The canons forbidding admission to the altar area are thus first of all not valid everywhere and secondly are already outdated in practice.

That women must not touch the holy objects is again enjoined in Antisidiorense (578 or later) in the 36th and 37th canons:

A woman may not with naked hand receive the eucharist; a woman may not take hold of the altar cloth [*palla dominica*] with her hand.[33]

According to DuCange, Augustine also recognized this prohibition.[34]

The collection of canons ascribed to St. Isidore of Seville repeats old rules without adding anything new.[35]

In the chapters of the Frankish kings, who formed the ecclesiastical and secular laws at the same time, we find for example two repetitions of canon 44 of Laodicea.[36] We find there the Capitula Ecclesiastica of Bishop Haito of Basle (807–23):

Everyone should take care that women do not approach the altar; even women consecrated to God may not intrude into any kind of altar service. If altar linens must be washed, they should be removed by clerics, given at the altar rails, and also be taken back there. And likewise offertory gifts, if they are brought by these women, are received by priests there and brought to the altar.[37]

That these prohibitions were not always adhered to is proved by the *relatio* of the bishops to the emperor Hludowicum (829): [38]

We have sought by all possible ways to prevent the illicit admission of women to the altar.[39] We have learned through a report of trustworthy people that in some provinces, in contradiction to the divine law and to canonical instruction, women betake themselves into the altar area, impudently take hold of the sacred vessels, hold out the priestly garments to the priests and—what is still worse, more indecent and unfitting than all this—they give the people the body and blood of the Lord and do other things which in themselves are indecent [*quae ipso dictu turpia sunt*]. Therefore, we have sought to prevent this, so that further liberties are not taken. But that women must not enter the altar area is written in the Council of Chalcedon [40] and in the decrees of Pope Gelasius.[41]

In this *relatio,* chapter 45 from the Council of Paris (likewise 829) is clearly quoted. But there we find an interesting expansion. After the words "which themselves are indecent," there follows:

It is most amazing how this practice, unpermitted in the Christian religion, could creep in; that is, how women, to whose sex it is in no way befitting to do what is contrary to the divine law, could ever allow themselves to do what is forbidden to secular males. Doubtless it occurred through the carelessness and negligence of some bishops. Therefore woe to us priests into whose hands the burdens of that priest have passed as they are described in Macch. 2: For they have indeed disregarded their duty which was delegated to them for the cult, and, while God's temple was without holy service, given themselves to carnal passions and illicit actions, so that women, without anyone preventing them, betake themselves into consecrated houses and therein have been able to introduce unpermitted things.[42]

One would be almost inclined to think when reading this that the actual reason for the statement "to whose sex it is in no way befitting" lies in the danger of "carnal passions and illicit actions." As a basis for the exclusion of women that would not be exactly convincing.

The reason adduced in the chapter of Theodulf, bishop of Orleans, is also remarkable: there, in the sixth chapter, we read:

When a priest celebrates the Mass, women in general should not approach the altar but remain in their places; and the priest should accept their gifts there in order to bring them afterwards to God; for the women should be conscious of their own weakness and the weakness of their sex; and therefore they must scrupulously guard that they do not touch anything consecrated to the service of the Church. The male laity must also scrupulously be on guard lest they endure the punishment of Uzza, who, because he wished to touch God's ark in extraordinary circumstances, perished by the hand of God.[43]

The reason is worth noting. The warning to women "to remain in their places" is either irrelevant to the question of the priesthood for women, wishing merely to ensure respectability, or it is characteristic of the Old Testament, an allusion to the arrangement of the forecourt in the old temple. In the latter case we know from Gal. 3, 28 that that is past.

In the same line as the respectability motif lies an amplification in the decretal of Pope Gregory IX to a canon of the Council of Mainz (888). The council forbids a priest to live in the same house with any woman, even his sister, because even in that case sins occurred (moreover the synods customarily say: live only with mother, sister, wet nurse).[44] This is very clearly a prescription aimed at celibacy. The decretals of Gregory IX continue immediately, without transition:

Also care must be taken that no woman presume to walk to the altar or to minister to the priest or to stand or to sit within the chancel.[45]

Both regulations are well known; but the immediate placement alongside one another seems to indicate that at least one of the reasons why it was thought that a woman should not be a priest was the danger of sin. Thomas also says this when he speaks *ex professo* on this matter. In the article "Does the grace of preaching wisdom and knowledge extend even to women?" he explains that women are not permitted to teach publicly, and he presents as a second argument: "So that the spirit of the men will not be seduced to sensuality." [46]

Hildegard Borsinger also explains it in this way; in reference to the prohibition of the ordination of deaconesses by the Gallic councils she says:

Explanations for this tenacious battle of the Frankish Church against an institution which was well developed in other places and worked blessedly are, in our opinion, to be found in the extravagances which arose in certain sects (e.g., Priscillianists), and further in the abuses of Syneisaktentum, the custom in the primitive Church of unmarried males living together with consecrated virgins, which degenerated more and more and induced the Church to make energetic attack against clerics and virgins living together in the same house.[47]

It might be noted in passing that the present writer often found the first reaction of people who discovered the topic on which he was writing to be: "So you too want some pretty collaborator in the rectory?" In other words, it seems to be very common to see a danger to celibacy in a female priesthood. That might under some conditions be a reason not to ordain women priests. But is it also a basis on which to say that a woman is "incapable"?

All this is not to say that this has been the chief reason for the exclusion of women from spiritual office. But it shows that, from early times, the need was felt to adduce more concrete, tangible reasons than merely the decision that "the sex is not competent." Was it feared that the latter would not be very compelling?

From a later period we find Leo IV's prohibition against women singing in church. This prohibition too stands in a series of regulations on chastity.[48]

The *Quinisextum* from Trullanum of 692 once again forbids women to speak in church during worship service.[49]

There is still extant an explanation from three French bishops, Licinius of Tours (520), Melanius of Rennes, and Eustochius of Angiers (it could be questioned whether they belong to the third or the fourth chapter of this book, and for this reason I quote them outside the chronological sequence). The bishops wrote a letter to two priests from Brittany who permitted women to assist them in the distribution of communion. The letter says:

> The complete novelty of this proceeding and the unheard-of superstition has disturbed us not a little, that such a contemptible sect which has demonstrably never existed in Gaul (until now) comes to the surface in our time, a sect which the Oriental Fathers call the Pepodian sect because Pepodius was the originator of this schism, a sect which presumes to have women associates at the divine sacrifice. We therefore command: Anyone who wishes to adhere to this error should be excluded by the Church community.[50]

According to Lafontaine there is no such decree of the Oriental Fathers. The mention of Pepodius is also an error: probably a confusion with Pepuza, the city of the Montanists. It is also clear here that the bishops are especially annoyed over the fact that the priests live together with these women and in one breath speak about the *pollutio* of the divine sacraments, because they are distributed by women, and utter their desire that priests live only with their mother, sister, or wet nurse.

From later times I have found nothing else official on the problem. But the most important texts cited in this and the preceding chapter have been taken into the Corpus Iuris Canonici. I have from time to time made mention of this in the footnotes, and it obviously also emerges in the glossaries and commentaries. A brief overview can be found in an article by F. Gillmann, "Weib-

liche Kleriker nach dem Urteil der Frühscholastik," which, however, concerns itself almost exclusively with the legal sources.[51]

The catechism of the Council of Trent for parishes has nothing
to say on the matter. The canon from the new Code of Canon
Law is very brief. The word "valid" is worthy of attention: "Only
a baptized male [*vir baptizatus*] can receive the sacrament of
holy orders validly" (Can. 968, § 1).

The *fontes* for Can. 968, § 1, all refer to the *baptizatus*. However, there has never been anyone in the Catholic Church who
held that the ordination of a woman was valid. This canon should
therefore be interpreted according to the old law, that is, in the
sense that the "valid" also has reference to the word "male." But
the canon of the code in itself still says nothing about "divine
law" or "ecclesiastical law." And the church can certainly impose
conditions as "ecclesiastical law" for the validity of the sacrament.[52]

In the year 1916 the Holy Office published a decree in which
it said, "The image of the holy virgin Mary clothed with priestly
vestments is to be reprobated."

Certainly the intention was to put an end to several unwelcome
excesses of the veneration of the *Virgo Sacerdos*. But as this problem comes under discussion later in chapter V, for the purpose
of this chapter a mere mention of the Holy Office's prohibition
suffices. A detailed description of the entire history of the matter,
before and after, is found in Laurentin.[53]

Evaluation of the Texts

What is to be said now to all this? Does it represent a sufficient
proof for the thesis that women cannot be priests? At first glance
that seems actually to be the case. By the prohibition of the
Council of Laodicea, woman seems to be banished from the area
of official cult. Pope Gelasius says so expressly and apparently
gives as his formal reason: "It does not belong to the female sex
to serve the holy altars." And many synods have repeated that.
Every abuse is rejected. "Be a woman even learned and holy, she
nevertheless may not presume to baptize others or to teach males
in the community assembly," says Gratian,[54] and these prescriptions prevailed as conciliar decrees, for they appear as such
in the so-called Fourth Council of Carthage.

But if the texts are examined exactly, the proof is not as strong
as might be thought.

Everything that was said earlier, in the chapter on the Fathers, is valid here. One must consider also how many provisions of ancient synods simply do not obligate us any more. Then how do we know that these in particular continue as valid?

Especially noteworthy is the "proof from the magisterium"; careful observation shows that many of the texts quoted actually refer to something completely different, to things which are in fact no longer forbidden. How can such material be used to construct a proof for keeping women away from spiritual office?

The touching of holy vessels and blessed cultic linens, entrance into the sacrarium during sacred service, removal of the altar linens for laundering outside the service, presenting the priestly vestments—all of this is now permitted without objection.

Thus, there is but little to be found which is relevant, and what there is consists merely of prohibitions which we have long considered outdated. Giner Sempere, especially, insinuates with his long series of quotations that there is a large body of convincing texts. In reality there is, besides a few pertinent texts (especially Gelasius), only a quantity of uninteresting material which only witnesses to the fact that in clerical circles women were not held in very high esteem.

Or is there—behind these now no longer valid and no longer convincing prohibitions, which of themselves can prove nothing— a basic view which is still obligatory: that woman is not suitable for hierarchical office?

The chapter on the Fathers already documented that at least one thing lay behind all this: a judgment on woman, her nature, which to a great extent—if not essentially—differs from the understanding which our times have of woman. Thus, before anyone should jump to the conclusion that a proof has been found, it must first be explained why it is believed that the basic conception of the Patristic and synodical times includes an authentic insight of the Faith in reference to woman which is actually different from their time-bound views. In other words, it should be demonstrated that this understanding of woman which we found in the quoted synodical and papal statements is more profound and more Christian than that which we found in the other contemporaneous passages on women and presented in the previous chapter.

In addition, texts such as that of Pope Gelasius or of the Council of Nîmes treat the subject of deaconesses.[55] And it is certain that, not only now but even at that time in other places, much of what is here forbidden was permitted as legitimate, especially for deaconesses. We have already mentioned access to the altar area for laywomen. Testimony of this for the deaconesses is also given in the "Testament of the Lord." [56] There were places where the deaconesses might dispense Holy Communion; it was certainly not merely an abuse, as Jungmann says.[57] In the "Testament of the Lord" it is even their duty to bring Communion to sick women.[58] K. H. Schäfer mentions that deaconesses in the West brought Communion to women and boys up into the sixth century. Until 829 (the Council of Paris) "female holders of benefices" brought Communion to the faithful.[59] Of course one can say that that was abolished; it was an abuse. Naturally that may be the case. But not everything which is abolished by synods is *eo ipso* an abuse; there must be a careful investigation of what the synods intended to abolish and why this happened and what was abolished right along with it. If there was merely or mainly a concern for the danger to celibacy, these suppressions stand in a completely different context, particularly as we have seen that much of what was abolished by the synods (the touching of holy vessels, etc.) has been reintroduced by us.

Even an expression like "a woman although learned and holy" startles us. The "although" could of course indicate that the prohibition is intended as universal and for all times and circumstances. If merely "a woman . . . may not presume" were said, it could be thought that it was meant only for the women of that time, who were not so learned (and not so holy?). But because it expressly says that this is true even for holy and learned women, it is also true for other circumstances. So it could be argued. But against this argumentation it can be objected that the very words "although learned and holy" point to a time limitation. In a time where women are just as learned as men, such a specification need not be added. Thus it can be concluded that the women of that time were considered in general as too stupid and not holy enough to exercise spiritual office, to "teach males in assembly." And it can be imagined that under these circumstances it would be thought better to exclude all women, even the few who might by chance have been capable. If this were true, the words "although learned and holy" would in the first place signify for our problem that the relevant sentence really treated of another subject than that which a contemporary statement on the situation presupposes.

A sentence like "The women must be conscious of their own

weakness and the feebleness of their sex" is likewise acceptable only with great difficulty to present-day sensibility. And the statement which this expression is supposed to support loses much of its weight!

A conciliar decision like the following also places the attitude of the first centuries in the Church in a questionable light. The Council of Compiègne (757) says in its twentieth canon:

> If someone has taken a woman and lived with her a long time and if the woman says that he has never had intercourse with her, and the man says he has, then the truth should be decided on the basis of the man's statement, because the man is the head of the woman.[60]

A contemporary ecclesiastical judge would not believe the woman immediately either, but only because the marriage is presumed to be consummated and not because the man is the head of the woman and therefore apparently more credible than she. Behind this there lies the rabbinic understanding of the witness of woman! In the same way Pseudo-Augustine also thought that woman could bear no witness.

Nevertheless it could be said with justice that the ordinary magisterium has never desired women priests. And the dogmatic theologians can call upon the constant practice of the church, upon various texts presented above, upon the Corpus of Canon Law and its commentary, upon the present Code of Canon Law, and upon one another—that is, upon various dogmatic theologians and canon lawyers. The designations in the manuals indeed diverge from "theologically certain" to "a matter of divine faith" (the latter of course depend heavily on the Pauline texts), but the content of the thesis remains the same: It is (at least) theologically certain that women *by divine law* cannot be priests, and thus are "incapable."

But it must really be asked, as we have often already, whether the word woman in the sensibility of our time still has the same content as it had in those texts which express the opinion of the magisterium. Of course it should not be denied that, possibly according to God's will, until recently women could not be ordained priests. But has woman remained the same? Does God also forbid it for the contemporary woman? Can texts from other times serve to prove that the woman of our time cannot become a priest?

It should be noted, in this connection, that the problem of the priesthood of women has never been acute until very recently. The Montanists were really anachronistic. Only for the past thirty to fifty years has a woman been able to become a physician, a lawyer, a judge, a minister of state, and so on. Rondet reports how even in 1909 an ecclesiastical book censor had deleted from a *Cours de semaines sociales* a sentence which advocated suffrage for women.[61] In a time in which women were thought of in this way the question of the priesthood for women, even if it was recognized in theory and existed in the manuals, was not yet really asked. All the texts of the magisterium and authors refer to a different problem from ours.

Since the problem—partly through developments in the Protestant camp—was first raised among Catholic dogmatic theologians, there have been no new statements of the magisterium. That seems to us to be quite remarkable. Certainly popes, Roman congregations, bishops, and so forth have not changed their opinion in this respect. But they have not found it necessary to express their opinion with new definiteness. The 1913 condemnation of the Marian image with priestly vestments clearly stands in the "climate" of opposition to woman's suffrage that we have just mentioned. This decision certainly does not contribute anything to the contemporary discussion of the problem.

Even Pius XII in his addresses to women, in which he expressly emphasized that the woman should not live only in the family but also might and should participate in public life in offices and professions, did not speak of denying the priesthood to women. One example is his address of 9 October 1945.[62]

On the 28th of August, 1949, he said:

Woman has left the reserve and the self-effacement of domestic life and to a large extent has made her own the places, functions, responsibilities, and rights which earlier were reserved exclusively for men. . . . Having reached her majority and become independent and possessed of the same rights as he, she is today the equal of man in the economy and in work, in science and art, in the liberal professions, in public employment and in the political and administrative affairs of the state and the community.[63]

On the 14th of October, 1956:

If at another time the work of the woman was limited to the house and its surroundings, today it expands into ever wider circles: into social and public life, the parliament, the courts, journalism, the liberal professions, the world of labor. May woman carry into all these fields her work of peace.[64]

Of course the Pope does not say "also in the sacerdotal office." But he does not forbid it. The ordinary magisterium thus in the recent decades in which the problem has become a real one has not spoken out against the priesthood of women, even in places where it could be expected.[65]

For the dogmatic theologians the task therefore lies in proving whether, why, and to what extent woman should occupy a different status in the ecclesiastical from in the secular world; or in proving that the old statements still have an obligatory character even in the altered circumstances.

One cannot help but recall how many opinions which were looked upon as unambiguous judgments of the ordinary magisterium nevertheless were altered later. This can be noted in recent sacramental theology. The point of view that the Church can decide on the validity of the sacraments and that the conditions for the validity of the dispensing of the sacraments were not specifically established by Christ has prevailed. Yet in these points too, dogmatic theologians thought for centuries that everything existed "by divine law" and was therefore unalterable. Did not the ordinary magisterium believe for centuries that a person could be reconciled to the Church only once in his life? Was not —to mention an example from another tractate of theology— the creation of Adam from the dust of the earth, and of Eve from the rib, stated by the magisterium? The prohibition on lending for interest was also a statement of the magisterium—until money took on another function in the economy. Is something similar perhaps true of woman, who now fulfills other sociological and psychological functions in society?

The burden of proof that this is not so, I believe, lies on those who try to defend the usual thesis against the priesthood for women. Another parallel must likewise be noted. Theology has always thought that only wheat bread and grape wine could be "valid matter" for consecration. And this has been considered proved with binding demonstrations from the ordinary magisterium, exactly like the *subiectum validum* for sacerdotal consecration. However, H. Bouëssé, for example, has already asked whether that is a *conditio sine qua non* for all times and places.[66] Schillebeeckx too speaks in very nuanced manner, although he inclines more to assume that this point was indeed established by Christ for all times.[67]

In conclusion: a view held universally by dogmatic theologians is binding on individual dogmatic theologians only if it is put forward as binding by all other theologians or if it is presented as so bound up with certain teachings of the faith that to deny it also endangers the underlying teaching of the faith. The first is not the case in our problem. Many dogmatic theologians call this thesis only "theologically certain," thus, to be precise, not binding as a *teaching of the faith*.[68] And no one proposes any teaching of the faith which would fall if this thesis were denied.

This, then, is our conclusion:

1. There are certain texts which justify our saying: the ordinary magisterium has until now been against the priesthood for women.
2. But, seen from a scholarly-theological viewpoint, it is not at all certain that this still has an obligatory character for our time. That may be the case, but it is not proved.

V Theological Speculation (Ratio Theologica)

It is striking that the Fathers undertook no real speculations on their thesis. They simply appealed to the fact that Jesus and the apostles commissioned no women. Or they referred to the Pauline texts. That is not speculative at all. Only where they appealed to the inferior status of woman did reflection emerge. In this of course they presupposed that the priest is a superior.

The actual basis for their thesis is thus the conviction that woman cannot have any leadership role—have no jurisdiction, we would say—and it is completely obvious to them that woman may not have this in either the religious or the secular area. The texts which we have cited from Augustine, Lactantius, and Chrysostom might be compared.

1. The Power of Jurisdiction

The same thing is true of Thomas, who attempts to give a genuine "ratio theologica." He does not appeal to the cultic, hallowing aspect of the priesthood (the *sanctificare* or *sacrificare* function), which becomes more prominent in latter times because the inability of women to rule is no longer so convincing, but exclusively to the aspect of the magisterium and of rule. His argumentation goes:

> For since a sacrament is a sign, not only the thing but the signification of the thing is required in all sacramental actions; thus it was stated above (q. 32, a. 2) that in Extreme Unction it is necessary to have a sick man, in order to signify the need of healing. Accordingly, since it is not possible in the female sex to signify eminence of degree, for a woman is in the state of subjection, it follows that she cannot receive the sacrament of Orders.[1]

Thomas is concerned merely with the *eminentia gradus* in the area of sign, not with *eminentia,* which should not be defined. To the objection that there were women prophesying in the Old Testament (Hulda in 4 Kings 22, 14) and that the "prophetic office" is superior to that of the priest, from which it could be concluded that a woman could also be a priest, he did not respond by disputing the superiority of the prophetic office (which we, fortunately or unfortunately, are perhaps inclined to do) or by saying (like Gratian) that such a thing could happen only in the Old Testament and not in the New, which is more perfect. Prophesying is no sacrament, but a "gift from God," and therefore "no external designation" is demanded for it, but only the thing itself. Then Thomas continues:

And since in matters pertaining to the soul woman does not differ from man as to the thing (for sometimes a woman is found to be better than many men as regards the soul) it follows that she can receive the gift of prophecy and the like, but not the sacrament of Orders.[2]

As we see, Thomas thus came to a logical development and systematization of various data from Patristic times. "In those things which pertain to the soul" woman is not different from man. Another passage states explicitly that woman too is created "in the image of God," that is, "in reference to the spiritual nature"; although the male is the "image of God" in another respect where the woman is not, inasmuch as the man is the "origin and goal" of the woman, just as God is the origin and goal of the entire universe.[3] It is also explicitly said that woman "in reference to the soul" can be better than many men. We will see later that Thomas believed that woman "in reference to the body" was in no way of equal value to the man, but far inferior. Perhaps he was of the opinion that a woman, on the level of "symbol," could not exhibit an "eminence of degree." Thomas does indeed seem somehow to have grasped that the entire woman is woman, for he applies the contrast of the sexes to the person:

The genus masculine refers to the hypostasis or person, whereas the genus neuter refers to the nature.[4]

But Thomas expresses no opinion on why woman can be a superior in the secular area but not in the religious. For to the objection that Deborah of the Old Testament was a judge he responded:

Deborah exercised secular offices, not priestly, just as today women can exercise worldly power [*possunt mulieres temporaliter dominari*].[5]

And he does not explain in any more detail just what constitutes the difference between secular and sacerdotal jurisdiction and why this distinction leads to specific conclusions denying spiritual jurisdiction to a woman. That however seems to be a very important question. For worldly office too demands an "eminence of degree on the level of symbol." Inasmuch as Thomas did not give an answer to this, his proof is very imperfect. According to Thomas himself woman even in the secular area is in the state of subjection! In fact, he says very generally: "The reason why [women] are in a subordinate and not a commanding position is because they lack sufficient reason, which a leader above all needs." [6] Manser believes that Thomas logically would have had to say that woman is unqualified for office in the secular area: "Even if Thomas in the above-mentioned passages speaks only of public-ecclesiastical offices and positions, it is nevertheless clear to everyone that the reasons which he adduces speak against any civil equivalence of woman with man." [7] In another passage Manser himself believes that Switzerland's denial of woman's suffrage is the "most reasonable" position.[8] Thus Manser resolves the contradiction by removing jurisdiction in temporal things. Professor Trooster of Maastricht permits the contradiction to remain, for he believes that it is the peculiar essential function of the man to be the head in the kingdom of God.[9] But it seems to us that we must really ask him why he believes that the function of the male is something other in the kingdom of God than it is in the secular area. The difficulty arises of itself in its most basic form: May the kingdom of God be compared to any other kingdom as if it were a kingdom of sin? In other words, are the kingdom of God and the kingdom of the world really so distinct from another that a completely different law prevails?

This is not the place to develop a complete overview of Thomistic teaching on woman. But one thing is certainly clear: in some respects Thomas has not proceeded beyond the views of the Fathers in reference to woman. For him, as for Augustine,

It was necessary for woman to be made, as the Scripture says, not as a helpmate in other works than generation as some say, since man can be more efficiently helped by another man in other works; but as a helper in the work of generation.[10]

Manser asserts that it is incorrect to say "woman according to Thomas existed only for breeding," for elsewhere Thomas says:

The human male and female are united, not only for generation, as with other animals, but also for the purpose of domestic life, in which each has his or her particular duty.[11]

But Manser is correct only insofar as these "other works," namely the education of children, are not precisely the same as breeding. But when Thomas says woman is the most frequent (not the best!) teacher of children,[12] he has not said anything essentially new. The question was whether Thomas had an understanding of other female tasks which are not immediately connected with childbearing. He certainly did not have, or express, such an understanding.

Anyone who so narrows the working scope of woman a priori must naturally answer with an unhesitating "yes" the question "Is being a woman an impediment to the reception of ordination?" Such a person believes men will be able to work much better together. In the area of sacerdotal tasks they need no help from women. Women are not created for this: "Not as help for other work, but as help in the work of generation."

That Thomas saw the "impediment of womanhood" merely in the priestly power of jurisdiction and not in the power of sanctification can be concluded from, among other things, the argument that he draws up to demonstrate that a woman can baptize validly. For the argument is not valid merely for baptism; it has a universal validity for all sacraments. In the article "Can a woman baptize?" he gives as the third objection:

In the spiritual regeneration water seems to hold the place of the mother's womb. . . . But he who baptizes seems to hold rather the position of father, which is unfitting for a woman. Therefore a woman cannot baptize.

He responds to this in the body of the article, "It ought to be said that Christ is the chief baptizer."

And, thirdly:

In carnal generation male and female cooperate according to the power of their proper nature; wherefore the female cannot be the active, but only the passive principle of generation.

But in spiritual generation they do not act, either of them, by their proper power, but only instrumentally by the power of Christ. Consequently, on the same grounds either man or woman can baptize in a case of urgency.[13]

If it is thus true that woman is not insufficient in the area of salvation in which the human acts "instrumentally by the power of Christ," because her nature does not act in its own power, then the question arises so much the more urgently why spiritual jurisdiction in the area of salvation does not belong to woman when after all secular jurisdiction is not denied her.

In the question of the validity of the Thomistic argumentation the question again emerges whether, perhaps, when he excludes woman from the sacerdotal office, he is speaking of another subject than we are when we speak of women.

Woman is indeed, for him, "something deficient and accidental." [14] For a precise interpretation of this expression see the two articles by A. Mitterer.[15] According to the intention of the "universal nature," which is dependent upon God, woman is not something which has miscarried, but she is such according to the intention of "individual nature," for the inner aim of the individual act of procreation of the male is precisely to beget one "similar to himself."

Who among us could still subscribe to such an idea! Or the idea that woman is here only for procreation! Or that she merely supplies the matter for the procreation of a new living being, nothing more than the earth for the seed! Woman is more than a field for the seed of the male in which (as in the seed kernels) the entire new being is already contained. From his false biological presuppositions on man and woman, and especially on the actual roles of the man and the woman in the act of procreation, Thomas arrived at a false understanding of the value of woman: a qualitative inferiority of woman, Mitterer correctly puts it, on account of genetic and functional inferiority.[16] A few texts may suffice.

Woman naturally is less in virtue and dignity than the male, for it is always more honorable to be active than to be passive.

And:

The discretionary power of reason naturally abounds more in man.[17]

Or:

The male is more perfect in reason and stronger in virtue.[18]

Further:

Women commonly are not perfect enough in wisdom that public teaching can be entrusted to them.[19]

And still worse:

Women have only a mediate contact with Christ: only the nuns know him immediately.

Woman is not immediately subordinate to God, but rather is subordinate to a man who is subordinate to God.[20]

The masculine sex is *nobilior* than the feminine, which is *ignobilior* and *vilior*.[21] Woman is less able to resist temptation.[22] The father is better suited for education, because he can instruct better with his understanding and can punish better with his bodily strength.[23]

Who can still agree with all this? At the very least a better proof is necessary. Nussbaumer does in fact assert that this agrees with the data of modern psychology;[24] but without giving evidence, that is not sufficient.

The Thomistic argument proceeds from the idea that woman does not possess "eminence of degree"; therefore it is to be concluded that the male does possess such eminence in order to be able to be a priest. We have just asked whether woman is still the same as in the time of Thomas. Perhaps it must also be asked whether the male has remained the same. Does he in our society still have the same "eminence of degree" which he had in Thomas's time? Much of what the man earlier was and produced is now no longer performed by him as man in his roles of husband or of father, but by the authorities, by the community—by a female type, that is. In a primitive society it is the man's job to protect against robbers and murderers; now this is done by the police, who of course are males but who act as an official authority, a group. In any case, the head of the family as such does not do it. He cannot. Likewise with sustenance; in the patriarchal period the father provided everything his own family needed; now, at most, he provides the money. Insurance provides our security in sickness; the man of course has paid for that himself, but it is no longer "on the level of a symbol"! On the level of a symbol, not he but the insurance company has "eminence of degree." His knowledge and his experience do not offer enough to the children; if they are to go through life well equipped, they need the school. His wife does the same work as he, or at least she could do it in the great majority of the masculine professions. And in the city he does not secure a home at all; that is done by the city offices for assigning homes or by other agents. "From matriarchy through patriarchy to bureaucracy," goes the formula.[25] The man is no longer leader, ruler, health bringer, etc., in the same measure as was earlier the case. Where he is still such, or attempts to be, or alleges himself to be, he becomes a distortion of this positively-valued title: he becomes a tyrant, and so on. The man is no longer so clearly the type of Christ. The community has become that. The farmer, large or small, was as a matter of fact the head. The contemporary factory worker or office employee is a number. And in government it is no longer the prince who rules but the majority of the ballots. Has the male remained the same? [26]

a. The Secular Jurisdiction of Women

When Thomas said, "The corruption of urbanity appears when a woman attains dominion," [27] he speaks of course in an Aristotelian, even a Patristic, manner, but he is not completely convincing. In the section which includes the words quoted above, he brings forth two arguments why abbesses could possess neither the "key of orders" nor the "key of jurisdiction." First, because according to Paul woman is "in the state of subjection" and therefore can have no spiritual power; second, because it is a "corruption of urbanity," etc. We have already discussed, in chapter II, the relativity of Paul's arguments. The second argument is likewise unconvincing. It is noticeable that, unlike Augustine, Thomas does not speak of the "unhappy home"; he talks not merely of the family but of "urbanity." Although Thomas elsewhere never mentions urbanity as a virtue (if we may trust the most important lexicons and indices of Thomas's writings), one may nevertheless conclude from a passage in which *urbanus* appears [28] that this virtue has reference not to the household but to civic life. If Thomas too had said only "unhappy home," one might have left it at that.

In this book it is not my intention to question the leadership role of the man in the family.[29] Papal statements, as for example that of Pius XI in the encyclical *Casti connubii,* are too clear for that.[30] Perhaps something more nuanced would be in order here, but that is not my present task. Thus, I shall also not touch the question of whether the man is head of his wife inasmuch as she too is a member of the family; nor am I discussing the question of whether the man is head of his wife insofar as she is a separate, free person who, although a member of the family, transcends this member-of-the-family existence. I am speaking only of the question of whether the man always and everywhere and under all conditions is the head of every woman—in other words, whether the man, merely because of his membership in the male sex, is the head of every woman, even if she is not his wife or if she is not married at all or does not wish to be. If this question should be answered in the positive, we could speak, with Thomas and Aristotle, of "corruption of urbanity"—but must this question really be answered in the positive? I believe that today this problem must not be presumed already long solved, as it was in earlier times. Thomas's understanding of woman appears to me too questionable. It cannot be seriously asserted that the phenomenon of a contemporary female minister of state is a "corruption of urbanity."

There is, moreover, a real question of how Thomas was able to say this when in other passages he recognizes that "women are able to rule in temporal matters." In this recognition of the secular jurisdiction of woman he is completely traditional. The Church has never rejected ruling princesses on the basis of their womanhood, neither in Byzantium nor in the West. Innocent III issued an explanation on the matter in the year 1202, as can be gathered clearly, if somewhat laboriously, from the wording of the Bull. It concerns a statement of arbitration of a French queen in a dispute between Cistercian monks and Hospitalers. One of the parties did not wish to hold to the statement. The pope wrote to the "Chancellor and Teacher Lotharius, Canon of Paris":

Although according to the rule of civil law women are excluded from such kinds of public functions, and although it states elsewhere that they—even if they enjoy a good reputation and are of good behavior, if they have taken on judicial activity, or if as rulers they have settled disputes between their freemen—are to be restrained from any judicial investigation so that no punishment at all against their justified contemners occurs from their allegations and also no exception is made from the contract; because alongside the recognized custom which is considered law, in parts of France—as is known—

such distinguished women exercise the regular power of
jurisdiction over their underlings, we through apostolic writing
leave it to your decision how far you admonish and instruct
the above-mentioned Hospitalarii, that they observe the
arbitration—particularly because it was empowered in the
presence of and through the concurrence of the bishops, as it
also was made carefully without any irregularity and freely
accepted by both sides—and moreover, should it be necessary,
to secure with it the punishment established in the contract,
under exclusion of appeal.[31]

One notices that the Pope looked upon the presence and assent
of the bishops as a happy coincidence, but not as essential for
the validity of the arbitrational dictum of the queen, for he says
only "especially"; and he accepts the jurisdiction of the queen as
"regular." Herewith the Pope decided that a woman can have
jurisdiction over men in the secular area, even over monks and
priests and over their abbot.

The Church has also always recognized secular princesses. The
current *Pontificale Romanum* has a proper consecration for a
reigning queen which is not the same as the consecration of
a queen who is the consort of the reigning king; [32] the consecration and coronation of the queen *ut regni dominae* is to a great
extent like that of a king. Thus, for example, the prayer at the
moment of crowning:

Know well that by this crown you partake of our [the
bishops'] service [*particem ministerii nostri*]. As we are
considered shepherds and guides of souls in the spiritual area,
so also should you in the secular area stand forth as a true
worshiper of God and a resolute defender of God's Church
against all calamities.

The queen thus is "particeps ministerii episcoporum."

Earlier the queen consort was anointed on the breast. In this
way God's blessing was imprinted in advance upon the future
successor to the throne under his mother's heart.[33] The royal consort was thus seen primarily as mother of the successor to the
throne—corresponding completely to the common understanding
of woman: she exists only for *generatio;* she is something only
inasmuch as she is a mother. But the Church too has progressed
beyond this understanding; it knows that a woman can also be
more. One would be almost inclined to think: where it is re-

quired and made possible by external circumstances, the Church immediately, without further consideration, granted woman much more than in other cases; here it became conscious of what it had always known, that woman can be completely equal to man. The Church points out that not only the king but also the reigning queen can possess the function of a representative of God: ". . . with our Savior and Redeemer Jesus Christ whose name and whose place is confided to you to bear . . ." And the queen is also mediator, specifically between clergy and people. The "Mediator between God and man" makes her a mediator between clergy and people.

Certainly neither king nor queen is a priest, a favorite thought of the eleventh-century reformers. But it is important that according to the Pontificale a woman can be the people's mediator. I shall enlarge on this theme later.

In all this we must remember that we are not concerned here with "things," with the sphere of *res:* we are working here in the sphere of *significatio.*

b. Have There Been Women with Spiritual Jurisdiction?

The actual progression beyond the traditional concepts of woman by the Church itself is still clearer when we see how much some abbesses were able to do without ecclesiastical objection. Authors speak of course of a quasi-episcopal power, "a *sort* of jurisdiction," [34] or they designate everything done by the abbess as "*dominativa* power," qualify her appointments and acts of jurisdiction as "designation of a person." But that cannot really correspond exactly to the way things were, because there is proof that the actual faculties of the abbesses lacked nothing which would have made the jurisdiction incomplete. There was nothing at all lacking. Thus one is forced to speak of a quasi-jurisdiction only if it is *presupposed* that a woman can have no jurisdiction. If the facts are taken soberly, it must be said simply: the abbesses had spiritual jurisdiction. If writers believe that in the light of these facts they must nevertheless still speak only in terms of, "as if it were a jurisdiction," it must be asked how these writers wish to define the concept "jurisdiction" in general. Their definition can only be: jurisdiction is that which woman cannot possess.

It is not the intention of this book to treat all those cases which could prove that women have had jurisdiction. For our purpose it is sufficient to focus on a few characteristic cases.[35]

A very clear case is that of the abbess of Quedlinburg, which is also important because Pope Honorius III confirmed the faculties of the abbess vis-à-vis the clerics who attempted to evade it. Even earlier the foundation was withdrawn from all episcopal jurisdiction and made immediately papal. In the year 1212 the abbess complained to the Pope that the canonesses and clerics subject to her jurisdiction whom she had suspended did not accept the suspension on the grounds that the abbess was not able to excommunicate them. The Pope responded:

> Our daughter beloved in the Lord, the Abbess of Bubrigen [Friedberg says in a footnote that this should be read as Quedlinburg in the diocese of Halberstadt] has set forth the following in a petition sent to us: Sometimes when she suspends her canonesses and the clerics who are subject to her jurisdiction [*clericos suae iurisdictioni subiectes*], because of disobedience and other lapses, from their office and benefice, they do not observe a suspension of this sort because they are strongly convinced that she cannot excommunicate; hence, their excesses remain uncorrected. So that the said canonesses and clerics show obedience and respect to the above named abbess and obey her good admonitions, we consign therefore to your discrimination to what extent you—according to previous admonition—wish to inflict on them ecclesiastical censure under exclusion of appeal.

The text was included in the decretals of Gregory IX.[36] Even if it is not said that the abbess herself could excommunicate— the abbot to whom the letter is directed should inflict the censure—the clerics are nevertheless to observe the suspension pronounced by the abbess.

It should not immediately be assumed that this is a genuine suspension or censure. It could also signify a withdrawal of the receipt of benefices or a forbidding of celebration—punishments, that is, which are part of the *potestas dominativa*—but in any case, the words of the Pope are quite obvious: "Clerics subject to her jurisdiction." The Pope thus has less difficulty with the *corruptio urbanitatis* than do Thomas and the Fathers. L. Hanser sees here an example of the cases where an abbess was an *Abbatissa nullius*.[37]

Pope Honorius III recognized female power over spiritual matters on still another occasion. In a letter he calls the "Abbess of Iotrens" simply "Head and mistress" of "priests and clerics" of the church there.[38]

Male canons who belonged to foundations of canonesses had to take a special oath of obedience to the abbess.[39] The abbess had the entire exterior and interior direction and administration of the congregation under her. She had to bestow all prebends, churches, benefices, offices, and canonicates in her church.[40] From the bull of Nicholas V (in the middle of the fifteenth century) to the foundation of Gandersheim it follows that the abbess had an "ordinary authority" in addition.[41] In the fifteenth century the abbess of Vreeden had to warn, suspend, or dismiss and discharge completely the male members of the foundation whenever they were negligent.[42] It is known that the abbess of St. Cecilia's in Cologne had jurisdiction and power of suspension over the canons.[43] She did have to be represented by a canon, called the abbess's chaplain, in cases of spiritual jurisdiction over men as well as in other formalities.[44] This fact seems to contradict our thesis on the possibility of female jurisdiction, but it should be noted that the canon was only her representative. The abbess's chaplain had to sit in judgment *in the name of the abbess.*[45]

The abbess of the Herford foundation appointed the entire clergy, the priests belonging to the cathedral church, the rectors of the independent chapels in the city, and so on. Herford was an abbey nullius. In the entire Middle Ages we know of no case in which the bishop by virtue of his right undertook any kind of official action in the area of this city. Hadrian IV, in the middle of the twelfth century, had renewed the older stipulations and declared the foundation free of any episcopal jurisdiction:

We forbid that in the said monastery any bishop outside the Roman pontiff exercise jurisdiction, and indeed in the sense that he never—unless he will be so invited by the abbess—may presume to celebrate solemn Masses there.[46]

That is exactly the opposite of contemporary canon law:

The local bishop must himself or through a representative visit the individual cloisters of nuns every five years which are subject to him or immediately to the Apostolic See. [can. 512, par. 1]

The "Lady of Herford" is designated as the Herford "ordinary." This was acknowledged by Paul III in a letter of 5 July 1549, which said in reference to the city:

> . . . nevertheless the abbess's right as proper judge to pronounce due penalties remains undisputed.[47]

Among monastic abbesses too there were similar cases. The most famous example is that of the abbess of the Cistercian monastery of Conversano, who has entered literature as the "monstrosity of Apulia."[48] After 1266 she was the successor of a Cistercian abbot who was abbot nullius. Her district was but small; nevertheless she appointed the priests for the service of her convent church and for the churches of the city belonging to the convent. On 19 July 1709 she procured a judgment by the Holy See against the clergy of the city, by which her legal prerogatives were confirmed:[49] she named the vicar-general, who ruled the area belonging to the abbey—in her name! The honors which must be offered to every newly consecrated abbess by the clergy were modified by the conciliar congregation in the above-mentioned judgment, but were in no way rejected as monstrous. Earlier the clergy had to betake themselves to the abbey in their choir robes; and while the abbess with miter and crozier sat under a baldachino in front of the outer monastery door, each individual member of the clergy had to file before the abbess, throw himself on his knees before her, and kiss her hand. The judgment supported the prescribed honors but changed a few details. The miter and crozier were first of all laid on a credence alongside the abbess, and the kissing of the hand no longer took place on the bare hand of the abbess but on the gloved hand or on the stole (!) of the abbess. Instead of throwing themselves on their knees before the abbess, the clergy could be satisfied with a mere bow.[50]

When the last abbess nullius of Conversano died in 1809, her territory was transferred to the bishop of Conversano. The government of Naples had already incorporated her district into that diocese in 1806, but it was canonically confirmed by Pius VII only in 1818[51]—itself a sign that Rome was not discontent with an abbess nullius.

There are others who had great power of jurisdiction—the abbesses of Fontevrault in France and of Essen in Germany, and an abbess in the republic of Lucca in Italy; the last was even called *episcopa* as a result of her extensive jurisdiction.[52] And according to Hallier the abbess of Fontevrault had "spiritual jurisdiction." [53]

A further case is that of the abbess of the Cistercian nuns of Las Huelgas near Burgos.[54] In the *Dictionnaire de théologie catholique* her own official "protocol" is quoted. We read there:

Lady, superior, prelate, legitimate administrator of the spiritual and temporal matters of the said royal monastery . . . as well as the convents, churches, hermitages affiliated with it, and the villages and places of its jurisdiction, manors and vassalages, in virtue of the apostolic bull and concessions with a jurisdiction that is plenary, privative, quasi-episcopal, nullius diocesis and with royal privileges: a double jurisdiction which we exercise in peaceful possession, as is publicly well known.

Further:

The power to act judicially, just as the lord bishops, in criminal, civil and beneficial cases, to grant dimissorial letters for ordination, faculties to preach, confess, exercise the care of souls, enter into religion, the power to confirm abbesses, to issue censures . . . and finally to convoke a synod.[55]

Of course, if it were absolutely necessary, especially in the granting of the faculties for confession by the abbess, one could speak of a mere "designation of person" and mean that the actual jurisdiction came from the Holy See, as the *Dictionnaire* does.[56] But in our opinion this is to construct a completely artificial solution after the fact, based only on the conviction that a woman can have no jurisdiction. The facts do not suggest such a construction; on the contrary. Only if it were clearly demonstrated elsewhere that "by divine law" a woman can have no ecclesiastical jurisdiction would such a concept be necessary as an emergency solution to explain a few minor, difficult cases. It certainly cannot be said: "A woman can have no jurisdiction, for look: even among the powerful abbesses there was only a 'designation of person' involved." Even to someone who examines the matter very carefully it is not clear why one should speak here merely of a "designation of person." Even Krebs must admit that appointments by the abbesses were not merely a matter of the abbess's right of patronage (although in other respects he sees the Pope as the actual bearer of jurisdiction in the case of the abbess nullius).[57]

Of course it becomes very difficult to discover why and to what extent these abbesses have lacked "eminence of degree on the level of symbol."

With all these examples before our eyes—especially those of Las Huelgas and Herford—it is no longer possible to speak of Conversano as a "monstrosity." Baronius, who coined the expression, probably knew only this one case and thus considered it a unique deformity.[58] But the cases, as we have seen, are not so few. So there can be no talk of a monstrosity; on the contrary, it must be simply accepted as a fact that women can have spiritual jurisdiction in the Church. As we saw, the abbesses were not only tolerated by Rome but were, in so many words, confirmed in their status.

Even the consecration formula for monastic abbesses is indicative. It includes a number of things reminiscent of the consecration of bishops and abbots. There are expressions like: "to govern the church" or "to govern and rule your church" (in the prayer *cunctorum* and in the Preface). "These words are quite strong," says Puniet.[59] Or: "Receive the complete, unlimited fullness of power to rule this monastery" (at the enthronement). Earlier, and even now in a few places, the abbess received the crozier.[60]

Even the double monasteries which stood under the guidance of the abbesses present the same image,[61] especially in the early Middle Ages (seventh to ninth centuries) in France; later in England. In Germany, however, it was the abbot who was the head of the double monastery.

The double orders are interesting. In the order of Fontevrault, founded in the twelfth century, the abbess was the general superior of the entire order. The founder, Robert of Arbrissel (c. 1177), appealed to John 19, 27: "Behold your mother." The order was sanctioned by Pope Paschasius II in 1106 and 1112. It was suspended only in 1790.[62] The abbess undertook the visitations, exercised penal jurisdiction even over the men, appointed the vicars-general in spiritual matters.[63] These vicars thus existed not for jurisdiction but for the power of ordination.

In other double orders the abbesses had in fact no more than a mere "dominative power." The Gilbertines were directed by a man.[64] The Brigittines stood under the direction of the local bishops.[65] But even St. Brigit referred to Mary as the head of the apostles after the resurrection. This argument thus is interesting because it says exactly the opposite of what we saw earlier in other passages: women cannot baptize, etc., because even Mary did not do that, or as Innocent III formulated it:

Although the most holy virgin Mary stood above and was also more excellent than all the apostles together, the Lord still did not confide to her but to them the keys of the kingdom of heaven. [See below at note 76.]

We return to Thomas's argument. As we have seen, his argument concerning the validity of the dispensing of baptism by a woman, if it is a valid proof at all, is a proof against the dispensing of any of the sacraments by a woman. As a matter of fact, he does not prove even from this angle the impossibility of a female priesthood. It is not the power of sanctifying that is his basis for declaring that a woman cannot be a priest. He argues from jurisdiction bound up with ordination: the woman is in "the state of subjection," and for this reason she cannot be a priest. Now the historical facts prove that she actually does not lack this jurisdiction. There have been women who have had ecclesiastical jurisdiction, and indeed so obviously that the same people who are convinced that a woman can have no ecclesiastical jurisdiction have had to contrive the solution of "designation of person," for in cases of "designation of person" very often those who designate give every appearance of giving jurisdiction as well—exactly like the abbesses. Thus these writers have implicitly admitted that it at least appears from without as if the abbess granted the jurisdiction.

But this makes the Thomistic demonstration very questionable: the aspect of the power of consecration offers no prospects, and the aspect of the power of jurisdiction is refuted by the facts. What remains? If the rejection of deaconesses is considered in this light, these texts (Pope Gelasius) lose at least a part of their strength. Even Gelasius cannot have held (in any case not as an authentic and infallible teacher of the Church) that a woman cannot baptize even in an emergency. In general, women were permitted much in the sacral area: emergency baptism, assistance at baptism (anointing with the holy oils), distribution of communion, wearing of the stole, singing of the gospel, etc. Only in the area of jurisdiction can stronger restraints be felt. Until the circumstances made it possible!

Even more questionable is the Thomistic proof in which we read that he himself knew that there were women who were no longer "in the state of subjection." Bear in mind that the "state of subjection" is the middle term on his syllogism. We have already seen the text; on 1 Cor. 11, 6, "It is shameful for a woman to have her hair cut off," he writes:

It appears to be contrary to this that the nuns have their hair cut off. . . . To which it can be answered, because they have taken the vow of virginity or have assumed widowhood, thus becoming betrothed to Christ, they are promoted to the dignity of men [*promoventur in dignitatem virilem*] whereby they are liberated from the subjection to men [*libertatae a subiectione virorum*] and are joined immediately to Christ.[66]

Ambrose attributes this "promotion" to faith, Jerome to the service of Christ, Thomas to vows. However that may be, these texts make comprehensible how the abbesses could have jurisdiction. As brides of Christ they were withdrawn from subordination to men. Of course Thomas himself did not draw this conclusion. For him:

Woman does not have the key of jurisdiction. . . . Rather, the use of the keys is committed to some women, for example, the need to correct subordinate women became of the danger which can threaten if men and women live together.[67]

But in his commentary on 1 Cor. 11 he went beyond his own position. He held that there was at least one group of women who were elevated "to male dignity" and "liberated from subjection to men": the nuns.

Writers on the question have, of course, known more or less about these actual powers of office of the abbesses and have sought to clarify these facts. Thus Thomas, as we have seen, said:

She does not have the key, but a certain use of the keys was committed to her.[68]

But Suarez correctly noted in this regard:

It is difficult to explain how the use of the key is committed to someone if the key itself is not committed; for no one can use something he does not have. Likewise, the use of jurisdiction can be committed to no one, unless the jurisdiction is committed; therefore, similarly . . . etc.[69]

Because Suarez gives a good overview of the attempted solution, let us follow him. In *De Censuris* he presents the problem that woman is "incapable of exercising spiritual jurisdiction, which belongs to the power of the keys." He quotes the passage from Thomas with which we began this chapter and many other commentators (the passage from Thomas in fact is in *IV Sent.*). He then proceeds further and says that this is "proved" from the chapter *Mulierem* 33, q. 5,[70] where it is stated that woman can neither teach nor administer justice. But these texts, he says, do not prove much, for there are no papal decrees but only statements of Augustine (Pseudo-Augustine!) and because they seem to treat the question not of absolute capability but of propriety. For this reason it is also stated there that woman cannot be a witness nor can she make any binding pledge (even he does not agree with this!). Rather, he believes, it can better be demonstrated from the chapter *De monialibus, de sent. excomm.*,[71] where it is said that an abbess cannot absolve her subordinate from a censure; thus, concludes Suarez, she can much less impose a censure, if she cannot absolve from it. It is also demonstrated in the chapter *Nova*, from *De poenit. et remiss.*, [72] which discusses several sacramental acts and preaching, and thus not jurisdiction. However, Suarez believed, an argument could be drawn from this text either by analogy or because the pope concluded in the end that the keys of the kingdom were not given to women, not even to the Holy Virgin.

And this is the a priori reason for this conclusion: in truth it is fittingness, because the feminine sex is not of itself appropriate to take on spiritual functions. Whence she is permitted neither to teach nor to rule over men (1 Tim. 2), although in religious orders there is granted to the word of the abbess a certain power of ruling which is morally necessary in orders of nuns, for that cannot honestly and decently be handled by men. This power nevertheless does not extend to proper acts of the keys, but only to acts of commanding, correcting, and instructing insofar as they fit in with paternal and, as it were, domestic rule, as all of the cited authors note, especially Victoria in great detail . . . and all the authors of Summas. This is corroborated by the fact that women cannot receive orders, as we will show below; this power, however, to apply censures presumes orders or at least the first tonsure. Finally, it is consonant with civil law where it is said that women are to be kept out of public offices and therefore cannot be judges.

Because Suarez apparently sensed that this solution—which was concerned merely with a domestic power—did not suffice, he made difficulties for himself from three texts from the Canon Law. We have already quoted these texts. In his solution he notes that in the Quedlinburg case it was not a genuine censure that was involved, but merely a "prohibition or a privation, which can also be called a suspension in the broader sense." The Pope also did not say that the censure which the abbess had imposed should be observed, but only her "precept and mandate," and the Pope commanded the abbot to force the obstinate man with a censure —thus intimating that the suspension pronounced through the abbess was no censure.

Beyond this, Suarez does not deny that a woman can have jurisdiction. He especially does not try to argue about "temporal jurisdiction." However, he says that the jurisdiction over clerics is never merely temporal. He implies that a woman by special law can indeed have jurisdiction over clerics (and thus spiritual jurisdiction), but never a jurisdiction so great that she can impose a censure. Indeed, he even believes that the Pope "in his absolute power" could also impart this power to women, an opinion which many other authors, such as Paludanus, Soto, Navarrus, and Ugolinus have also advocated, for that would not be "contrary to divine law." [73] But the Church, as a matter of fact, has never gone that far "because it is not fitting." And "if it is not directly against divine and natural law, it is nevertheless not completely compatible with them." [74] According to Suarez, then, a woman is not excluded from spiritual jurisdiction "by divine or natural law."

In *De religione* he refers to the above passages and amplifies a few. What the abbess exercises over her nuns is simply an "act of religious dominion, which derives in the real sense not from the power of the keys but from vows." What she exercises in reference to clergy he explains according to the content of the act either as a "jurisdiction which is bound up with ecclesiastical property and which is sometimes extended to clergy, insofar as it relates to the act of making prescriptions (he means, for example, 'that they should not celebrate Mass,' thus a quasi-suspension) and to reprimand them; for these acts of themselves concern not spiritual but corporal matters," or as a "designation of person" to whom the Pontiff gives jurisdiction, specifically when her acts are properly spiritual. In order to explain the "designation of person" more closely, he gives an example: "An example is the faculty of choosing a confessor by whom the penance is given."

In this way an abbess can also excommunicate, thus impose a censure, "at least through her officials." [75]

That is, as we have already said, a paltry solution. We do not wish to reproach Suarez, for perhaps he did not know that there were so many opposing facts in this matter. But how could *we* today say that all this was either only "domestic power" or "designation of person"? Is it really credible that the Pope gave jurisdiction to so many persons of whom he had never heard? The theory of quasi-jurisdiction or dominative power seems to imply a dangerous juridicism which is not entirely without meaning, but which has meaning only if it is already established that a woman can never have jurisdiction or impart it. For Suarez, who was convinced that a woman cannot be a cleric (and thus a bearer of jurisdiction), that was an explanation. But if one wishes to investigate whether it is true that a woman is "in the state of subjection" in the Church, and whether the Church has at all times and in all places held and taught that, then this explanation is insignificant. It is, indeed, only an after-the-fact interpretation that can be useful if the thesis is established, which is not accomplished here by the facts themselves.

The historical facts on the question of female jurisdiction are only very seldom mentioned by our authors. One passage from the *Corpus Iuris Canonici* is again and again adduced, in which Innocent III prohibited abbesses from conferring the vow of virginity, hearing confessions, and singing the gospel. The other passages from the *Corpus Iuris Canonici* are apparently unknown to them. Although it is thus true that Innocence III forbade these three functions to abbesses, it must at least be taken into consideration that our other texts and even more the historical facts make the Thomistic thesis of the "state of subjection" of woman very questionable.

Innocent III wrote to the bishop of Burgos:

Certain novelties, about which we wonder not a little, have recently come to our ears: apparently abbesses in the dioceses of Burgos and Valencia bless their own nuns [*moniales proprias benedicunt*], and in matters dealing with misdeeds they also hear their nuns' confessions, and when they read the gospel they presume to proclaim publicly. Since this is equally unseemly and absurd and can in no case be permitted by us, we commend to your discretion, by apostolic writing, to see to it that this not happen any further, to prohibit it firmly by reason of apostolic authority, for although the most blessed virgin Mary stood above and was also more excellent than all the apostles together, the Lord still did not confide to her but to them the keys of the kingdom of heaven.[76]

By the first (*moniales benedicere*), the vow of virginity is meant. In the course of history this usurpation of power was often protested.[77]

The second (*confessiones audire*) is not attested to further. There are examples which seem similar, but doubt is cast on them. One passage in the Rule of Basil which seems to refer to it is probably speaking of the presence of the abbess at the confession of reverence.[78] The Rule of St. Donatus speaks of non-sacramental confession of guilt.[79] The same is true for the few statements from the life of St. Burgundofara.[80] Finally there is the Chapter of Charlemagne (789), which says:

> It is said that, contrary to the custom of God's holy Church, several abbesses bless men with the laying on of hands and with the sign of the cross on the head and that they also invest virgins with a priestly blessing. Know, holy Fathers, that this must be forbidden completely by you in your dioceses.[81]

As Giner Sempere proves, however, this is concerned with a mere blessing, not, as has been thought, with the laying on of hands in reconciliation.[82]

On the third point, the singing of the gospel (*evangelium praedicare*), we already know that it has continued to exist in the Carthusian order.

And the argument is therefore interesting because elsewhere—in an order approved by another pope—the supreme power lies with a woman, and the founders of the order appeal to the fact that Mary according to John 19, 27, was the mother of John; thus he was subject to her, just as, according to Brigit, Mary was the chief of the apostles! To conclude these paragraphs we must quote a text which I believe best gives the real background of the Thomistic proof, and in any case is a witness to the widespread attitudes toward woman of the Thomistic time. The reader must himself judge whether in the light of these attitudes it is not necessary to investigate the question of the female priesthood in another manner, and whether the argument from authority can be valid in this problem.

Guido of Baysio ("Archdeacon") writes in his *Rosarium* (1298–1302):

Add: say that [woman] may not be ordained as is said above; and the reason is that ordination can be given only to full members af the Church, for it is given to bring forth grace in another. However, the woman is not a full member [*perfectum membrum*] of the Church, but only the man.

Here we have the same ideas as in Thomas, except that we know of no text from the latter which speaks thus of the membership of woman in the Church. Thomas does, however, speak of her membership in the state; she is, according to him, not a full citizen, but only through her husband.[83] Later on in the same *Rosarium* we find:

I say besides that woman has been the effective cause of damnation, because she was the source of the transgression of the commandment and Adam was deceived by her, and that she therefore could not be the effective cause of salvation, while ordination is the effect of grace in another, and thus of salvation. But woman could be the material cause of salvation. Because woman is taken from man, even a virgin must rather be in a material way a mother of salvation, and that is true: because for women their sin was the material cause of our salvation, namely the holy virgin Mary, from whom in a material way Christ our salvation proceeded, and thus Goffredus established that woman, if she were ordained, would not receive the sacramental character of orders.[84]

The only question is, from what viewpoint should such a text be read: as witness of the tradition that women cannot be ordained priests (as Giner Sempere reads it), or as an example of the kind of background against which this tradition creates its concepts? This background is extremely weak if not explicitly false, on account of the integral role of the motherhood of Mary.

One would be inclined to retort: just as Christ our salvation proceeded not only *materially* from Mary (*materialiter Christus salus nostra procedit*), so also did salvation in general come not only materially from a woman. Mary's maternity is indeed proof that salvation can also proceed effectively from a woman. Why can woman be the effective cause of nonsalvation but not an effective (instrumental) cause of salvation? Whence this discrepancy between her salvific power and her nonsalvific power? Not from original sin, for her nature is not altered thereby; in any case it is difficult to see why *woman* has lost her saving power through original sin and *man* has not. The whole idea rests on a biological misinterpretation, as Mitterer has decisively proved.

The following is still to be noted: the important later dogmatic theologians have added nothing new. It is thus superfluous to go into their theological rationale more closely. Joseph A. Wahl gives an overview of the arguments from Bonaventure, Cajetan, Dionysius the Carthusian, Durand, Scotus, De Soto, Billuart, Vasquez, and a few more.[85]

Suarez merely refers to *IV Sent.*, dist. 25—we already know the Thomistic commentary on this passage—and to the sentence ⸻ He adds nothing beyond this.[86] In

es danger but is sacrament.[87]

ie fears two things: most holy sacrament, appen, perhaps that) carnal desires. This canons; the first from it primitive-tabooistic and so on, as though male involuntary nocperienced them even qualification, unfit for

ie track to see in this sychological area why the idea that a woman can also ⸻ it has never prevailed. But to prove it, completely new research is needed.

2. The Bridegroom

Theologians have sought other proofs besides the arguments from the lower status of woman, most especially considerations which derive from the idea that the priest, or more precisely the bishop, is the bridegroom of his bride, the congregation, or diocese, just as Christ is the bridegroom of his bride, the Church. That is the major proposition of the argument. The minor proposition adds: a woman cannot fill the role of the bridegroom on account of her sex. Thus, goes the conclusion, she cannot be a priest either, at least not a bishop.

This argument can be found, curiously enough, among Protestants too, for example, Professor Haitjema of the Calvinist theological faculty of the University of Groningen. He holds that Christ rules his Church through office.[89] The office is, of course, according to old Reformation principles, not hierarchical, but he nevertheless believes several corrections must be made. Although the source of office is the *coetus fidelium,* the Church is seen more and more, according to Haitjema, as the Church of the Word, as Church of the three divine institutions: Scripture, sacrament, and office. Christ rules the congregation through Spirit and Word, and in this uses the officebearer as his organ.[90] Office thus exists not only to care for Church order, which is already present through Christ in a Church which already exists; it should equally serve to build up and gather together the congregation, that it might appear as the congregation of Jesus Christ, prepared without blemish or wrinkle as the bride is adorned for her bridegroom. Therefore a woman cannot be a bearer of office. The relation of Christ and the Church is presented with an almost sacramental significance in Scripture in the symbol of marriage; and thus in office too there should be a reflection of this: the representation of Christ, the bridegroom of the congregation.[91]

This idea is brought forward by Swedish Lutheran thinkers, especially H. Riesenfeld.[92] Of course "Romanizing" attitudes are ascribed to him. In general such ideas are found only among the "high church" Protestants. For the others, Christ, who is present wherever two or three are gathered together in his name, has no need of representation.[93] This is certainly consonant with Reformation thinking. Whether in Protestantism there is nevertheless still room for a representation—perhaps even a sacramental representation—of the Lord in the Church, need not be investigated further here. Certainly, however, what Congar wrote in 1953 seems to us today to be incomplete:

Since the Protestant Reform entirely rejected the hierarchical priesthood and every properly sacerdotal title of the ministry and of the Church, forbidding women access to the ministry can only be a question of expediency.[94]

On the Catholic side of course this argument is also familiar. It is only noteworthy that it emerges in literature so late. It is found in the Middle Ages in the writings of Bonaventure:

The other levels of ordination are steps to the episcopacy insofar as one has proved himself in one's office. But the bishop is the spouse of the Church. If then woman cannot be admitted to the episcopate, but only man—otherwise he would not be the spouse of the Church—only men can be admitted to the preceding levels of ordination as well.[95]

To our knowledge it was first developed in recent times by Engelbert Krebs in an article in *Hochland*. In fact he did not quote any writers who had used it before him. He argues as follows: The bishop at his episcopal consecration receives a wedding ring which pledges him as the visible vicar of the bridegroom Christ to his Church. To be a bridegroom, however, is man's work, and thus in the office of the priest there lies a mystical connection to maleness, which makes it conceivable that Christ entrusted this male office to men once and for all.[96] Hick, in his book on woman in Paul,[97] writes in somewhat the same spirit, as does A.-M. Henry in his article "Le mystère de l'homme et de la femme," [98] and many others.

This aspect of the problem was seldom stressed by the great theologians of the Middle Ages. In none of the classical arguments does this aspect play even the slightest role, although it was well recognized that the bishop could be seen as the bridegroom of his diocese.[99] We need only remember the struggle over the election of Pope Formosus at the end of the ninth century, which was portrayed by his opponents as invalid because he had already been bishop of another diocese and thus had deserted his bride.[100] In the battle against simony too there was an awareness that the bishop could be called the bridegroom of his diocese. Emperors who bestowed dioceses for money were considered procurers, fathers who gave their daughters over to prostitution.[101] But in the question of female priesthood the thought of referring to this aspect arose only very rarely.

Even in recent times the idea has not found as great approbation as could be expected. Although, for example Diekamp,[102] like Lercher,[103] refers to Krebs, neither has taken over this idea, but instead something else from the same article (see section 3 of this chapter). Schmaus does not acknowledge the idea either, although he presumably used Krebs's article, as we shall see later.

The validity of this argument seems quite questionable to me. In several writers, moreover, the proof seems to be situated not only in the argument, as we have seen it formulated in a syllogistic fashion above, but at the same time in the jurisdictional aspect. It is not always stated clearly, "Only men can be bridegrooms," but rather, "Only men can represent Christ, insofar as Christ as the bridegroom is the head of his bride, the Church." Then the jurisdictional aspect comes into play.

Now to get to the matter. Surely several things must be asked of the major premise: first, whether the bridegroom function of the bishop to his congregation is something which touches and expresses the essence of office or is only a metaphor, an image to express symbolically certain aspects of office without expressing the reality itself. It certainly expresses very beautifully the totality of his contribution to his diocese, the exclusivity of his love, his care, his loyalty, sacrifice, finality, solicitude etc. But is it a real symbol, presenting the essence itself? Is it the kind of image that is itself a concrete embodiment of the essence? In other words, *is* the bishop the bridegroom of his diocese, or can he only be compared to one? But if he actually is a bridegroom, how could he then be replaced? A real marriage is indissoluble. And although the old canons are against it,[104] the displacement of a bishop is not impossible, as the practice of the Church proves.

Pope Innocent III sensed this difficulty and rescued himself with the help of a "trick": as God can separate a marriage, so too Christ's vicar, the Pope, can displace bishops. It was not the "canonical constitution" which gave the Pope this faculty, but the "divine constitution."

> As no man can dissolve a legal marriage between man and woman, for the Lord says in the gospel, "What God has bound together let no man put asunder," so too can the spiritual marriage bond between the bishop and his Church, considered to have been begun in the nomination, validated in the confirmation, and consummated in the consecration, be dissolved only by the authority of him who is the successor of Peter and the representative of Jesus Christ.[105]

So we have to make a choice. Either the bridegroom relationship of the bishop to the diocese is not an image which is the concrete embodiment of the essence, or the Pope can dissolve *matrimonia rata et consummata*—sacramental marriages—with permission to enter a new marriage. Innocent III himself clearly tended toward the second possibility.[106]

For Thomas the bishop was not at all so univocally a bridegroom of the diocese. For he appears to insinuate a comparison with soluble eternal vows rather than with insoluble marriage.[107] It was often said later that bishops have a double marriage: a soluble one with their diocese and an insoluble one with the Church. What a soluble marriage means, however, remains very questionable.

The marriage is a concrete embodiment of the bride and bridegroom relationship between Christ and the Church, as Schlier has explained very neatly and explicitly when commenting on Eph. 5.[108] But is this just as true of the episcopal office and its relation to the diocese in the same sacramental-symbolic way? That, it seems to me, has not yet been proved.

It is noticeable that Paul designates himself with an explicitly female qualification in Gal. 4, 19, where he writes: "My children, for whom I am again in labor (Vulgate: *parturio*) until Christ shall have been formed in you." He appears not to have considered the bridegroom aspect so essential. He can also characterize himself in other ways.

Laurentin still refers to 1 Cor. 4, 15, and Phil. 10,[109] which texts are, however, not convincing because of the double meaning of γεννᾶν (fatherly and motherly).[110] Laurentin also mentions a certain tendency "to consider sacerdotal functions as maternal functions" since the twelfth century, and later in the French school as well as in Scheeben. But he dismisses this tendency as artificial and relies on Bonaventure, who says, "The priest is neither father nor mother—*Sacerdos nec pater nec mater*." [111] But is it really so artificial? The manner of expression of Gal. 4, 19, is certainly clear enough! And on the matter of "not father" —there are plenty of Pauline passages where Paul does call himself father and speaks of his children: 1 Cor. 4, 14; 2 Cor. 12, 14; Phil. 10; 1 Cor. 3, 1; 2 Cor. 6, 13; Phil. 2, 22.

One would rather tend to say, "The priest is not only father and not only mother, but simultaneously father and mother."

On the bridegroom role of the bishop, it must further be said that Paul also calls himself the "marriage arranger" for the community: 2 Cor. 11, 2. This concept of the "marriage arranger," which Paul also uses for Christ himself in Eph. 5, immediately after the assertion that Christ is the bridegroom of the community,[112] seems to us to express the kernel of the episcopal office no less clearly than does that of the bridegroom. The bishop of course is also "representing" Christ, he makes him present, but in an equally true sense the bishop is not Christ himself and it is his function to lead the Church to its bridegroom Christ. This of course says nothing *per se* about the possibility of a female marriage arranger, but it makes clear that it is still far from obvious that the bishop must be designated according to his essence as bridegroom.

It is already striking in the Old Testament that Israel was described as both male and female: Israel may appear now as daughter and now as son, and also as bride.[113] The images are exchangeable; one alone does not express the essence itself with great stringency.

According to Joachim Jeremias, the bridegroom metaphor for the Messiah is unknown in the body of Jesus's preaching, though it is also familiar in the primitive Christian literature. Jesus does not compare the community of salvation with the bride but rather with the wedding guests.[114] Schlier also, in his excursus on the "sacred marriage" in his commentary on Ephesians, says that the Old Testament texts do not contain more than images, comparisons. In the synoptics, Jesus of course is the "bridegroom," but the community are wedding guests or bridesmaids. In Paul, the apostle in 2 Cor. 11 is the marriage arranger (father of the bride?). There remain, then, only the passages from the Apocalypse and, in Paul, Eph. 5.[115] But, it might be remarked, if the community is to be seen ultimately as the bride of Christ, then projecting the image onto the bishop necessitates its own proper proof. And Eph. 5 does not speak of the bishop in any case. J. J. von Allmen correctly notes: "It is very obvious that St. Paul never considers the Church his own spouse." [116]

Thus one is truly justified in expecting a more precise proof that the bishop is the representative of Christ, that also in this regard he plays the role of the bridegroom and portrays it sacramentally and symbolically, and that the image of the bridegroom is of a different order from other images, as for example the shepherd, the leader of the army, the marriage arranger, father, and so on, which can also be used to characterize the episcopal office.

Be that as it may—ultimately the bishop is really the representative of Christ and thus also of Christ as bridegroom of the Church—the heart of the question lies in the minor premise. Can a woman really not fulfill this role of bridegroom? Is sexuality decisive here?

We have seen Ambrose, Jerome, and Thomas say that the believing woman or the woman living in a religious order is raised to the status of the male. It must be assumed that she certainly remains a woman. Thus, what is meant is that at least biological sexuality has become irrelevant to what a woman can become and how she is to be evaluated. (For the question of whether there is a psychic-spiritual femininity and to what extent that is relevant, see below.) One other thing is certain: the relation between bridegroom and bride in this context is not sexual in the biological sense; the children of God are born "without blood, without the will of the flesh, nor from the will of man" ($\theta\dot{\epsilon}\lambda\eta\mu a$ here has the meaning of sexual drive).[117] The relation has a meaning which transcends the biologically sexual. But is there sense then in asking about the biological sex?

If, in the Old Testament, Jahweh was called the bridegroom of the covenant people, Schoonenberg correctly notes,[118] it was not in order to sexualize the image of God but to personalize it; [119] the Bible expressly rejects any sexualizing of the image of God (the prohibition of the golden calf, which was earlier a bull and symbolic of male procreative power). Of course we always speak of God as father—but is not that also just a manner of presentation? According to Quell, the word "father" in scriptural usage means primarily "bearer of authority," [120] and is thus not chiefly sexual—unless one wants to characterize woman as "incapable of jurisdiction." Beyond this, the Church has in fact used other styles of portrayal. The Fathers already speculated on the passage from the Psalms, "from the womb I have begotten you," and John speaks of him "who is in the bosom of the Father." The passage from Isaiah (49, 14 ff.) also comes to mind: Jahweh compares his love with that of a mother in the sense that his love is still greater. In short, God transcends all sexuality.

But it will be answered that Christ was after all a man, and the bishop is the representative of Christ, not God. Obviously that is correct, but then the question arises whether Christ was *so* much male that he cannot be represented by a woman. Bonaventure is definitely negative:

For in this sacrament the person who is ordained
characterizes Christ as mediator; and because the mediator
was only of the male sex and also can be characterized only
by the male sex, only males can receive ordination, for they
alone can represent [Christ] on the basis of their nature and,
if they have received the character of ordination, can also
bear its sign in completion [*actu*].[121]

It must nevertheless be said that a woman can in any case
represent the aspect of "like a hen" (Luke 13, 24). And if one
still wishes to respond to the question in the negative, how can
one still say that woman is of equal value to man or even that
woman is redeemed? The ὁμοούσιος ἡμῖν does not hold true for
males alone. Christ took on the complete human nature, the Fathers argue, or else it would not all be redeemed, "for what was
not taken on is also not redeemed." [122]

That was true first of all for metaphysical completeness—body
and soul—but must it not be asked whether it is not also true of
the feminine? And if the feminine is also taken on by Christ,
how can the female not also represent him? This is formulated
by an Anglican as follows:

Since there is in our Lord Jesus Christ himself, both as man
and as God, the perfect expression of all that is best both in
man and woman, . . . to represent him perfectly in human
priesthood both man and woman are needed.[123]

And an Orthodox writer states that in Christ there is no exclusivity, but all humanity: each finds himself in Christ. He is the
universal archetype of the human, the second Adam who includes all in himself, as the first Adam enclosed the undifferen-
tiated male and female within himself before the birth of Eve.[124]

To put it differently, *if* there are really feminine virtues (more
on this later), how can virtues be called Christian if Christ himself did not realize them? But if he did realize them, they, and
thus he too, can be represented by a woman.

Christ, much as he was a real male,[125] did not complete the
biologically sexual in his life. And it must be asked whether this
uncompleted masculinity in the male is really so exclusively something of the man that it cannot be realized by a woman. That is
of course a matter that cannot be settled here. But sociological
and psychological investigations force us to put the question seriously. It is still not at all agreed what is transtemporally typically

male and what transtemporally typically female. The best-known authors who have investigated this are Ruth Benedict and Margaret Mead. A few citations must suffice to indicate that a real problem lies before us here. Ruth Benedict says:

> Man is not committed in detail by his biological constitution in any particular variety of behavior. [The behavior of man and woman is rather dependent on the sociological and cultural circumstances.] [126]

Margaret Mead says that there are no changeless structures which are ordered according to the sexes:

> We are forced to conclude that human nature is almost unbelievably malleable, responding accurately and contrastingly to contrasting cultural conditions.[127]

What is biological naturally remains the same, but apart from that essential differences appear. Man as well as woman can be motherly, and both can be rough, aggressive, "masculine." Or the man can be motherly and the woman masculine and fatherly: "The woman the dominant, impersonal, managing partner, the man the less responsible and the emotional dependent person." [128]

One should be very careful about calling a certain property, tendency, or style of conduct typically masculine or typically feminine:

> If we look the world over, we find that the capabilities of both sexes have been attached, sometimes to one sex, sometimes to the other.[129]

The Dutch psychiatrist J. H. van den Berg also says that we must not see certain psychic properties as necessarily bound up with biological data.[130]

Edith Stein too proposes the task of investigating whether the various types into which women are differentiated contain a single and immutable nucleus which could be characterized as a "species" of woman: [131]

> The question of the species woman is the principal question of all the questions on women. If there is such a species, then no alteration of the conditions of life, of economic and cultural relationships like her proper activity will be able to change anything. If there is no such species, . . . then under certain

conditions the carryover of the one type into the other is possible. This is not so absurd as it might appear at first. The concept already has support in that bodily difference is considered constant, but the spiritual is viewed as infinitely variable.[132]

She herself does not try to say the question is unanswerable.[133] But she limits herself almost completely to outlining the method according to which one would have to proceed.[134]

The question is linked, we think, to whether the human spirit is differentiated according to sex. We believe with Schoonenberg that the question cannot be answered with a straightforward yes or no. God (and the angels?) are not differentiated sexually.

Sex comes "from below." Thus the *anima* as the material form is certainly differentiated sexually; but at the same time the *anima,* as transcending materiality, is also asexual. The person (and we are actually speaking of that, not of the soul) *has* masculinity or femininity and is distinguished by it, projects it—and at the same time he *is* man or woman. For this reason, according to Schoonenberg, the position of authority of the male and the subordination of the woman do not lie on the highest level of intrahuman relationships. The inequality of the sexes manifests itself where the persons do not yet deal with one another completely as persons: in the sphere of law, where human communities are still "organization" and "society," and not yet completely "community." [135]

Schoonenberg adds that the position of man and woman on the plane of organization and society is quite variable, depending on cultures and times. The relationships within the family, as Peter and Paul see them, are, according to him, not specifically Christian but rather time-conditioned. But—he continues—in the sacramental-ecclesiastical area there are no such variations, for these structures are established by Christ himself. When he investigates further the background of these directives of Christ, however, he begins not quite logically to refer to psychological and sociological phenomena.[136] It will be clear to the reader that I cannot agree with him on this last point. Why would these variations exist in the secular area and not in the sacramental-ecclesiastical? It can only be imagined to what remarkable situations that could lead. Besides, it appears to me to be too much of a Scotist, voluntarist way of thinking.

On the question of whether a woman can fill the role of the

bridegroom, the following must be considered. First, no one has ever concluded that the congregation should consist solely of women. And writers have always considered the biological sex irrelevant where it was a matter of the virginity of the male members of religious orders. Friedrich Wulf has explained [137] that it can in fact be justly said that the priest represents the bridegroom-Christ and the members of religious orders the bride-Church, but that that is only a kind of emphasis, because both are the representation of the same eschatological reality. The male priest is also a member of the faithful, a member of the bridal Church. He can thus—at least as a member of the community—fill the role of bride. According to Wulf, it would be impossible to call an individual person, either man or woman, the bride of Christ. The ascetical literature which has done so, based on 1 Cor. 7, is one-sided. The Fathers and others such as Bernard have never done that; Bernard even explicitly rejected it. Only as member of the religious community and the Church are man and woman in a bridal relationship to Christ. But the man is indeed in this role!

As the male can also stand in the bridal role, Schoonenberg's words, although he has something else in mind, are valid:

> The relation of the Church to her bridegroom is proper to every Christian, for the Church does not hover over us but exists in us. We are often inclined to ascribe the marital relationship with Christ only to the soul. But Paul mentions specifically the body: "the body is for the Lord and the Lord for the body" (1 Cor. 6, 13).

The second section which presents the relationship as mutual shows the marital character of our belonging to Christ:

> Here indeed is the same mutuality of belonging to one another in the body which Paul proclaims between man and woman in 1 Cor. 7, 4.[138]

If the male can thus fulfill the bridal role in the community, it must also be asked why the woman cannot fulfill the role of bridegroom. Obviously that is not apparent of itself. But it should be investigated. Especially if one considers at the same time that the feminine is not so facilely defined as is customarily thought; if one considers that in Christ the entire human nature, including its feminine aspects (if these do exist), was assumed; if one considers that according to Paul and the Fathers—in their best moments—the religious significance of the sexes, as they prevailed in the Old Testament, is surmounted fully by Christ; if one considers that in any case the biologically sexual is irrelevant for the bridegroom relationship between Christ and the Church; if one considers that the new era, where "they marry not and are not given in marriage" does not simply break in upon us abruptly but is actualizing itself already little by little in this world. This last especially seems to us to bring up many questions. For if it is true—the passage from Jerome almost suggests even a disappearance of the contrast between man and woman— it could be thought that this happens in precisely the same measure in which the sphere of the *sacramentum et res* disappears and the *res* prevails in its totality. That, however, would mean that as long as there is a sacramental office (as long as the *sacramentum et res* is there for the *res,* as long as the *res* has not yet entirely realized itself), so long and in that measure a distinction between the sexes is still significant for office.

With this, I think, we are at one of the central questions of the entire problem. "Office" and "distinction of the sexes" belong to the time in which we still live: to the sacramental time. We return to the reflections of Thomas, who looked for the necessity of the male priest merely in the area of the *sacramentum et res,* not in the sphere of the *res* itself. As Schoonenberg also formulates it: "The concept of office implies the plane of interhuman relationships insofar as they are still 'objective.' " [139]

The same idea is worked out by A.-M. Henry [140] and Laurentin [141] in somewhat different terminology. Henry, moreover, says that every woman is a new man, because she is "another Christ." But that, according to him, is "the spiritual order, where the difference of sex no longer counts." [142] But on the plane of symbol there is a difference. And therefore man and woman, although they have the same vocation, have a differing mission.[143]

Laurentin approaches the question from the viewpoint of the Church. The Church is simultaneously "Jesus Christ distributed and communicated" and "the spouse of Christ." Under the first aspect the Church is male; "recapitulated in the man Christ, its chief, its head, it is represented by men: the bishops and the priests." Under the second aspect (communion) it is essentially female, the bride of Christ and mother of Christians; as a type it has a woman, Mary.[144]

Thus we stand before the question of whether on the level of symbol too man and woman are of equal value, or, to use a better expression, whether man and woman can fulfill the same sociological functions—the roles of bridegroom and bride.

The answer to this question depends, we think, on what is actually believed to be characteristic of man and woman. Now that, as we have seen above, is still far from settled, at least for the woman of our time. For even if it were established that there is a transtemporal species woman (to use Edith Stein's terminology), it could still be true that this transtemporal species woman would say nothing on the problem of whether a woman can fulfill a certain sociological function. Then it would follow that even were it established that a woman in earlier times could certainly not represent Christ, that would still say nothing on this possibility for our time.

Secondly, one comes to an answer to this question in the sense that the woman can fill only the role of the bride, which is not to suggest that the woman is less than the man, as Thomas quite candidly does. For the woman would, at least on the plane of symbols, stand only on the level of Mary, not on that of the God-man, while the man would stand on both levels—on that of Christ and, as a member of the bride-Church, on that of the Mother of God.

Henry in a logical manner also comes to that, so that he even says:

> The man represents the Christ, that is to say, the Word of God who takes flesh . . . , the Wisdom in whom everything has been conceived and ordered; the woman represents the humanity toward which God bends and comes to snatch it back from the quagmire of evil, of sin, of opposition to the Spirit.[145]

These are certainly strong words! Woman is close to being once again, as she was to the Fathers, the type of sin, of the flesh. A contemporary theologian is startled at this. Even if Henry intends to do no injustice to woman, because he is speaking only on the level of mission, not on that of vocation, it is our impression that this subsequent correction makes no great amends. At bottom he does say exactly what Thomas said.

Laurentin looks only at the de facto representation exercised only by males. He does not explain the "why." He gives some kind of post factum explanation—the dichotomy: "Jesus Christ distributed and communicated" vis-à-vis "the spouse of Christ"— but he does not show why it must be so.

If woman cannot be "another Christ" even on this point, she seems to lack something which cannot be remedied by modifying the statement to say that that is true only on the plane of symbol. For I believe that in this case males can once again— even if only in secret—pray with the rabbis, "I thank you that you have created me a man," which Paul in Gal. 3, 28, rejected for all time.

Obviously there are different missions in the Church. And obviously there are differences between the sexes. But how does one know that these two tension lines, "man–woman" and "suited for office–not suited for office" run parallel? We might illustrate what we mean with two detailed quotations from Karl Barth:

We have seen that the systematizations to which we might be tempted in this connexion do not yield any practicable imperatives. Different ages, peoples, and cultures have had very different ideas of what is concretely appropriate, salutary and necessary in man and woman as such . . . the distinctions are given [according to Barth they are knowable only through the law of God; pp. 7 f.] and it would be totally perverse to wish to blur them.[146]

The command of the Lord does not put anyone, man or woman, in a humiliating, dishonourable, or unworthy position. It puts both man and woman in their proper place. Interpretations may vary as to where this place is, for the Lord is a living Lord and His command is ever new. It is certainly foolish to try to make an inflexible rule of the particular interpretation of Paul in this instance. It is undoubtedly the case that women may also not wear veils and actually speak in the assembly. But this is not the most important point to be gathered from I Cor. 11 and 14 in the present context. The essential point is that woman must always and in all circumstances be woman; that she must feel and conduct herself as such and not as a man.[147]

Thus: there are certainly differences between the sexes, but how does one know that they signify anything about suitability or unsuitability for spiritual office? Ultimately even Henry and Schoonenberg can only adduce the psychosociological differences between man and woman for their demonstrations.[148] And Laurentin has only the data of Scripture and tradition and the fact that Christ was a man as verification.[149] But Christ was also a Jew and a free man, and Goyim and slaves can nevertheless be priests.

It must not be said here that being a Jew or a Gentile is something different from being a man or woman and that therefore the Jewishness of Christ says nothing on the question of whether a non-Jew can represent him, but sex does indeed import something. For sexual difference is also rejected in Gal. 3, 28; its significance is denied. And finally, when it is said that a Gentile can be a priest, it is true only because baptized Gentiles are the "new Israel according to the Spirit." But is not the believing woman in the same way a man? Very much in the sense of the texts we have quoted from Ambrose, Jerome, and Thomas, Edith Stein writes:

> Because Christ incorporated ideal human perfection, in which all narrow-mindedness and lack are elevated, the merits of male and female nature united and weaknesses canceled, his true disciples are likewise elevated more and more above the limits of their nature. Thus we see in saintly men feminine tenderness and kindness and truly maternal care of the souls entrusted to them; in saintly women we see masculine courage, constancy, and determination.[150]

Thus our understanding of Gal. 3, 28 is indeed of significance for our question—even if, as we have seen in Schlier, it is indirect and qualified—for if being a Gentile no longer matters for the question of whether someone can be a priest because the Gentiles are the new Israel, then also being a woman does not matter, because in Christ every woman is elevated to the masculine level.

In this context too the old question returns: are secular offices not on the level of symbol? Would not the distinction between vocation and mission, between hierarchy and communion, also obtain in the secular area? Or between the sphere of justice and organization and that of community? But if that is no hindrance to admitting women to secular office, what reason can be given as a hindrance to spiritual office?

Perhaps theology must simply rely on the facts of secular psychological-sociological development. That did no harm in the problem of slavery or in the attitudes toward witches, the burning of heretics, tolerance in general, suffrage for woman, and so on.

3. *The Begetter of the Life of Grace*

The arguments of Thomas and those deriving from the concept of the bridegroom are, as we have seen, more concerned with the aspects of "teaching" and of "leading." Now we will consider the argumentation from the viewpoint of "sanctifying."

This is formulated in the clearest and briefest way by Odo Casel, though only incidentally and in another context. He starts from the supposition that the natural talents of the priest are not suppressed but are included in ordination. He says: The idea of woman is to portray the power of obedience of the spiritual creature to God; she is the image of the soul, the Church, the bride of God, receptive and loving. The man is an image of the divine principle as the procreator, the life awakener; for this reason, only masculine nature can be "taken up" into the ordination of the priest as mediator of divine life.[151]

M. Schmaus too suggests the same thoughts. The intrinsic reason why only baptized males can be ordained is, according to him, not to be seen in a natural inability of woman for the sacerdotal vocation, but in the tasks of the priesthood which correspond more to the essence of the male. The priest is in a special manner the instrument of Christ. It is obvious that that baptized person who serves Christ in a special manner, as the instrument of his salvific operation, also participates in his natural qualities. The fact that the Son of God took on human nature in its masculine form is not based in the essence of God, for God stands beyond all sexual differences. Rather, it has its basis in the work of Christ. The Son of God become man had to fulfill the task laid upon him by the Father in the public eye of the earth and for the whole world. The public eye is the work place of the man; woman works in obscurity. Further, there lies in the male character a hint of the type of Christ's mission, to bring lost life back to the world. To beget life is a masculine thing. In this natural relationship there lies a correspondence to the fact that the Son of God, whom the Father granted to have life in himself as the Father bears it in himself, begot in mankind divine life in its fullness. So too in the priest his character as male signifies a natural allusion to his mission to proclaim the message of the kingdom of God in the public eye of the world, to dispense the sacraments, and thus to mediate divine life to creation perfected in the power of Christ. The business of woman is rather to take up life and to preserve it. That signifies no lesser competency of woman. What is most valuable in the kingdom of God is not the fullness of power of office bestowed for service, but divine life mediated through the power of the office.[152]

The Old Catholic bishop of Deventer (Netherlands), Msgr. P. J. Jans, argues in the same manner, with express reference to Schmaus.[153]

Engelbert Krebs's article, which we have already mentioned several times, works out the same argument in the following way:

> The priest stands in the stead of Christ. It is his office to beget from humanity children of God for heaven (1 Cor. 4, 15). To beget life is, in humanity, the business of the male. Christ brought new life to humanity. For this reason he appeared among us as a male, because his work was man's work. "Just as the Father has life in himself, so he also gave to the Son to have life in himself" (John 5, 26). Thus the mystery postpones itself into the lap of divinity. That is the most characteristic quality of God: that he does not receive his life but has it in himself. And the eternal word, which proceeds eternally from him, has, as its essential image, likewise life in itself. Therefore the first in the Godhead is not called Mother but Father. For any mother merely protects and hands on received life. And the eternal essential image is Son and not Daughter, for the Father has also given to him "to have life in himself." God is without doubt exalted above all sexuality. But if we ask who among humans reflects in at least some respect that most characteristic quality in God—that is, to hand on nonreceived life—then it is the male and father on earth, while the woman and mother reflects more that kind affection and care for life at hand, as is also proper to God (Is. 49, 15; Mt. 23, 37).[154]

As we have already seen, Diekamp and Lercher follow him, although they also stress the arguments from Krebs omitted by us:

> The masculine sex rather than the feminine is more suited to teaching, since from its own psychic strengths it is more likely to be equal to the demands of mental work; . . . it is more suited to ruling, since it more than the female sex follows steadily the direction of reason and not of feeling.[155]

The "since" clause is not at all illuminating, so we will not enter further into these last arguments. The one thing that must be said to these is that they are too time- and culture-conditioned to be the foundation for a divine law.

As Schmaus too follows Krebs (he often uses the same statements word for word), we shall discuss the two together.

Schmaus's assertion on public activity seems likewise much too time-conditioned. If it were true, it would also be perverse to have women ministers of state and so on. Pius XII in any case thought quite differently about the activity of women in the public arena. He even commanded it! [156]

Let us go on to the idea that procreation is a male affair and that the woman merely receives life and cherishes it; or, as Krebs says, the mother only hands on received life. There is much to question here. Can it really be said that the mother receives life? She receives indeed; however, it is not life but semen. Life is begotten by man and woman together. One gets the impression that Schmaus and Krebs are still speculating on the proceedings in the begetting of human life from an Aristotelian-Thomistic attitude. Mitterer's entire criticism is thus also valid for them.[157] What they say in this reference is simply wrong. In the Dutch and German languages it is said very significantly when a woman has born a child, "She has given life to a child." *She!*

Now it could be replied that the man is nevertheless the more active partner, that he initiates the coming into existence of the child, although the child is begotten by two parents, and that Schmaus is thus correct. But his argument does not have as its middle term the activity of "being the first" but of "awaking life," "handing on life which he carries in himself as not-received." That is certainly not true. The male alone does not give life, and the woman does not give the life of the male to the child, but the two hand on their common life.

But the inadequacy of the argument comes to light most clearly if we consider more closely the trinitarian reflections of the writers. What we present here should certainly not be understood as our own concept; we merely wish, arguing from Schmaus's standpoint, to reduce his ideas ad absurdum.

The argument proceeds by saying that Christ and the priest mediate the divine life of grace, that is, they proclaim the kingdom of God and dispense the sacraments. Now the handing on of the life of grace is the same thing as what we call the imparting or sending of the Holy Spirit. If we then proceed to say that the economic trinity is the immanent trinity,[158] we come to the remarkable fact that according to Krebs and Schmaus the Son sends the Spirit (the life lets life proceed from itself) as *non-received* life. "The Son of God, whom the Father has granted to have life in himself, as the Father bears it in himself, generates the divine life (= the Spirit) for men." But that is incomprehensible. The Son does not have life in himself *as* the Father has it in himself, for he has it as imparted, whereas the Father has it as unimparted. Schmaus's statement contains—*salva reverentia*—a contradiction, I believe. If the Father has *granted* the Son to have life in himself, it can no longer be said that the Son has it as the Father bears it in himself. In fact, Schmaus himself says in his volume on the trinity: "The second person is characterized as the reception of the divine essence and as the handing on of it to the Holy Spirit." [159]

It is certainly better to adhere to the Council of Florence:

> As everything which belongs to the Father the Father gives to his only-begotten Son in generation with the exception of his Fatherhood, so the Son also has the quality that the Holy Spirit proceeds from the Son, eternal from the Father. [160]

The fact that the Son generates the Spirit for men comes from the Father (the economic trinity is the immanent trinity).

"To hand on nonreceived life"—that, according to Krebs and Schmaus, is the task of Christ and of the male. It is not accurate for the male, for the woman too hands on "nonreceived" life; she does not receive the life but the semen of the man, and both man and woman give their own life together (perhaps it can even be said: *tamquam unum principium*—as one pair of parents—even if in a different sense than it is meant for the trinity) to the child. Nor does it hold true for Christ. It is written of him not only: "Just as the Father has life, so has he also given the Son to have life in himself" (John 5, 26), but likewise, "*You* have *given* him power over all flesh, to give eternal life to all whom you have given him" (John 17, 2); and: "For I have given them the words which *you gave* me" (John 17, 8); and: "I have given them *your* word" (John 17, 14); and: "The glory which *you* have *given* me I have given to them, that they may be one even as we are one" (John 17, 22). And what is true of the priest? He does not hand on nonreceived life, but he can act only insofar as he himself is empowered to do so. Once one begins to think in this direction, one can hardly avoid seeing here a parallel to woman instead of to man!

This is not the place to go further into this trinitarian reflection. What has been said is sufficient as a question mark to the argument proposed by Krebs and Schmaus.

Just as woman was "in the bosom" of man (Adam) and came forth from him as "like to him," and as *both* generate the child through their life—to be sure, in such a way that Eve receives from Adam so that she brings forth the child—so also, it might be said, does the sending of the Spirit, the generating of the life of grace, take place. We can discover no argument here for the male character of the priest. Or, in other words, everyone will admit that the woman is "another Christ" as "receiving from the Father"; but, one might think, she is in her natural womanhood just as much the image of Christ as "breathing the Holy Spirit." Why then should she not be the person who portrays the mediation of grace in her nature? One gets the impression that Krebs and Schmaus have merely played with the word "generate."

It is certainly quite unusual to see the reflection of the Son in woman; usually it is the reflection of the Holy Spirit that is looked for in woman. There are Fathers who even call the Holy Spirit "the rib of the word." [161] And certainly that too makes sense. But do not the correct psychological and sociological understandings of the generation of children force us to take such considerations seriously?

A second ground for questioning the argumentation of Krebs and Schmaus we believe must be deduced from the very traditional teaching on the dispenser of the sacraments.

According to Schmaus it is the task of the male priest to dispense the sacraments, and thus to mediate the divine life to a creation perfected in the power of Christ. Here again we come upon the noteworthy fact that on the one hand he speaks of "giving the life" which the male has in himself (and the woman apparently does not), but on the other hand he does add "in the power of Christ." The second, however, appears to be more accurate than the first. Traditional teaching does indeed say with Thomas on the question of whether a woman can baptize validly:

In spiritual generation no one (that is neither male nor female) operates on his own power, but only as an instrument through the power of Christ.[162]

Joseph A. Wahl, who discusses this article of Thomas, over-looks the logical consequences. In the pertinent article he has read only that woman must not baptize "publicly," just as she must not speak "publicly" in the Church.[163]

What is specific for the dispensing of the sacraments is thus according to Thomas not that the dispenser hands on his own life which he has in himself, but that he has been allowed to cogenerate life. The instrument is effective insofar as it is brought to act by the principal cause.

It is to be noted that the Thomistic argument is not valid only for baptism but for all sacraments and also for proclamation. Therefore it is not evident that only the male should be the person assigned to dispense the sacraments. He it is who imparts to the woman that she can hand on life together with him. He is therefore analogous to Christ inasmuch as Christ is the high priest; while the woman is analogous to Christ inasmuch as he operates through the earthly priest. To formulate it in another way: in marriage the woman is the analogue of the ecclesiastical priest, the man the analogue of Christ as high priest. How then can the male be seen as the earthly priest? One would even be inclined to see the woman as priest insofar as the priest dispenses the sacraments.

Perhaps here we may mention a statement by Karl Barth which concerns a much different subject but is nevertheless also relevant in our context. When he considers why Christ should have no earthly Father, he amplifies:

Willing, achieving, creative, sovereign man, man as an independent fellow worker with God, man in the impulse of his *eros,* who as such, where God's grace is concerned, simply cannot be a participator in God's work,[164] is *a parte potiori* man the male. . . . Willing, achieving, creative, sovereign man as such cannot be considered as a participator in God's work. For as such he is the man of disobedience. As such, therefore, if God's grace is to meet him, he must be set aside. But this man in the state of disobedience is *a parte potiori* the male. So it is the male who must be set aside here, if a countersign is to be set up as the sign of the incarnation of God. In this sign the contradiction of grace is directed against the male because he is peculiarly significant for the world history of human genius. What happens in the mystery of Christmas is not world history, not the work of human genius.[165]

What we believe is the following: if in the sacraments it should also be indicated that salvation is not wrought by men themselves but must be received unclaimed as a free gift of God, why has it not been asked whether woman would perhaps not better represent this aspect?

Put in a trivial manner: if it is not against the symbolism of the sacraments and of masculinity that males can receive them, how is it then against the symbolism of the sacraments and of femininity for women to dispense them?

It is important to consider that we have discovered here something significantly feminine, not only in the Church as bride, as receiving, but in the Church as imparting, as dispensing life. Or in the terminology of Laurentin: not only in the Church as "communion," but in the Church as "hierarchy." In Schoonenberg's terminology: not only in the Church as "community," but also as "organization." How is it possible that this idea has never been raised before, although it certainly seems to be not seriously off the track? Perhaps because the need has never been felt; in earlier times woman just could not be a priest. And, second, because the role of woman in the generation of the child was seen falsely, as though she received the child from the father and only carried it ("protected," says Schmaus) and gave it birth. That this is not true need not be demonstrated again. Only one point do we wish to stress: it should not be thought that this is so merely on the biological level; it is just as true on the psychological plane. Alice Scherer writes: "Man and woman are both receptive and creative together as much in reference to one another and to the world as in reference to their creator." [166]

And it has been the merit of Mitterer to have put this forward clearly in a theological context. Mitterer himself said nothing in his article of the logical consequences of his thesis for a feminine priesthood. In this respect we hope to enlarge the reflections.

We do not argue against Krebs that the Church, the bride, is sacerdotal. More on that later. We have only stated that the sacerdotal function—to obtain from Christ the power to bestow the spirit—suggests the role of the woman in marriage rather than of the man.

But the following conclusions could be drawn. The priest is of course primarily the representative of God to the people, but he is also the representative of the people to God. Pius XII in his encyclical "Mediator Dei" especially stressed the first,[167] but he did not deny the second; and the reason why he emphasized the first so strongly was simply that he wished to prove that the people did not delegate the priest, but that the priest was commissioned by the apostles and by the hierarchy. The fact thus remains that the priest is also the deputy or representative of the people, the bride-Church.

One would tend from this to ask as well why the person who represents the bride really ought not be a woman. The priest is not merely the mediator of the divine life (we have already seen that this aspect too does not immediately suggest the male!), but also the representative of the bride to the bridegroom. In the priesthood (ultimately in the Pope) the Church, the bride, finds her socially visible, juridically tangible culmination. Why is it always presupposed that that must be a male? At least the idea that the community must always find its representative in a man should be analyzed and argued more closely. Apart from all the other considerations of this book, it seems to me that the central point of the problem is not whether a woman can say, "This is my body," but whether a woman can conduct and lead the celebration of the Anamnesis as president and representative of the community—that is, whether a woman can represent the congregation in the religious area (for until now it still has not been proved that this question can be answered differently for the religious area than for the secular).[168]

If we understand Karl Rahner correctly, he also sees this point as the heart of the matter. Corresponding to his distinction between the two aspects of the Catholic priesthood (the cultic priest, in whom man's word to God is made visible, and the prophetic priest, in whom God's word to men is visible), he says that woman is capable of being the bearer of the prophetic Spirit, but cannot exercise the cultic priesthood which by virtue of its essence follows natural orders.[169] In other words: woman can indeed mediate from "above" to "below," but not from "below" to "above.' The latter, according to Rahner too, is the central problem.

It is not the task of this work to answer the questions which it demonstrates must be raised. But the question becomes even more urgent when it is remembered that there is an ancient tradition (see Thomas), cited by Pope Leo XIII, which says that Mary in her *fiat* to the angel spoke in the name of all humanity.[170]

And in the secular area the fact remains that the Church has never protested against reigning queens; in fact it even speaks at their coronation of their position as mediator, as we have seen above.

And the dogma of Mary as Mediatrix of all graces has no meaning at all if it does not also signify that Mary stepped forward in a mediatory fashion toward Christ in the name of the Church.

But here we arrive at the next subtopic.

4. Mary Was Not a Priest

As we have seen in the preceding sections time and again, the fact that Mary was not a priest has long been seen as a proof that women could not be priests. Even today the fact that the Mother of God was not a priest is raised by writers.

However, the problem of the priesthood of the Mother of God is a long way from being ready for the "solved" file, as is demonstrated simply by the almost unsurveyable quantity of new articles on this theme.[171] It is not possible to sketch out even in rough outline the most important aspects of the problem here. Laurentin, with an amazing display of material from all centuries, shows that according to all the writers Mary "is superior to sacramental priests." But at the same time it is established that "Mary did not receive the sacrament of orders . . . , she did not receive formally the power to celebrate the Mass." The entire task thus consists in bringing these two statements into harmony with one another.[172] Almost every writer attempts to make his solution in this way, perhaps by saying that Mary was a priest "in a more eminent way," or "improperly" or "properly but as a servant or assistant" (*proprie sed tamquam ministra vel socia*), etc.[173] Thus Mary was a priest in some way. If we then investigate why it was necessary to seek these solutions, the reason is naturally found in the fact that no one wants to say that Mary possessed the "ministerial priesthood" (the second statement). Asking further why no one has ventured this far, Laurentin has only one answer:

One reason only is ever forthcoming: Mary is not capable of the sacrament of orders "on account of her female sex." [174]

These are strong words, but according to Laurentin's basic investigations, quite justified words: "one reason only . . . ever." In other words, the Fathers and later writers would gladly have ascribed the priesthood to Mary but they did not venture to because Mary was a woman.

Granted that a very strong argument of tradition against the priesthood of women is involved—one thing is nevertheless certain: the power of the argument "Mary was not a priest" for the dogmatic thesis that a woman cannot be a priest is thereby invalidated. For the thesis of the theologians and Fathers that a woman cannot be a priest can no longer be proved by the argument that "Mary was not a priest" if their thesis itself was the *only* reason (une seule raison) why they always said that Mary was not a priest. Obviously both can be true together, but the first cannot be used to prove the second and the second at the same time be used to prove the first.

Still a second difficulty exists in this proof of the Fathers and theologians. For if, for the sake of argument, we were to grant that Mary *was* in no way a priest—does it then follow that no woman *can* be a priest? That would follow only if one could really say with Rondet and many others:

Mary is woman; it is in Mary that one must learn the role of woman in the history of the world." [175]

Actually, if the *factual* condition of the most holy virgin in her earthly life were the norm for what a woman could be or could do, then a woman could never be a priest. But is that true? First it would have to be proved that that was really true specifically for the priesthood. For it must, for example, also be said that Mary never had sexual intercourse, but no one would say here: "It is in Mary that one must learn the role of woman in the history of the world." Sexual intercourse, according to Thomas, is for women also a *bonum excellens*.[176] Mary also had no secular profession and exercised no public office; she acted only in obscurity. But it does not follow from this that every woman should remain at home (even if so esteemed a writer as M. Schmaus seems to say that; Pius XII said something very different!). The letter of Timothy seems of course to intimate that (1 Tim 2, 15), but Rondet correctly comments on that:

Christianity has liberated woman, restoring her dignity and her supernatural vocation, but has it not also for a long time confined her to the roles of spouse and mother? [177] Paul accented the submission of the woman to her husband more than was just.[178]

To say simply that Mary was not a priest and, that thus no woman ever can be is certainly not sufficient. It must be investigated exactly why her not being a priest is relevant while other actual circumstances from her life are not.

A third difficulty also works against Rondet's statement, "It is in Mary that one must learn the role of woman in the history of the world." For this is to presuppose that woman can become only what she can read in Mary as her prototype, while the man has as his prototype the God-man himself. Would it not be better to consider Mary as the prototype of the creature in general, thus of both women and men, not as the prototype of woman alone? Would it not be better in light of Gal. 3, 28 to seek for man also a norm for what he can be in a man who is not God-man? This is not irrelevant; in fact it has often been done. Several Fathers name in this context St. Joseph or even the apostle John, as Laurentin indicated.[179] Recently too P. Evdokimov did that in the noteworthy book *La femme et le salut du monde;* he sees John the Baptist as the archetype of the male.[180] And the double orders of Fontevrault, of which we spoke in greater detail earlier, venerated specially the apostle John alongside Mary.[181] Let us remember that the founder of this order, explaining the superiority of the abbess over the male members, pointed especially to John 19: "Behold your mother—behold your son."

The theologians would answer: yes, that is true on the level of the *res*, but not on the level of the *sacramentum et res;* on the level of the *res* woman is just as oriented to the God-man as is the man, but not on the level of the *sacramentum et res*. But then all the difficulties which we raised earlier return. It would mean that woman does occupy a lower place in some things; the man could again recite the rabbinic prayer.

If Epiphanius of Salamis and the Apostolic Constitutions fear that the institution of the female priesthood necessarily went together with the adoration of female deities, and see therein a proof that women should not be priests, then their own arguments can be turned back on them: if women, at least in the area of public cult, are oriented only to Mary, the tendency will arise among them to deify Mary. But if it is made clear to them and the world that women can be "another Christ" even in the cultic area, then the need for Marian maximalism disappears of itself.

5. *The Situation of the Primitive Church*

Karl Rahner, in a lecture in the summer of 1959, raised the point that Christianity has the right to remain imprisoned in certain historical situations of its origins, and that therefore woman could not become a priest.

It was clear from the beginning that this was merely an attempt to come to grips with the problem and did not pretend to be a final solution. Even the circumstances—it was an unprepared response to an unexpected question—make it clear that Rahner must not be held to this solution. The questions which are asked here are thus not intended in any way to invalidate this response as if it were his. We are concerned with the value of the argument itself. Moreover, Prof. Trooster of Maastricht has also referred to this aspect independently.[182]

The idea itself is clear. There is a *jus divinum* in the Church which is not founded in the essence of things; *jus divinum* is not the same as *jus naturale;* there is a *jus divinum* which arises from actual circumstances, and thus is qualified more by history than by essence.[183]

Rahner mentioned several other examples. The New Testament, for example, was composed in Greek. But that is not in any way to be understood as following from the essence of the Greek language; it was contingent and might have been different. Nevertheless the Church can no longer change this fact. A second example: the Church celebrates its liturgy with wheat bread and grape wine. It can certainly be said that if Jesus had lived in Germany he would have used rye bread and beer at the last supper. So according to Karl Rahner's attempt at a solution, the male priesthood cannot be derived from the essence of the sexes. And it can certainly be accepted that the Church in its primitive phase merely took over the contemporaneous contingent ethos and thereby "canonized" it for all times.

As the first and most serious question to all this, we must point out that the establishment of the contingent has still not been proved in the matter of the priesthood. For there are many things which for centuries appeared to belong to matters which were established by the Church as permanent but which were later discovered not to have been; this is the case in sacramental theology, as for example the alteration of the thesis on the "special establishment" of the sacraments by Christ. It is true that this thesis was changed on the basis of historical data; it was seen that, de facto, in several points this fixing of the contingent which had always been assumed had not occurred. And for our case there is no historical material that would say to us: where an establishment of the contingent is seen, there was none in fact. However, this example is not brought up with that intention, but merely to show that the perception of what is fixed for all times is changeable. And, de facto, there are also things which actually seemed valid in the primitive Church and thus might suggest that an establishment of the contingent was involved but which were nevertheless later abandoned. Our example from chapter II comes to mind: the *Quaedam capitula ad religiosam sectae nostrae disciplinam pertinentia.* Much of what has been considered *jus divinum positivum* has gradually turned out to be *jus ecclesiasticum.*

For this reason a tighter proof must be demanded that the thesis of the primitive phase of the Church also says something decisive on this point. And as long as no really binding statement of the magisterium exists, one can have recourse only to Scripture and tradition, for according to this understanding, metaphysics, psychology, and sociology are not decisive. But we have already seen in the preceding chapters how many difficulties the arguments from Scripture, tradition, and magisterium leave still unanswered.

Several difficulties also appear, we feel, against the principle as such. If the selection of males was really only time-conditioned and contingent, as this thesis asserts, then indeed very unpleasant consequences could be drawn. This attempted solution proceeds from the idea that Jesus, if he had lived in another time and in another land, could also have chosen women. This attempt thus grants that there could be another time in which woman could be completely appropriate for spiritual office. This speculation must thus come to grips with the following: it is then possible that the Church and its spiritual office stand fixed in a social ethos—that of the first century—which stands diametrically opposed to the ethos of the century in which the Church now lives. That seems to us to be an idea difficult to cope with.

Rahner's two examples also raise still further problems. The New Testament was composed in Greek, which could well have been different; it has in fact consequences even in our time. We will always have to go back to the Greek manner of expression if we wish to express our faith anew or orient ourselves anew to revelation. But is that an example for other cases? In this case it simply happened that way. Revelation is past and finished, and it did happen in *this* way and not another. It would be nonsense to think that the Church could, although she used the Greek language in the past, change it later in order to express her decisive self-understanding in later times. If a lawgiver expresses himself in a certain way, with these certain words and expressions, he can never try to express *this* law and *this* way of promulgation in a different way. What has happened remains for all eternity a happening in this and not in another way. And if what has happened in this way is normative for later times, the way is also normative. But that is still not *eo ipso* an example which of itself says anything about other matters. Only if it is clear from some other place that the Church has expressed an aspect of her self-understanding in the male priesthood—perhaps from an anlysis of biblical theology of office and of woman—only in that case may it be said that there is a parallel here.

For the example of the material of the eucharist, it can be said that it is perhaps no longer an example at all. John McHugh in an article in *Verbum Domini* has shown that it is very doubtful whether Jesus used wheat bread at the Last Supper at all. According to McHugh, it would more likely have been barley bread. And he refers to the significance of this thesis for the missions.[184] But apart from the question of whether Jesus used wheat bread or not—is that really normative for all times? It seems to be not so certain. H. Bouëssé has already questioned it, as we have seen earlier (chapter IV, note 66).

VI Postscript

In the preceding pages I hope to have made clear that there is still much to be done for a genuine proof either pro or contra. Some things are still far from clarified, at least not in the measure that the thesis of the dogmatic theologians could be said either to be certainly proved in a sober, methodical fashion, or to be certainly incorrect.

It was not my intention to reduce to nothing the difference between man and woman, which certainly always exists even if it be alterable. I have only sought to investigate whether this distinction—which earlier was clearly exaggerated to a fault and was portrayed as fixed in this manner for all times—is relevant for the question of whether woman is excluded from ecclesiastical office.

As F. Leenhardt has correctly said, the unsuitability of woman for the contemporary pastoral office is obvious. But that is at least partly because the pastoral office in its traditional forms is formed by man.[1] This book, then, was not written to come to the aid of those young women who would like to be ordained to the priesthood *now*, as St. Catherine of Siena perhaps wished to in an earlier age.[2] For such young women desire to be something which they can have experienced affectively only as something typically masculine. The theoretical and speculative considerations which they would employ, perhaps along the lines of this work, can change nothing, for the affective experience also counts on the psychological plane. Thus they have, in my opinion, somewhat unhealthy desires. Their demands point to the fact that they have still not been able to identify with their own sex. God preserve us from such unbalanced priests.

It is therefore too early for us to try to portray concretely what it would be like if a woman stood at the altar or sat in the confessional. For *we* too know the spiritual office only as masculine and would feel uncomfortable in such performances. But would that always remain the case? Are there no slow changes?

One of the Dutch women pastors, Domina Van Wilsum, tells how a child in her congregation visited relatives in another congregation. When the male pastor from this other congregation called at the home, the child said in amazement, "How can this man be a pastor? That can't be right; he's a man!" [3]

But the question is not whether woman can exercise the masculinely formed pastoral office but whether the pastoral office must be only male and can be only male. Women would in any case have to fill the pastoral office in a feminine way. Very relevant here is Barth's exposition that the content of the command of the Lord in 1 Cor. 14, 37, is just this: that a woman always must conduct herself as a woman:

The command of the Lord, which is for all eternity, directs both man and woman to their own proper sacred place and forbids all attempts to violate this order. The command may be given a different interpretation from that of Paul, for it is the living command of the living Lord. Yet if it is to be respected at all, it cannot even for a moment or in any conceivable sense be disregarded in this its decisive expression and requirement. [4]

The present work was undertaken out of an admittedly un-Augustinian and un-Thomistic, yet justified masculine humility, out of the doubt whether we men can work better with one another than with the help of women; whether we men do justice to the fullness of the tasks of office; whether we really can represent sufficiently the "fullness of Christ's divinity." [5]

Perhaps there were times in which the male could fulfill these tasks. But just as the individual male—according to C. G. Jung —with his growth to adulthood expresses, or should express, more and more his anima aspect (the feminine in him), while in the female the animus should increase in influence,[6] so it may be thought that, in a Church and in a humanity growing to the fullness of the eschaton, men should also be making more place for women, and women should become more fitted to represent the man Christ. This inversion of course does not lie on the biological, physical level (for that would be a perversion), but on the psychic and spiritual. But who would assert that the representation of Christ must realize itself on the biological, physical plane?

That was the background of this work. Has the author been successful in bringing more clarity? He would be content if he could say with Augustine: [7]

In many ways the question has been compressed. Everything I have said I have said so that the difficulty of the question would be magnified. You see that [this question] is valid, and almost insoluble.

Translators' Afterword

Translators' Afterword

It is little more than a decade since Father van der Meer wrote the first version of this book, but even in those few years there have been deep changes of attitudes in church and society which have affected the possibility of the ordination of women.

The first is the massive impetus of Vatican Council II, which took place from 1962 to 1965, immediately after Dr. van der Meer completed his research. In Vatican II the Catholic Church publicly committed itself in the most official and solemn way possible to a thorough reform and renewal of its own structures. The Decree on Ecumenism, for example, issued by the Pope and all the Catholic bishops gathered together, stated in a very clear, even blunt, fashion:

Christ summons the Church, as she goes her pilgrim way, to that continual reformation of which she always has need. (art. 6)

Finally, all are led to examine their own faithfulness to Christ's will for the Church and, wherever necessary, undertake with vigor the task of renewal and reform. (art. 4)

Catholics' . . . primary duty is to make an honest and careful appraisal of whatever needs to be renewed and achieved in the Catholic household. (art. 4)

Such a thoroughgoing reform of course includes that key element in the Church, the priesthood; the Council devoted not only a large section of its Constitution on the Church to the priesthood and its renewal, but even composed an entirely separate document on the meaning and renewal of the priesthood. The need to carry out this reform grew critical in the next few years, as tens of thousands of priests all over the world left the active priesthood.

One serious attempt to face the problem was the intense study of the priesthood sponsored by the American Catholic bishops (see page xxii of the Translators' Foreword). Another was a recent investigation by members of several Catholic and Protestant ecumenical institutes in Germany of what they described as "one of the problems of the greatest import within and between the Christian confessions today, . . . the problem of church ministry." They noted that progress toward a rapprochement between the churches will take place "only if the symptoms and causes of the crisis are precisely analyzed, and if, through a reflection on the basis of the common foundation of the Christian churches, a decision is made to reform the understanding and structure of church offices." [1]

Clearly such an openness to change will be needed for any serious discussion of a topic as significant as the ordination of women to the priesthood. Outside an era committed to the reform and renewal of the Church in general and the priesthood in particular, the issue of the ordination of women priests would likely remain an academic question. But in the post-Vatican II era such a reform is a real possibility.

The second area of great change in the past decade is the status of women. Several times in the present book the author has paused to ask, "Are we perhaps speaking of something different today when we use the word *woman?*" There are many women today who would not only assert that our understanding of woman has changed but who would rise to speak directly to Father van der Meer's point that

The unsuitability of woman for the contemporary pastoral office is obvious. But that is at least partly because the pastoral office in its traditional form is formed by men. This book, then, was not written to come to the aid of those young women who would like to be ordained to the priesthood *now.* For such young women desire to be something which they can have experienced affectively only as something typically masculine.

The female voices would be raised not only in America but also in Western Europe—particularly in the Scandinavian countries, the Netherlands, Germany, and England—and they would find an echo in the Marxist countries and even in unexpected places such as some of the Islamic lands.

Within the past decade the orientation of the feminist movement has turned from an attempt to adapt to the established norms and structures, to an attempt to work out an approach to living based on the "feminine experience." No longer is the masculine—or the feminine—role in contemporary society seen as a norm or ideal; the completely human, it is asserted, can only be discovered once the sexual and professional roles imposed by society are exposed and analyzed. The present priesthood, obviously, is one of the many roles which have been formed to a great extent by such extrinsic forces.

The women who have only recently begun to enter the American Catholic seminaries have all been formed by—and have in their turn helped to form—many of the new attitudes and values of the contemporary feminist movement. They come with professional backgrounds in social work, education, and journalism; they know who they are in a way that would not have been possible a mere decade ago.

But besides the fact that such women would not exercise the priesthood in anything but a womanly way, it is argued that these feminine approaches and values are sorely needed in today's priesthood and that the priesthood cannot be reformed and renewed without both female theologizing and female experience. This last, of course, suggests that the ordination of women must come not as a result of a renewal of the priesthood but as a preliminary to a real renewal. Otherwise even a newly reformed priesthood will be another masculine model "unsuitable for women."

The structure of the Catholic Church today as compared to the structure of a Women's Liberation group is relevant here. It should be noted too that there are women theologians who see the women's movement as a religious movement with religious values and goals.

The structure of the Church is, of course, mainly hierarchical. In a feminist group, on the other hand, the leadership floats: a typical group will rotate its leadership position to give each member a chance for responsibility and for growth. Similarly, routine chores will be shared. Each person will be aided in the performance of her or his responsibilities not by an internalized theology of hierarchical authority but by the freely expressed supportive attitude and atmosphere within the group.

Such a structure is clearly foreseen in the concepts of co-responsibility promoted by Cardinal Leo Suenens of Belgium;

the emphasis on mutual support and solidarity likewise finds a vital point of contact with Vatican II's stress on the Church as the People of God; the reforms in the Catholic liturgy promote a greater sense of community. The Church in many ways is heading, although slowly, toward the steps already taken in women's circles.

A team ministry in which the members bring not only their differing talents but their special training and varying experiences to a leadership community which acts by consensus rather than by unilateral authority; a parish in which a parish council truly representative of the constituency assumes responsibility for major policy decisions and planning; a church community which provides opportunities for genuine service to the world and its unfortunate; a religious community which encourages each member to develop and express in freedom his or her growth in the joy of God's grace—all this is dimly seen in the future of the Catholic Church, though it is already breaking through into the world within the new feminist movement. A renewed priesthood within such structures would hardly be the traditionally "masculine" one that Dr. van der Meer rightly warned women today not to hanker after.

A church in which the nature of authority has changed drastically will, according to feminist theologians, liberate both men and women to discover the fully human in them, the male and the female. Tenderness and strength, an ability to feel and an ability to think, receptiveness and assertiveness will grow within each individual, who will thus more nearly attain the full range of human virtues exemplified in Jesus Christ.

At the same time, the paths toward a common humanity, beginning as they do too often today at stereotyped poles of aggressive masculinity and passive femininity, will come from almost opposite directions. This polarity means that the leadership and the guideposts for women must be far different from those for men. Women priests would therefore seem to be an absolute necessity as spiritual directors, moral and ascetic theologians, and, perhaps most important, models for women.

Within just the past few years there has been a shift from arguing only that there are no real impediments to the ordination of women—an argument which many people believe is finally completed in the present book—to an assertion that there are strong positive reasons for ordaining women priests in the Catholic Church.

Notes

Notes

Translators' Foreword

1. *Wir schweigen nicht länger! We Won't Keep Silence Any Longer* (Zurich, 1964). This is a collection of essays in either German or English by a number of Catholic women—Swiss, German, and American—who deal with the status of women in the Catholic Church. It includes a petition by Dr. Heinzelmann addressed to the Preparatory Commission of Vatican Council II concerning the place of woman in the Roman Catholic Church, and resolutions on the same subject passed by St. Joan's International Alliance at its 1963 and 1964 conventions. ("St. Joan's Alliance grew from the Catholic Woman's Suffrage Society founded in London in 1911, the only association of Catholics to work for woman's suffrage . . . , and enjoys consultative status with the United Nations.")

2. "De positie van de vrouw in de Rooms-Katholieke Kerk," *Do-C* (Documentatie Centrum Concilie) paper no. 194 (1965).

3. Much of the following is taken from a summary of the German Lutheran situation in Margaret Sittler Ermarth, *Adam's Fractured Rib* (Philadelphia, 1970), pp. 71–85.

4. Raymond Tiemayer, *The Ordination of Women* (Augsburg, 1970), pp. 34 f. John Reumann, in Krister Stendahl, *The Bible and the Role of Women* (Philadelphia, 1966), p. ix, also mentions Holland.

5. World Council of Churches, *Concerning the Ordination of Women* (Geneva, 1964), p. 3.

6. Van der Meer also treats this matter: "There are now, at least in the Scandinavian churches, women on whom the bishops have imposed hands and upon whom the Mass vestments have been conferred. . . ." (see chap. I).

7. Stendahl, *The Bible and the Role of Women* (Philadelphia, 1966).

8. Stendahl traces the history on pp. 2–4.

9. *Genesis III*, vol. 1, no. 4 (Philadelphia, Nov.–Dec., 1971), p. 3.

10. Tiemeyer, *Ordination of Women*, p. 16.

11. Ibid., p. 41.

12. *The Lambeth Conference 1958* (London, 1958), p. 2.112.

13. "34. The Conference affirms its opinion that the theological argu-

ments as at present presented for and against the ordination of women to the priesthood are inconclusive.

"35. The Conference requests every national and regional Church or province to give careful study to the question of the ordination of women to the priesthood and to report its findings to the Anglican Consultative Council (or Lambeth Consultative Body) which will make them generally available to the Anglican Communion." *The Lambeth Conference 1968* (London, 1968), pp. 39–40.

14. "In reply to the request of the Council of the Church of South East Asia, this Council advises the Bishop of Hong Kong, acting with the approval of his Synod, and any other bishop of the Anglican Communion acting with approval of his Province, that if he decides to ordain women to the priesthood, his action will be acceptable to this Council, and this Council will use its good offices to encourage all Provinces of the Anglican Communion to continue in communion with these dioceses." Resolution of the Anglican Consultative Council meeting in Limura, Kenya, 23 February to 5 March 1971 (*Ecumenical Press Service*, 11 March 1971, p. 5).

15. *Genesis III*, vol. 2, no. 1 (Philadelphia, May/June, 1972). Since the preparation of this translation there has appeared an excellent summary of the customary arguments pro and con by two Episcopal women: Emily C. Hewitt and Suzanne R. Hiatt, *Women Priests: Yes or No?* (New York, 1973). The book includes a chronology and documentation of the question in the Episcopal Church.

16. Stendahl, *The Bible and the Role of Women*, p. 2.

17. Paragraph 41: "Secondly, it is obvious to everyone that women are now taking a part in public life. . . . Since women are becoming ever more conscious of their human dignity, they will not tolerate being treated as mere material instrunemts, but demand rights befitting a human person in domestic and public life."

Paragraph 15: "Human beings have the right to choose freely the state of life which they prefer, and therefore the right to establish a family, with equal rights and duties for man and woman, and also the right to follow a vocation to the priesthood or the religious life."

18. Heinzelmann (see n. 1 above), p. 11.

19. Already in its 1963 resolutions St. Joan's International Alliance affirmed "its belief that the dedicated work done by so many women for the Church would be more firmly based if they had some outward sign of the official support and blessing of the Church. As a concrete suggestion St. Joan's International Alliance submits that, if in the future, diaconal status duties are to be entrusted as an independent ministry, this ministry be open to both men and women." Heinzelmann (see n. 1 above), p. 111. In 1970 Jeanne Barnes began a Deaconess Movement within the American Catholic Church. The movement's newsletter, *The Journey* (Mary B. Lynch, ed., 4852 N. Kenwood Ave., Indianapolis, Ind. 46208), now has a circulation of over 400. Canada too has its own newsletter, *Diakonos*. Carrying this idea of an organization with a newsletter into the area of a movement for women priests, Sister Valentine Buisseret (Dominicaine, 33 rue Auguste Gevaert, 1070 Brussels, Belgium) announced in 1972 the founding of an international Association of Women Aspiring to the Presbyteral Ministry.

20. Page 54.

21. *National Catholic Reporter,* 30 April 1971.

22. "At a meeting of the Canadian Catholic Conference in spring of 1971, sixty-five of Canada's seventy-five bishops met with sixty women in a dialogue workshop on the status of women. A set of recommendations were submitted to the hierarchy for consideration and were accepted in principle 64 to 1. The recommendations were the following:

(1) Declare clearly and unequivocally that women are full and equal members of the church, with the same rights, privileges and responsibilities as men.

(2) Make strong immediate representations to the forthcoming synod of bishops, asking that all discriminatory barriers against women in canon law and tradition be removed.

(3) Ordain qualified women for the ministry.

(4) By whatever means deemed appropriate, encourage the presence of qualified women on all bodies dealing with matters which concern all church members.

(5) That all practical measures be taken to ensure that the attitude of the clergy toward women, sexuality and marriage respect the inherent dignity of women." Ibid.

23. "Episcopal conferences should undertake serious studies of their own national cultures and of church law and practice in order to eliminate any form of infringement on the rights of women in civil or ecclesiastical life.

"This study should investigate the entire area of implications of women's rights in both civil and church society. It should be complemented but not replaced by a study of an international commission established by the Holy Father, as suggested by Cardinal Flahiff. These studies should investigate the possibility of advancing qualified women to the service of the church (I shall submit to the synod secretariat a separate memorandum on this point).

"Women are not to be excluded from service to the church, if the exclusion stems from questionable interpretation of scripture, male prejudice, or blind adherence to merely human traditions that may have been rooted in the social position of women in other times." *National Catholic Reporter,* 5 November 1971.

24. *National Catholic Reporter,* 20 October 1972.

25. *Journal of Ecumenical Studies,* vol. 9, no. 1 (Winter, 1972): 239–41. The quoted report was issued by the Worship and Mission Section of the Roman Catholic/Presbyterian-Reformed Consultation. The Theology Section of the same Consultation issued a statement on "Ministry in the Church," including the following pertinent passage: "Because of the growing consensus among Roman Catholic and Reformed theologians that there is no insurmountable biblical or dogmatic obstacle to the ordination of women, and because of our common insights into the present and future needs of the people of God, we conclude that ordination of women must be part of the Church's life. . . . Since the problems and potentialities of the entry of women into the ministry of the Church, ordained as well as unordained, and indeed the full involvement of women in the whole of society, are in many ways common to all our churches, it is of the utmost importance that this issue be dealt with ecumenically as well as by each individual church.

Therefore, we recommend that an ecumenical commission composed of women and men be constituted by our churches: to study the role of women in church and society, especially the involvement of women in offices and leadership functions, both clerical and lay, to recommend corrective and innovative actions and programs in these areas, and to monitor their implementation." *Journal of Ecumenical Studies,* vol. 9, no. 3 (Summer, 1972): 593–95.

Chapter I

1. Joseph A. Wahl, *The Exclusion of Woman from Holy Orders,* Studies in Sacred Theology, 2d series, no. 110 (Washington: Catholic University of America, 1959).

2. H. Rondet, "Éléments pour une théologie de la femme," *Nouvelle revue théologique* 79 (1957): 915–40.

3. G. Philips, "La femme dans l'Église," *Ephemerides theologicae lovanienses* 37 (1961): 597–603.

4. *Summa Theologiae* suppl., q. 39, a. 1 (taken from *4 Sent.* d. 25, q. 2, a. 1).

5. E. Krebs, "Vom Priestertum der Frau," *Hochland* 19 (1922): 196–215.

6. A. M. Henry, "Le mystère de l'homme et de la femme," *Vie spirituelle* 80 (1949): 463–90; cf. also, "Pour une théologie de la féminité," *Lumière et vie* 8 (1959): 100–128.

7. René Laurentin, *Marie, l'Église et le sacerdoce,* Etude théologique (Paris, 1953), vol. 2, esp. pp. 69–83.

8. Franz Xaver Arnold, *Woman and Man, Their Nature and Mission,* trans. Rosaleen Brennan (New York: Herder and Herder, 1963).

9. Cf. the literature in chapters III and IV, esp. de Labriolle, Daniélou, Gillmann, Giner Sempere, Lafontaine.

10. Cf. J. E. Havel, "La question du pastorat féminin en Suède," *Archives de sociologie des religions* 4 (1959): 116–30; interesting factual material is also found in D. Zähringer, "Die Frau am Altar und auf der Kanzel?" *Erbe und Auftrag* 36 (1960): 304–15.

11. M. E. Thrall, *The Ordination of Woman to the Priesthood* (London, 1958); L. Magistra, "The Ministry of Woman," *Theology* 63 (1960): 281–85; cf. also ibid., pp. 377 f., 387 f., 472 f.; E. L. Mascall, *Woman and the Priesthood of the Church* (London, 1960).

12. P. Evdokimov, *La femme et le salut du monde* (Paris, 1958).

13. P. J. Jans, "Mann und Frau in ihrem Verhältnis zum kirchlichen Amt," *Internationale kirchliche Zeitschrift,* 52 (1962): 145–56.

14. Cf. J. Daniélou, "L'ordination des femmes en Suède," *Etudes* 305 (1960): 398 f.

15. E. Hertzsch, "Das Problem der Ordination der Frau in der evangelischen Kirche," *Theologische Literaturzeitung* 81 (1956): 379 f.; cf. also Zähringer (n. 10 above).

16. Zähringer, p. 304.

17. Charlotte von Kirschbaum, *Der Dienst der Frau in der Wortverkündigung,* Theologische Studien 31 (Zürich, 1951), p. 3.

18. Edith Stein, *Die Frau, Ihre Aufgabe nach Natur und Gnade*, Edith Steins Werke 5 (Freiburg-Louvain, 1959), pp. 42 f.; cf. pp. 105 f.

19. Karl Barth, *Church Dogmatics* (hereafter cited as *CD*) III/4 (Edinburgh, 1961), pp. 151 f.

Chapter II

1. *Didascalia* 3, 6: F. X. Funk, *Didascalia et Constitutiones Apostolorum* I (Paderborn, 1905), p. 190. The Constitutiones Apostolorum add nothing essential.

2. Epiphanius, *Adversus Haereses;* Migne, *Patrologia Graeca* (hereafter cited as *PG*) 42, c. 744; *Die Griechischen christlichen Schriftsteller* (hereafter cited as *GCS*) (Leipzig, 1897 ff.), 37, p. 477.

3. Ambrosiaster, *Comment. in Ep. ad 1 Tim. 3, 11; PL* 17, c. 496.

4. Diekamp-Hoffmann, *Theologiae dogmaticae manuale*, vol. 4 (Paris, 1946), p. 426.

5. Pohle-J. Gummersbach, *Lehrbuch der Dogmatik*, vol. 3 (Paderborn, 1960), p. 581.

6. Karl Rahner, *Theological Investigations* (Baltimore, 1963), vol. 2, pp. 319 ff.

7. Stein, *Die Frau* (see chap. I, n. 18, above), p. 108.

8. Not always, but often; cf. Strathmann's article μάρτυς in G. Kittel, *Theological Dictionary of the New Testament* (Grand Rapids, Mich., 1967), vol. 4, pp. 492, 497.

9. Hans Kosmala, "Gedanken zur Kontroverse Farbstein-Hoch," *Judaica* 4 (1948): 234. Cf. Hermann Strack and Paul Billerbeck, *Kommentar zum Neuen Testament aus Talmud und Midrasch* (hereafter cited as Billerbeck) (Munich, 1922), vol. 3, pp. 157, 467.

10. Oepke's article γυνή in Kittel, vol. 1, p. 782.

11. Billerbeck, vol. 3, p. 468.

12. Kosmala, pp. 235 ff.

13. Oepke, p. 782.

14. Billerbeck, vol. 3, p. 468.

15. Kosmala, p. 227.

16. Billerbeck, vol. 3, p. 467.

17. Ibid., p. 217.

18. Ibid., p. 251.

19. Ibid., p. 560.

20. Ibid., p. 559–60.

21. Ibid., vol. 2, p. 441.

22. Denzinger—Schönmetzer, *Enchiridion Symbolorum* (hereafter cited as Denz.-Schönm.) (Freiburg, 1965), p. 1752.

23. Wahl, *The Exclusion of Women* (see chap. I, n. 1, above).

24. Ibid., p. 12.

25. Oepke, p. 787; cf. J. Leipoldt, *Die Frau in der antiken Welt und im Urchristentum* (Leipzig, 1954), p. 190; Lietzmann-Kümmel, *An die Korinther I-II*, 4th ed., Handbuch zum Neuen Testament 9 (hereafter cited as HNT) (Tübingen, 1949), pp. 75, 190.

26. E. B. Allo, *St. Paul, Première Épître aux Corinthiens* (Paris, 1934), p. 258.

27. Leitzmann-Kümmel, pp. 75, 190.

28. Ambrosiaster, *Patrologia Latina* (hereafter cited as *PL*) 17, cols. 240, 259.

29. R. Cornely, *Commentarius in Si Pauli Epistol.* (Paris, 1890), 2, p. 444.

30. Origen, *Catenae in 1 Cor.*, quoted in P. de Labriolle, *Les sources de l'histoire du Montanisme* (Fribourg, 1913), pp. 55 f.

31. *PL* 30, c. 878.

32. *PG* 66, c. 938.

33. *PL* 68, cc. 663–64.

34. *In Luc.* 24, Lib. 10, 165: *Corpus Christianorum* (hereafter cited as *CCh*) Series latina 14, p. 393.

35. *PL* 191, c. 1672.

36. *Summa Theologiae* II–II, q. 177, a. 2; III, q. 55, a. 1, ad 3; cf. III, q. 67, a. 4; *in 1 ad Cor.* 14, lectio 7.

37. E.g., L. Lercher, *Institutiones theologiae dogmaticae* IV-2, pars altera, 3d. ed. (Innsbruck, 1950), pp. 316–17.

38. Ph. Bachmann, *Der erste Brief des Paulus an die Korinther*, ed. E. Stauffer, 4th ed. (Leipzig, 1936), pp. 346, 425.

39. Else Kähler, *Die Frau in den paulinischen Briefen, unter besonderer Berücksichtigung des Begriffes der Unterordnung* (Zürich, 1960), pp. 45–46.

40. L. Hick, *Stellung des hl. Paulus zur Frau im Rahmen seiner Zeit* (Cologne, 1957), p. 181.

41. Ibid., p. 181.

42. *PL* 191, c. 1630; cf. c. 1672.

43. *In 1 ad Cor.* 11, lectio 3.

44. *Adversus Haereses* 3, 11, 9: *PG* 7, c. 891.

45. H. Greeven's article "Frau" in *Religion in Geschichte und Gegenwart*, 3d ed. (Tübingen, 1956), vol. 2, c. 1069.

46. G. Friedrich's article on προφήτης [κτλ] in Kittel, vol. 4, p. 851.

47. Allo, pp. 254–55.

48. Lietzmann-Kümmel, p. 53.

49. P. Tischleder, *Wesen und Stellung der Frau nach der Lehre des hl. Paulus*, Neutestamentliche Abhandlungen (hereafter cited as, NTA) 10, nos. 3–4 (Münster, 1923), p. 140.

50. J. Daniélou, "Le ministère des femmes dans l'Eglise ancienne," *Maison Dieu* 61 (1960): pp. 73–74.

51. Kähler, pp. 43–67.

52. Ibid., p. 171.

53. Kirschbaum, *Der Dienst der Frau* (see chap. I, n. 17, above), p. 24.

54. Barth, *CD* III/4, pp. 168–81; cf. III/2, pp. 309 ff.

55. Kähler, p. 170.

56. Ibid., p. 169.

57. Ibid., p. 160.

58. Allo, p. 259.

59. The dispute began, one could say, with G. Delling, *Paulus' Stellung*

zu Frau und Ehe, Beiträge zur Wissenschaft vom alten und neuen Testament, 4th ser., no. 5 (Stuttgart, 1931).

60. F. a. P. Salá, *Sacra Theologiae Summa,* 2d ed., Biblioteca de Autores Christianos 73 (hereafter cited as BAC) (Madrid, 1953), vol. 4, p. 710.

61. For further references see chapter III.

62. Wahl, pp. 14 ff.; Lercher, p. 316; Diekamp-Hoffmann, p. 426.

63. Cf. H. Haag, ed., *Bibellexikon,* 2d ed. (Einsiedeln, 1968), pp. 1316 ff.

64. Kähler, p. 76.

65. Ibid., p. 84.

66. Ibid., p. 77.

67. Delling, p. 111, is of course of another opinion.

68. Ibid., p. 112.

69. Lietzmann-Kümmel, p. 190.

70. Hick, p. 182.

71. Tischleder, p. 173.

72. Greeven, p. 1069.

73. F. J. Leenhardt and Fritz Blanke, *Die Stellung der Frau im Neuen Testament und in der alten Kirche,* Kirchliche Zeitfragen 24 (Zürich, 1949), p. 42.

74. Barth, *CD* III/4, p. 156.

75. Rondet, "Eléments" (see chap. I, n. 2, above), p. 926.

76. F.-R. Refoulé, "Le problème des 'femmes-prêtres' en Suède," *Lumière et vie* 8 (1959): 80 f.

77. A. J. Rasker, "De vrouw in het ambt," *In de Waagschaal* 11 (1955): 152.

78. Hick, pp. 188 f.

79. Daniélou, "Le ministère des femmes," p. 74. His interpretation of λαλεῖν as "prédication de la parole" has already been questioned by us above.

80. In disagreement with me are Kähler, pp. 151 ff. and Leenhardt, p. 45.

81. Kähler, p. 170.

82. Tertullian, *De cultu feminarum,* passim.

83. Y. M.-J. Congar, "La femme dans l'Église," *Recherches de sciences Philosophiques et Théologiques* 37 (1953): 763.

84. Thrall, *Ordination of Woman* (see chap. I, n. 11, above), p. 13.

85. Refoulé, pp. 65–99.

86. Ibid., pp. 82–83.

87. Ibid., pp. 84–85.

88. Ibid., pp. 85 ff.

89. H. von Campenhausen, *Die Begründung kirchlicher Entscheidungen beim Apostel Paulus,* Sitzungsberichte der Heidelberger Akademie der Wissenschaften, Philosophisch-historische Klasse, Jhrg. 1957 2. Abh. (Heidelberg, 1957).

90. Ibid., pp. 22 f.

91. Lietzmann-Kümmel, *op. cit.,* at the appropriate place.

92. Billerbeck, vol. 3, p. 468; cf. Kähler, p. 81; Campenhausen, p. 24.

93. Billerbeck, vol. 3, p. 561.

94. Sessio 5, canon 1 ff. Denz.-Schönm. 1510 ff.

95. Campenhausen, p. 29.
96. Refoulé, p. 90.
97. K. H. Steck, "Authorität und Freiheit in der Theologie," *Evangelische Theologie* 14 (1954): 389 f.
98. Cf. Kähler, pp. 67 ff.; Havel, "La question du pastorat" (see chap. I, n. 10, above), pp. 122–23.
99. Interview with Karl Barth in *In de Waagschaal* 3 (1948): 376.
100. Refoulé, p. 92.
101. Ibid., p. 94.
102. Ibid., pp. 94–95.
103. Campenhausen, p. 15.
104. *PL* 17, c. 210.
105. *Ad. Quir.* 3, 44: *PL* 4, c. 725.
106. C. J. von Hefele, *Conciliengeschichte*, 9 vols., vol. 8 and 9 by J. Hergenröther (Freiburg, 1855–90); trans. by H. Leclercq as *Histoire des conciles d'après les documents originaux*, 9 vols. (Paris, 1907–) (hereafter cited as Hefele-Leclercq); vol. 2, p. 118.
107. Ibid., n. 2.
108. Ibid., p. 124.
109. Ibid., p. 900.
110. L. Vischer, *Die Auslegungsgeschichte von 1 Kor 6, 1–11*, Beiträge zur Geschichte der neutestamentlichen Exegese 1 (Tübingen, 1955), p. 13.
111. Ibid., pp. 21–43 passim.
112. *Ad. Quir.* 3, 44: *PL* 4, cc. 725 ff.
113. Hefele-Leclercq 2, p. 119.
114. Ibid., p. 894.
115. *PL* 84, c. 206.
116. *PG* 41, cc. 1022–23; *PG* 42, c. 823.
117. F. Böckle, "Bestrebungen in der Moraltheologie," in *Fragen der Theologie heute*, ed. J. Feiner, J. Trütsch, and F. Böckle (Einsiedeln, 1957), pp. 439 ff.; Karl Rahner, "Bemerkungen über das Naturgesetz und seine Erkennbarkeit," *Orientierung* 19 (1955): 239–43; Karl Rahner, "Über das Verhältnis des Naturgesetzes zur übernatürlichen Gnadeordnung," *Orientierung* 20 (1956): 8–11; cf. also J. David, "Wandelbares Naturrecht," *Orientierung* 20 (1956): 171–75; J. Fuchs, "Positivistisches Naturrecht?" *Orientierung* 20 (1956): 113–15, 127–29. The more recent discussions concerning natural law will be presumed to be familiar to the reader.
118. Rahner, *Orientierung* 20 (1956): 10.
119. H. van Oyen, "Man en vrouw volgens de Bijbel," *Wending* 9 (1954–55): 317.
120. C. J. H. Vaessen, "Die Stellung der Frau, theologische Betrachtungen nach der Lehre der Heiligen Schrift und des kirchlichen Lehramtes," Dissertatio ad obtinendum lauream in sacra theologia, Promotor Prof. Mag. H. Häring, O.P. (unpublished dissertation), Pontificium Athenaeum Angelicum (Rome, 1956), p. 57.
121. Kähler, pp. 138 ff., 198 ff. See this chapter, sec. 2, for statements by Barth and Charlotte von Kirschbaum.
122. H. Schlier, *Der Brief an die Epheser* (Düsseldorf, 1957), pp. 252–80.

123. *Summa Theologiae* II-II, q. 32, a. 8, ad 2; q. 177, a. 2; q. 67, a. 4; suppl., q. 39, a. 1.

124. Cf. ibid., II-II, q. 177, a. 2.

125. Schlier, p. 253, n. 1.

126. Ibid., p. 254.

127. Ibid., pp. 227–28; on the whole matter cf. also H. Schlier's article on κεφαλή in Kittel, vol. 3, pp. 673 ff.

128. V. Heylen, "Het hoofd van het gezin," *Tijdschrift voor Theologie* 1 (1961): 309–28; this quotation is from the "sommaire," p. 328.

129. He mentions, naturally enough, virgins and widows.

130. Kähler, pp. 48–67.

131. *Summa Theologiae* suppl. q. 19, a. 3, ad 4.

132. Above all Delling; see above n. 59 of this chapter.

133. Rondet, p. 926; cf. p. 932.

134. For the references, see above nn. 9 ff. Also cf. in general J. Jeremias, "Die gesellschaftliche Stellung der Frau," in J. Jeremias, *Jerusalem zur Zeit Jesu* (Göttingen, 1958), pp. 232–50.

135. Billerbeck, vol. 1, p. 299; cf. vol. 3, p. 469.

136. Kosmala, p. 234.

137. Billerbeck, vol. 1, p. 137; vol. 3, pp. 561, 626, 645.

138. Ibid., vol. 3, pp. 370, 427, 442. Further references are in Delling, pp. 49 ff.

139. Delling, p. 49.

140. Oepke, pp. 781–82; also cf. van Oyen, pp. 305 ff.

141. Oepke, p. 782; cf. Billerbeck, vol. 3, p. 558.

142. Kosmala, pp. 231–32.

143. Billerbeck, vol. 3, pp. 610–11.

144. Kosmala, pp. 230–31.

145. E. A. Synan, "The Covenant of Husband and Wife," in *The Bridge*, A Yearbook of Judaeo-Christian Studies 4 (Newark, 1962), pp. 149–70; esp. p. 154.

146. Oepke, p. 776; cf. Kosmala, pp. 227–28; H. Lietzmann, *An die Galater*, 2d. ed., HNT 10 (Tübingen, 1923), p. 23.

147. Kosmala, p. 227, with references.

148. Also cf. K. Rengstorf, *Mann und Frau im Urchristentum* (Cologne, 1954), p. 11.

149. H. Schlier, *Der Brief an die Galater*, 11th ed. (Göttingen, 1951), p. 130.

150. Oepke, p. 785.

151. J. von Allmen, *Maris et femmes d'après Saint Paul*, Cahiers théologiques 29 (Neuchâtel-Paris, 1951), p. 36.

152. Hick, pp. 78 ff.

153. Billerbeck, vol. 1, p. 318; vol. 2, pp. 23 ff.; cf. Kähler, p. 27.

154. Daniélou, "Le ministère des femmes," p. 70.

155. Leenhardt, p. 14.

156. Kosmala, pp. 233 ff.

Chapter III

1. Joseph A. Wahl declared that it was, stating that the matter was too clear to require much discussion. However, he has not convinced me. See above, chap. I, n. 1.

2. P. de Labriolle, *Les sources de l'histoire du Montanism, textes grecs, latins, syriques* (Fribourg-Paris, 1913).

3. *PG* 41, c. 880.

4. Hefele-Leclercq, vol. 2, p. 35. In general cf. *DThC* 10, cc. 2355–70, article on Montanism.

5. For example, Wahl, pp. 39 ff.; Lercher (see chap. II, n. 37, above), p. 316; Diekamp-Hoffmann (see chap. II, n. 4, above), pp. 426–27; P. Gasparri, *Tractatus canonicus de sacra Ordinatione*, vol. 1 (Paris, 1893), pp. 75 ff.; S. Many, *Praelectiones de sacra Ordinatione* (Paris, 1905), pp. 176–94.

6. *PG* 41, c. 848; *GCS* 31, p. 211.

7. *PG* 41, c. 858.

8. *PG* 41, cols. 880–81.

9. *PG* 41, cols. 948–49.

10. *PG* 42, cols. 740 ff.; *GCS* 37, pp. 475 ff.

11. P. H. Lafontaine, "Le sexe masculin, condition de l'accession aux ordres, aux IVe et Ve siècles," *Revue de l'Université d'Ottawa*, Section spéciale 31 (1961), p. 143, n. 12.

12. Ibid., pp. 145 ff.

13. *PG* 41, c. 643.

14. *PG* 104, c. 706.

15. I. F. Sagüés, *Sacra Theologiae Summa*, BAC 90 (Madrid, 1952), vol. 2, p. 887.

16. H. Achelis and J. Flemming, *Die syrische Didaskalia* (Leipzig, 1904), pp. 76 ff.; F.–X. Funk, *Didascalia et Constitutiones Apostolorum*, vol. 1 (Paderborn, 1905), pp. 188 ff.

17. Achelis and Flemming, p. 81; Funk, pp. 198 ff.

18. Achelis and Flemming, p. 85; Funk, pp. 208 ff.

19. Achelis and Flemming, p. 80.

20. Ibid., p. 276.

21. Ibid., p. 279.

22. *DThC* 15, pp. 134–35.

23. *PL* 2, c. 56; *Corpus scriptorum ecclesiasticorum latinorum* (hereafter cited as *CSEL*) (Vienna, 1866–), vol. 70, p. 53; *CChr* series latina 1, p. 221.

24. *CChr* series latina 1, p. 277.

25. Ibid., 1, pp. 291–92.

26. Ibid., 2, p. 1219. For English see *The Ante-Nicene Fathers* (Buffalo, 1885), vol. 3, p. 446.

27. *CChr* series latina 1, p. 688.

28. Ibid., 2, c. 1030.

29. *CSEL* 1, p. 343. For English see *The Fathers of the Church*, vol. 40 (New York, 1959), pp. 117–18.

30. Cf. *DThC* 15, pp. 134–35.

31. *PL* 17, c. 253.
32. Ibid., c. 273.
33. Ibid., c. 494.
34. Ibid., c. 496.
35. Ibid., c. 460.
36. *PG* 7, cols. 580 f.; cf. ibid., c. 592.
37. *PL* 42, c. 30.
38. *PL* 53, c. 596.
39. *PL* 3, c. 1164; for the text correction *"non* sine sacramento solitae," instead of "sine sacramento solitae," see *CSEL* 3 b, c. 818, and de Labriolle, pp. 63 ff.; and for the interpretation cf. Lafontaine, p. 142, n. 11, and *Bibliothek der Kirchenväter,* 2d. ed. (hereafter cited as *BKV*) (Munich, 1928), vol. 60, pp. 379 ff. For English see *Library of the Fathers* (Oxford, 1843), vol. 15, pp. 69 ff.
40. *PG* 62, cols. 543 ff.
41. *PG* 13, c. 242; cf. *PG* 14, c. 772.
42. *PL* 34, p. 387.
43. Quoted in de Labriolle, pp. 55–56; cf. the edition by J. A. Cramer (Oxford, 1841), p. 279.
44. *PG* 7, c. 891.
45. *PG* 61, cols. 216–17.
46. *PG* 20, c. 473.
47. Quoted in de Labriolle, pp. 105 ff.
48. *PG* 39, cols. 988–89.
49. *Corpus Iuris Canonici,* c. 4, C. 30, q. 3; Emil Friedberg, *Quinque compilationes antiquae nec non collectio canonum Lipsiensis* (Leipzig, 1882), 1, pp. 1101 f.; cf. Ph. Jaffé, *Regesta pontificum Romanorum ad a. p. ch. n. MCXCVIII* (Leipzig, 1851), vol. 1, p. 696; *PL* 151, c. 529.
50. Daniélou, "Le ministère des femmes" (see chap. II, n. 50, above), p. 80.
51. *PG* 74, c. 881.
52. *CSEL* 50, p. 51.
53. *PL* 112, c. 100.
54. *PL* 191, cc. 1630–31.
55. *PL* 192, c. 340.
56. *PG* 31, cc. 240–41.
57. *PL* 34, cc. 204–5.
58. Ibid., c. 206.
59. *PG* 12, c. 158.
60. *PL* 32, c. 866.
61. *PL* 35, c. 1395.
62. *PG* 12, cc. 296–97.
63. *PG* 35, cc. 993 ff.
64. *PG* 54, c. 600.
65. *PL* 26, cc. 536–37.
66. *PL* 34, cc. 452–53; for text correction cf. *CSEL* 28, cc. 376–77.
67. Ibid., c. 293.
68. Hefele-Leclercq, vol. 2, p. 446.
69. *PG* 14, c. 1278.

70. *PL* 30, c. 714.

71. *PL* 111, cols. 1605–6.

72. *PG* 33, c. 356.

73. *PG* 35, c. 997.

74. Hefele-Leclercq, vol. 3, p. 216; J. D. Mansi, *Sacrorum conciliorum nova et amplissima collectio* (Florence, 1757–98). New edition and continuation under the title, *Collectio conciliorum recentiorum ecclesiae universiae* (Paris, 1899–1927), vol. 9, p. 913.

75. *PG* 46, c. 993.

76. Odo Casel, *Jahrbuch für Liturgiewissenschaft* 10 (1930), review of Johannes Quasten, *Musik und Gesang in den Kulten der heidnischen Antike und christlichen Frühzeit* (Münster, 1929), p. 293.

77. "Instructio ad Vic. Ap. Sutchuen," in *Codicis Iuris Canonici Fontes* (Vatican, 1939), 4598, vol. 7, p. 139.

78. "Motu proprio De musica sacra instauranda 1903," in, ibid., vol. 3, p. 613.

79. "Instructio de musica sacra," in *Acta Apostolicae Sedis* (Rome, 1909 ff.), vol. 48 (1958), p. 658.

80. *PG* 20, c. 476; for English see *The Fathers of the Church*, vol. 19 (New York, 1953), pp. 323–25.

81. *PL* 34, cc. 395 ff.

82. *Summa Theologiae* I, q. 92, a. 1.

83. *CSEL* 32, p. 325; *Corpus Iuris Canonici*, c. 9, C. 36, q. 2; Friedberg, vol. 1, p. 1291. For the excommunication see canon 27 of the Council of Chalcedon; Hefele-Leclercq, vol. 2, pp. 814–15; *Corpus Iuris Canonici*, c. 1, C. 36, q. 2; Friedberg, vol. 1, p. 1290. For further punishments see *Corpus Iuris Canonici*, c. 34, C. 27, q. 2; Friedberg, vol. 1, p. 1073.

84. *PL* 6, c. 1046.

85. Ibid., c. 421.

86. *PG* 51, cc. 230–31.

87. *PG* 43, c. 88.

88. *PL* 30, c. 732; cf. also c. 878.

89. *PL* 35, cc. 2244; cf. *Corpus Iuris Canonici*, c. 17, C. 34, q. 5; Friedberg, vol. 1, p. 1255.

90. *Corpus Iuris Canonici*, C. 15, q. 3, Gratianus; Friedberg, vol. 1, p. 750.

91. *CSEL* 28, p. 395; cf. *Corpus Iuris Canonici*, c. 14, C. 33, q. 5; Friedberg, vol. 1, p. 1254.

92. *PG* 66, c. 938.

93. *PG* 82, c. 310.

94. *PG* 95, c. 1005.

95. *PG* 119, c. 156.

96. *PL* 30, c. 878.

97. *PL* 68, c. 664.

98. *PL* 103, cc. 232–33.

99. *PL* 15, cc. 1936–37; cf. *CSEL* 23, 3, pp. 514 ff.; *CChr* series latina 14, pp. 390 ff.

100. *PG* 14, cc. 1009–10.

101. *PL* 76, c. 1194.

102. *PL* 118, cc. 481–82.
103. *PL* 38, c. 1108.
104. *GCS* 1, 1, pp. 354–55.
105. *PG* 13, c. 1819.
106. *PG* 72, c. 941.
107. *PL* 15, c. 1629; *CSEL* 23, 3, pp. 167–68.
108. *PG* 61, cc. 315–16.
109. *PG* 95, c. 685.
110. *PG* 118, cc. 857–58.
111. *PG* 125, cc. 38–39.
112. *PG* 74, c. 689.
113. Ibid., c. 692.
114. *PL* 70, c. 1338.
115. *PL* 75, cc. 982–83.
116. *CSEL* 32, 1, p. 153; cf. *Corpus Iuris Canonici,* c. 18, C. 34, q. 5; Friedberg, vol. 1, p. 1255.
117. *PG* 7, c. 1245.
118. *PL* 22, cc. 1152–53.
119. *PL* 35, c. 1513; cf. *CChr* series latina 36, p. 153; *BKV* 8, pp. 256–57.
120. *Summa Theologiae* I, q. 93, a. 4, ad 1.
121. *PL* 15, cc. 1844 ff.; *CSEL* 23, 3, p. 514; *CChr* series latina 14, pp. 390 f.
122. *PL* 26, cc. 531 ff.
123. One should compare this, for example, with the dates from paleontology, which indicate the oldest prehominid forms gave evidence of a much more outspoken sexual dimorphism. P. Teilhard de Chardin, *Der Mensch im Kosmos* (Munich, 1958), p. 196.
124. *Expositio super 1-am epist. ad Cor. cap. 11.* lectio 2, cura R. Cai O.P., 8th ed. (Turin-Rome; Marietti, 1953), vol. 1, p. 347.
125. Cf. *DThC* V, cc. 457–520; still important is H. Wallon, *Histoire de l'esclavage dans l'antiquité,* 2d ed. (Paris, 1879), esp. part 3, pp. 256–388.
126. *PG* 54, cc. 593 ff.
127. *PG* 54, cc. 600 ff.
128. K. H. Rengstorf's article on δοῦλος in Kittel, vol. 2, p. 272; cf. E. B. Allo, *St. Paul* (see chap. II, n. 26, above), p. 173; *DThC* V, p. 463; A. Steinmann, "Zur Geschichte der Auslegung von I Kor 7, 21," *Theologische Revue* 16 (1917): 340–48. The second interpretation has the context in its favor, for in this chapter Paul says every time: remain in the condition in which you were when you came to believe. Most exegetes now opt for this interpretation. It remains nevertheless true that the exegesis of μᾶλλον χρῆσαι in this case is not simple. "Be a better slave" would imply an asceticism, a moralizing mentality, which one does not easily expect in Paul.
129. *PG* c. 156. It is therefore not clear how Allo, p. 173, can reckon Chrysostom with the other direction.
130. *PL* 41, cc. 643–44.
131. *PL* 34, c. 624.
132. *PL* 41, c. 644.
133. *PL* 34, c. 590.
134. For documentation see *DThC* V, pp. 463 ff.

135. Wallon, pp. 318 ff.

136. For the consequences cf. H. D. Wendland's article "Sklaverei und Christentum," in *RGG* (3d ed.), vol. 6, pp. 101 ff. Bibliography is included. Cf. also *DThC* V, pp. 463–64.

137. One need only consult indices under the terms *servitus* and *servus;* for example: *Indices in Summa Theologiae et in Summa contra Gentiles,* extractum ex tome XVI editionis leoninae (Rome, 1948), 324b, 675b, 676a.

138. *DThC* V, p. 486.

139. Quoted in ibid., p. 515.

140. Ibid., p. 475.

141. A very good overview is found in A. Kalsbach's article, "Diakonissin," in *Reallexikon für Antike und Christentum* (1941–   ), vol. 3, pp. 917 ff.; cf. *Lexikon für Theologie und Kirche,* 2d ed. (1930–   ), vol. 3, p. 327; *DThC* IV, pp. 685 ff.; Lafontaine, pp. 156–82; Daniélou, "Le ministère des femmes," passim; F. Gillmann, "Weibliche Kleriker, nach dem Urteil der Frühscholastik," *Archiv für Katholisches Kirchenrecht* 93 (1913): pp. 239–53; Many, pp. 176–84, 188–94; Hefele-Leclercq, vol. 2, pp. 446 ff. (as far as Arausicanum I); Santiago Giner Sempere, "La mujer y la potestad de orden," *Revista española de Derecho Canónico* 9 (1954): pp. 851–59.

142. Hefele-Leclercq, vol. 2, pp. 446 ff., n. 1.

143. K. H. Schäfer, "Kanonissen und Diakonissen," *Römische Quartalschrift für christliche Altertumskunde und für Kirchengeschichte* 24 (1910): 60 ff.; cf. E. Martène, *De antiquis Ecclesiae ritibus* (Antwerp, 1736–38), vol. 2, pp. 197 ff.

144. Hefele-Leclercq, vol. 1, pp. 615 ff. Daniélou denies this of course, but he has Kalsbach, who is very authoritative in this matter, opposed to him; Daniélou, p. 86.

145. Hefele-Leclercq, vol. 2, pp. 803–4.

146. Ibid., pp. 446 ff.

147. Ibid., p. 1039.

148. Ibid., p. 452.

Chapter IV

1. P. de Labriolle disputes St. Epiphanius' claim that the Montanists ordained women; cf. P. de Labriolle, *La crise montaniste* (Paris, 1913), pp. 510–11. G. Bardy, however, thinks it did happen; cf. *DThC* X, p. 2368. For a discussion of the whole matter see Lafontaine, "Le sexe masculin" (see chap. III, n. 11, above), p. 145, n. 22.

2. *D. Martin Luthers Werke.* Kritische Gesamtausgabe (Weimar, 1888), vol. 6, p. 407. Cf. E. Hertzsch, "Das Problem der Ordination der Frau in der Evangelischen Kirche," *Theologische Literaturzeitung* 81 (1956): 380.

3. Quoted in *RGG* (2d ed.), vol. 2, p. 722.

4. Denz.-Schönm. 1768, 1776.

5. Giner Sempere, "La mujer" (see chap. III, n. 141, above), pp. 841–69.

6. *PG* 5, c. 1078; cf. Jaffé, *Regesta* (see chap. III, n. 49, above), vol. 12, p. 6; Mansi, *Sacrorum conciliorum* (see chap. III, n. 74, above), vol. 1, p. 653.

7. Cf. Jaffé.

8. Cf. Mansi, vol. 1, p. 690. Likewise, Giner Sempere, p. 848.

9. Jaffé, 12, p. 9.

10. *DThC* X, p. 2360.

11. J. Quasten, *Patrology* (Utrecht-Brussels, 1950–53), 1, p. 279.

12. *PG* 5, c. 1136; cf. Jaffé, *op. cit.*, 1², p. 9; Mansi, pp. 689–90. The Council of Laodicea forbade the same to subdeacons. However, according to Hefele-Leclercq that is not a general prohibition but is applicable only in the case of a solemn entrance. Hefele-Leclercq, vol. 1, p. 1011; cf. *Corpus Iuris Canonici*, D. 23, c. 26; Friedberg (see chap. III, n. 49, above), vol. 3, p. 86.

13. *Corpus Iuris Canonici*, D. 23, c. 25; Friedberg, vol. 1, p. 86.

14. See above, end of chap. III, and below, this chap., "Evaluation of the Texts."

15. Canon 1306 stipulates absolutely no limitations; current canon law, therefore, thinks otherwise.

16. Hefele-Leclercq, vol. 1, p. 1020; Mansi, vol. 2, pp. 571, 581.

17. "Ut mulieres omnes ecclesiae catholicae, et fideles a virorum alienorum lectione et coetibus separentur; vel ad ipsas legentes aliae, studio vel docendi vel discendi, conveniant. Quoniam hoc apostolus iubet." Hefele-Leclercq, p. 987; Mansi, vol. 1, pp. 633–34.

18. "Il est prescrit aux femmes fidèles à l'Eglise de ne prendre aucune part aux réunions des hommes étrangers; il leur est interdit de se joindre aux femmes qui font des lectures, pour s'instruire et enseigner elles-mêmes. Cela est défendu par l'Apôtre." Lafontaine, p. 150.

19. "Le concile . . . s'en prit à l'enseignement public offert par les femmes." Ibid., p. 149.

20. Giner Sempere, p. 844.

21. *PL* 20, c. 155; *CSEL* 1, pp. 99–100.

22. Hefele-Leclercq, vol. 2, p. 93. Mansi was not aware of the canons of Nîmes; cf. Hefele-Leclercq, vol. 2, pp. 91 ff.

23. Ibid., p. 93, n. 9.

24. Lafontaine, p. 150.

25. L. Duchesne, ed., *Liber pontificalis*, 2 vols. (Paris, 1886, 1892), vol. 1, p. 227.

26. *PL* 59, c. 55; cf. *PL* 67, c. 309; Jaffé, 1², p. 85; Mansi, vol. 8, p. 44.

27. Mansi, vol. 9, p. 855.

28. Hefele-Leclercq, vol. 3, p. 186; Mansi, vol. 9, p. 793.

29. Giner Sempere, p. 849.

30. Hefele-Leclercq, vol. 3, p. 180.

31. Ibid., p. 209.

32. J. A. Jungmann, *Missarum Sollemnia*, 4th ed. (Vienna, 1958), vol. 2, p. 13, n. 42; p. 464, n. 3.

33. Hefele-Leclercq, vol. 3, p. 220; Mansi, vol. 9, p. 915; Jungmann, p. 471, n. 43; p. 472, n. 47. Jungmann also cites Caesarius of Arles, *PL* 39, c. 2168.

34. Ch. DuCange, *Glossarium ad scriptores mediae et infimae latinitatis*, 3 vols. (Paris, 1678), vol. 3, p. 170.

35. *PL* 84, cc. 49, 133, 207, 581, 805.

36. *Monumenta Germaniae Historica,* Legum Sectio 2 Capitularia regum francorum (Hanover, 1883), vol. 1 (Quarto-Ausgabe), pp. 55, 102.

37. Ibid., p. 364.

38. Ibid. (Hanover, 1897), vol. 2, p. 32; cf. *PL* 97, cc. 821–22.

39. The editor notes in the text: Conc. Paris, lib. I, c. 45; abbrev. Mansi 14, 565.

40. The editor notes: Laodic. 44; Mansi 2, 571, 581.

41. The editor notes: Gel. decr. 26; Mansi 8, 44.

42. Hefele-Leclercq, vol. 4, p. 67; Mansi, vol. 14, p. 565.

43. Mansi, vol. 13, p. 996; cf. ibid., vol. 19, p. 705.

44. Hefele-Leclercq, vol. 4, p. 691; Mansi, vol. 3, p. 167.

45. *Corpus Iuris Canonici,* c. 1, X, de cohabitatione clericorum et mulierum, III, 2; Friedberg, vol. 2, p. 454.

46. *Summa Theologiae* II-II, q. 177, a. 2.

47. H. V. Borsinger, *Die Rechtsstellung der Frau in der katholischen Kirche* (Leipzig, 1930), p. 42.

48. *PL* 115, c. 681.

49. Hefele-Leclercq, vol. 3, c. 572.

50. De Labriolle, pp. 266 ff.; Lafontaine, pp. 152–53; de Labriolle, "Mulieres in Ecclesia taceant, Un aspect de la lutte antimontaniste," *BLAC* 1 (1911): 291–92; P. Browne, "Die Sterbekommunion im Altertum und Mittelalter," *Zeitschrift für Katholische Theologie* 60 (1936): esp. p. 709.

51. F. Gillmann, "Weibliche Kleriker nach dem Urteil der Frühscholastik," *Archiv für katholisches Kirchenrecht* 93 (1913): 239–53.

52. *Acta Apostolicae Sedis* (Rome, 1916), vol. 8, p. 146.

53. R. Laurentin, *Marie, l'Eglise et le sacerdoce* (Paris, 1952) vol. 1, pp. 521 ff.

54. *Corpus Iuris Canonici,* D. 4, de consecratione, c. 20; Friedberg, vol. 1, p. 1367; cf. D. 23, c. 29 in part one; Friedberg, vol. 1, p. 86. The texts in reality are from canons 99 and 100 of the so-called 4th council of Carthage: the Statuta Ecclesiae Antiqua; cf. Hefele-Leclercq, vol. 2, p. 120.

55. Kalsbach's article on Diakonisse in, *Reallexikon für Antike und Christentum* (1941 ff.), 3, pp. 917 ff.

56. *Test. Dom.* 1, 23.

57. Jungmann, p. 479, n. 94.

58. *Test. Dom.* 2, 20; cf. Josephine Mayer, *Monumenta de viduis diaconissis virginibusque tractantia,* Florilegium Patristicum 42 (Bonn, 1938), p. 32.

59. K. H. Schäfer, *Die Kanonissenstifter im deutschen Mittelalter* (Stuttgart, 1907), pp. 31, 59.

60. Hefele-Leclercq, vol. 3, p. 943; Mansi, vol. 12, p. 657; cf. *Corpus Iuris Canonici,* c. 3, C. 33, q. 1; Friedberg, vol. 1, p. 1150.

61. Rondet, "Eléments" (see chap. I, n. 2, above), p. 932.

62. *Katholiek Archief* 2 (1947–48): 53–60.

63. *La documentation catholique* 28 (August, 1949), cc. 1089–96.

64. *Herder-Korrespondenz* 11 (1956–57), p. 105.

65. Cf. also the address of 12 September 1947: ibid. 2 (1947–48), pp. 75 ff.; of 24 April 1952: ibid., 6 (1951–52), pp. 398–99; of September 1957: *Katholiek Archief* 12 (1957), pp. 1165–76; of 2 July 1958: ibid. 13

(1958), pp. 913–20; John XXIII's address of 1 March 1959: ibid. 14 (1959), pp. 606–8.

66. H. Bouëssé, "De la nature des sacrements chrétiens," *L'année théologique* 8 (1947), esp. pp. 201–9; afterwards Bouëssé repeated these thoughts in *Le Sauveur du monde 4, L'économie sacramentaire*. Doctrina sacra 4 (Chambéry-Paris, 1951), pp. 59–68.

67. E. Schillebeeckx, *Christus, Sacrament van de Godsontmoeting*, 3d ed. (Bilthoven, 1959), p. 115, n. 54.

68. E.g., Lercher, *Institutiones* (see chap. II, n. 37, above), p. 315.

Chapter V

1. *Summa Theologiae* suppl., q. 39, a. 1; this text is taken over from Thomas's work, *In 4 Sent.* d. 25 q. 2, a. 1.

2. Ibid. suppl., q. 39, a. 1, ad 1.

3. Ibid. 1, q. 93, a. 4, ad 1.

4. Ibid. III, q. 52, a. 3; I, q. 32, a. 2, ad 4; cf. G. M. Manser, "Die Ehe," *Divus Thomas* 24 (1946): 121–246, esp. 123.

5. *Summa Theologiae* suppl., q. 39, a. 1, ad 2.

6. *In I ad Cor.* lectio VII, 1, p. 402.

7. Quoted in A. Nussbaumer, "Der hl. Thomas und die rechtliche Stellung der Frau," *Divus Thomas* 11 (1933): 150; in the same sense see Manser, pp. 128 ff.

8. Manser, p. 130.

9. S. G. M. Trooster, "De leek in huwelijk in gezinsleven (III), VI Man en vrouw," *Katholiek Archief* 14 (1959): 565.

10. *Summa Theologiae* I, q. 92, a. 1; cf. I, q. 98, a. 2; suppl. q. 41, a. 1. Already in 1930 Hildegard Borsinger raised her criticism in her book, *Die Rechtsstellung der Frau in der katholischen Kirche* (Leipzig, 1930), p. 50. The argument against her interpretation by Nussbaumer, pp. 138 ff., is not convincing.

11. *Summa Theologiae* I, q. 92, a. 2; cf. Manser, pp. 126–28.

12. *IV Sent.* d. 27, q. 1, a. 1; q. 3, concl. 2.

13. *Summa Theologiae* III, q. 67, a. 4.

14. Ibid. I, q. 92, a. 1, ad 1.

15. A. Mitterer, "Mann und Weib nach dem biologischen Weltbild des hl. Thomas und der Gegenwart," *Zeitschrift für katholische Theologie* 57 (1933): 491–556; Mitterer, " 'Mas occasionatus' oder zwei Methoden der Thomasdeutung," ibid 72 (1950): 80–103; cf. also the article by A. Nussbaumer and G. Manser cited in note 7.

16. Mitterer, "Mann und Weib," p. 519.

17. *Summa Theologiae* I, q. 92, a. 1, ad 2.

18. *ScG* 3, 123.

19. *Summa Theologiae* II-II, q. 177, a. 2.

20. *In 1 ad Cor. 11.* lectio III, 1, p. 349.

21. *Summa Theologiae* III, q. 31, a. 4, ad 1.

22. Ibid. II-II, q. 156, a. 1, ad 1; suppl., q. 62, a. 4, ad 5.

23. *ScG* 4, 122.

24. Nussbaumer, p. 146.

25. A. Ziegler, "Das Bild der Frau von heute," *Orientierung* 23 (1959): 68.

26. On the whole issue cf. H. Schelsky, "Der Vater und seine Authorität,' *Wowa* 8 (1953): 663 ff. Also, Vaessen, "Die Stellung der Frau" (see chap. II, n. 120, above), pp. 263 ff.

27. *Summa Theologiae* suppl., q. 19, a. 3, ad 4; *in 1 Tim*. 2. lectio III; *in 4 Pol*. 2. lectio III.

28. *Summa Theologiae* II-II, q. 123, a. 5, ad 2.

29. Cf. A. Ziegler, *Das natürliche Entscheidungsrecht des Mannes in Ehe und Familie* (Heidelberg-Louvain, 1958).

30. *AAS* 22 (1930), pp. 549–50; cf. pp. 567–68.

31. *Corpus Iuris Canonici*, 4, X, de arbitris, I, 43; Friedberg (see chap. III, n. 49, above), vol. 2, p. 231.

32. *Pontificale Romanum*. De benedictione et coronatione reginae ut regni dominae.

33. A. Wintersig, "Zur Königinnenweihe," *Jahrbuch fur Liturgiewissenschaft* 5 (1925): 150–53.

34. P. de Puniet, *Le Pontifical romain* (Louvain-Paris, 1931), vol. 2, p. 136.

35. For the following pages we have depended heavily on the unpublished dissertation of Vaessen (see above), pp. 151 ff.

36. *Corpus Iuris Canonici*, 12, X, de maioritate et oboedientia, I, 33; Friedberg, vol. 2, p. 201.

37. L. Hanser, "Abbatissae nullius," *Studien und Mitteilungen zur Geschichte des Benediktinerordens und seiner Zweige* 43 (1925): 219.

38. *Corpus Iuris Canonici*, 14, X de excessibus praelatorum et subditorum, V, 31; Friedberg, vol. 2, p. 841.

39. Schäfer, Kanonissenstifter (see chap. IV, n. 59), p. 103.

40. Ibid., p. 143.

41. K. H. Schafer, "Kanonissen und Diakonissen," *Römische Quartalschrift für christliche Altertumskunde und für Kirchengeschichte* 24 (1910): 89.

42. Schäfer, *Kanonissenstifter*, p. 144.

43. Schäfer, "Kanonissen," p. 54.

44. Schafer, *Kanonissenstifter*, p. 146.

45. Ibid.

46. A. Cohausz, *Herford als Reichsstadt und papstunmittelbares Stift* (Bielefeld, 1928), p. 25.

47. Ibid.

48. E. Krebs, "Priestertum der Frau" (see chap. I, n. 5, above), pp. 214–15; Hanser, p. 220. The expression "Monstrum Apuliae" was coined by Baronius.

49. "Abbesses," *DThC* I, p. 21.

50. Borsinger, *Rechtsstellung der Frau* (see chap. IV, n. 47, above), p. 55.

51. Hanser, p. 220.

52. F. Ferraris, *Bibliotheca canonica iuridica moralis theologica* (Rome, 1844), vol. 1, p. 28.

53. M. F. Hallier, *De sacris electionibus et ordinibus ex antiquo et novo ecclesiae usu* (Paris, 1636), p. 519.

54. Borsinger, pp. 57–58.

55. "Abbesses," *DThC* 1, p. 21.

56. Following Suarez here; see below. *DThC* I, pp. 21–22.

57. Krebs, p. 215.

58. Borsinger, p. 55.

59. De Puniet, vol. 2, p. 134.

60. L. Eisenhofer, *Handbuch der katholischen Liturgik* (Freiburg, 1933), vol. 2, p. 429.

61. Cf. S. Hilpisch, *Die Doppelklöster* (Münster, 1928).

62. M. Heimbucher, *Die Orden und Kongregationen der katholischen Kirche* (Paderborn, 1907), vol. 1, pp. 327–29.

63. Borsinger, p. 65; *DThC* 1, p. 21.

64. Hilpisch, p. 73.

65. Borsinger, p. 63; Hilpisch, pp. 78–85.

66. *In 1 ad Cor. 11.* lectio II, *op. cit.,* 1, p. 347.

67. *Summa Theologiae* suppl. q. 19, a. 3, ad 4.

68. Ibid.

69. F. Suarez, *De Religione,* Tract. 7, lib. 2, cap. 9, ed. Vivès (Paris, 1860), vol. 16, p. 148.

70. Friedberg, vol. 1, p. 1255.

71. Ibid., vol. 2, p. 903.

72. Ibid., p. 886.

73. Many other authors think otherwise, however; cf. *DThC* II, pp. 2125–26.

74. F. Suarez, *De Censuris,* Disp. 2, sect. 3, ed. Vivès (Paris, 1861), pp. 22 ff.

75. Suarez, *De Religione,* p. 148.

76. *Corpus Iuris Canonici,* 10, X, de poenitentiis, V. 38; Friedberg, vol. 2, p. 886.

77. Cf. the Capitulare Caroli Magni, Mansi, vol. 13, app. 3, c. 174.

78. Giner Sempere, "La mujer" (see chap. III, n. 141, above), p. 859; cf. *DThC* I, p. 20.

79. Giner Sempere, pp. 860–61.

80. Ibid., pp. 862–63.

81. Mansi, vol. 13, app. 3, c. 174.

82. Giner Sempere, pp. 863 ff.

83. Mitterer, "Mann und Weib," pp. 534 ff.; Nussbaumer, p. 150.

84. Quoted in Giner Sempere, pp. 846–47, and Gillmann, "Weibliche Kleriker" (see chap. IV, n. 51, above), p. 253, n. 1.

85. Wahl, *Exclusion of Women* (see chap. I, n. 1, above), pp. 45–56.

86. Suarez, *De Censuris,* Disp. 51, sect. 2, p. 565.

87. F. Suarez, *Disput. in 3am partem,* Disp. 87, sect. 1, ed. Vivès (Paris, 1861), vol. 21, p. 922.

88. The Missale Romanum appears to consider it still useful to state expressly that the priest may celebrate despite "de defectibus dispositionis corporis," 9, 5. For a general discussion cf. also J. Fuchs, *Die Sexualethik des heiligen Thomas von Aquin* (Cologne, 1949), pp. 50–53, 249–53.

89. Th. L. Haitjema, *Nederlands Hervormd Kerkrecht* (Nijkerk, 1951), p. 142.

90. Ibid., p. 11.

91. Ibid., pp. 148–49.

92. Refoulé, "Femme-prêtres en Suède" (see chap. II, n. 76, above), pp. 76–77.

93. Ibid., pp. 78–79.

94. Congar, "La femme dans l'Eglise" (see chap. II, n. 83, above), p. 764.

95. *In IV Sent.* dist. XXV, art. II, q. 1 (ed. Quaracchi, 1889), tom. IV, p. 649.

96. Krebs, "Priestertum der Frau" (see chap. I, n. 5, above), p. 209.

97. Hick, *Stellung des hl. Paulus* (see chap. II, n. 40, above), p. 179.

98. Henry, "Le mystère" (see chap. I, n. 6, above), pp. 488 ff.

99. Bonaventura, *In IV Sent.* dist. XX, p. II, q. 3 in corp. (ed. Quaracchi, 1889), tom. IV, p. 534.

100. K. Bihlmeyer and H. Tüchle, *Kirchengeschichte,* 12th ed. (Paderborn, 1948), vol. 2, pp. 59–60.

101. Cf. *Humbertus Cardinalis libri 3 adv. Simoniacos.* lib. 3, cap. 5, 11. Monumenta Germaniae Historica Libelli de Lite 1 (Hanover, 1891; editio nova, 1956), pp. 203–4, 211–12.

102. Diekamp-Hoffmann, *Theologiae dogmaticae* (see chap. II, n. 4, above), p. 426.

103. Lercher, *Institutiones theologiae* (see chap. II, n. 37, above), p. 316.

104. Nicea, canon 15: Hefele-Leclercq, vol. 1, pp. 597–98; Chalcedon, canon 5: Hefele-Leclercq, vol. 2, pp. 783–84.

105. *Corpus Iuris Canonici,* 7, X, de translatione episcopi, 1, 4; Friedberg, vol. 2, p. 100.

106. Denz.-Schönm. 769.

107. *Summa Theologiae* II-II, q. 184, a. 7, and q. 185, a. 4.

108. H. Schlier, *Der Brief an die Epheser* (Düsseldorf, 1957), pp. 252 ff.

109. R. Laurentin, *Marie, l'Eglise et le sacerdoce* (see chap. I, n. 7, above), vol. 1, p. 93, n. 119.

110. F. Büchsel's article γεννάω [κτλ] in Kittel, *Theological Dictionary of the New Testament* (see chap. II, n. 8), vol. 1, p. 665.

111. Laurentin, *Marie, l'Eglise et le sacerdoce* (see chap. I, n. 7, above), vol. 2, p. 79, note 62.

112. Schlier, p. 266.

113. G. Quell's article πατήρ in Kittel, *op. cit.,* vol. 5, p. 972, n. 145.

114. J. Jeremias, *Die Gleichnisse Jesu* (Göttingen, 5th ed., 1958), p. 159, n. 2; cf. also pp. 43–44, 100.

115. Schlier, pp. 264 ff.

116. J. von Allmen, *Maris et femmes d'après Saint Paul.* Cahiers théologiques 29 (Neuchâtel-Paris, 1951), p. 16.

117. G. Schrenk's article θέλημα in Kittel, vol. 3, p. 59.

118. P. Schoonenberg, *Het geloof van ons Doopsel,* vol. 1: *God, Vader en Schepper* ('s-Hertogenbosch, 1955), p. 202.

119. I therefore do not agree with Henry, who believes that God is to be understood as male; p. 467.

120. Quell, p. 970.

121. *In IV Sent.* d. XXV, a. II, q. 1 (ed. Quaracchi, 1889), tom. IV, p. 650.

122. M. J. Rouët de Journel, *Enchiridion Patristicum,* 19th ed. (Freiburg, 1956), p. 1018.

123. R. W. Howard, quoted in Thrall, *Ordination of Women* (see chap. I, n. 11, above), p. 15; cf. also H. Thurn, "Animus und Anima," *Geist und Leben* 26 (1953), pp. 50–51.

124. P. Evdokimov, *La femme et le salut du monde* (Paris, 1958). Dutch translation, *De vrouw en het heil der wereld* (Rotterdam, 1962), p. 274.

125. P. Schoonenberg, *Het geloof van ons Doopsel,* vol. 3; *De mensgeworden Zoon van God* ('s-Hertogenbosch, 1958), pp. 161 ff.

126. Ruth Benedict, *Patterns of Culture* (Boston, 1934), p. 14.

127. Margaret Mead, *Sex and Temperament* (New York, 1935), p. 191.

128. Ibid., p. 190.

129. Margaret Mead, *Woman, Society, and Sex* (New York, 1952), p. 23.

130. J. H. van den Berg, "Man en vrouw," *Wending* 9 (1954–55), p. 275.

131. Edith Stein, *Die Frau* (see chap. I, n. 18, above), p. 109.

132. Ibid., p. 121.

133. Ibid., p. 125.

134. Ibid., pp. 122 ff.

135. Schoonenberg, vol. 1, pp. 203 ff.

136. Ibid., vol. 3, p. 162.

137. F. Wulf, "Der Zölibat des Weltpriesters und die Jungfräulichkeit des Ordensstandes," *Geist und Leben* 35 (1962): 51–55.

138. P. Schoonenberg, "Het huwelijk in heilshistorisch perspectief," *Streven* 15, no. 1 (1962): 502.

139. Schoonenberg, *Het geloof van ons Doopsel,* vol, 3, p. 53.

140. Henry, pp. 479–80.

141. Laurentin, vol. 2, pp. 74 ff.

142. Henry, p. 477.

143. Ibid., pp. 479–80.

144. Laurentin, vol. 2, pp. 74 ff.

145. Henry, p. 484.

146. Barth, *CD* III/4, pp. 154–55.

147. Ibid., p. 156.

148. Henry, p. 488.

149. Laurentin, vol. 2, pp. 70 ff.

150. Stein, p. 44.

151. O. Casel, "Katholische Kultprobleme," *Jahrbuch für Liturgiewissenschaft* 7 (1927): 110–111.

152. M. Schmaus, *Katholische Dogmatik* IV/1 (Munich, 1952), pp. 594–95.

153. P. J. Jans, "Mann und Frau in ihrem Verhältnis zum kirchlichen Amt," *Internationale Kirchliche Zeitschrift* 52 (1962): 145–56.

154. Krebs, p. 207.

155. Lercher, p. 316.

156. See the addresses of Pius XII cited above in chap. 4, nn. 58 ff.

157. Mitterer, in both articles (cf. above, note 15), passim.

158. Karl Rahner, *Theological Investigations* (see chap. II, n. 6, above), vol. 4, pp. 77–104.

159. M. Schmaus, *Katholische Dogmatik* (Munich, 1948), vol. 1, p. 428.
160. Denz.-Schönm. 1300–1302.
161. Methodius v. Olympos, *PG* 18, c. 73; cf. Damascenus, *PG* 94, cc. 814 f. Further texts are provided by Daniélou, *Théologie du Judéo-Christianisme* (Tournai, 1958), pp. 191–92.
162. *Summa Theologiae* III, q. 67, a. 4.
163. Wahl, p. 47.
164. When Barth excludes participation, he is exclusively in the spirit of the Reformation. The Council of Trent had specifically defined *co-operari* (Denz.-Schönm. 1554). But one could well say that woman is better suited to symbolize this *co-operari* that man, who more aptly symbolizes *operari;* woman is the *adiutorium* of man. And in our situation the concern is about *co*-operation!
165. Barth, *CD* I/2, pp. 194–95.
166. A. Scherer, *Die Frau, Wesen und Aufgaben.* Wörterbuch der Politik 6 (Freiburg, 1950), p. 2.
167. *AAS* 39 (1947): 538; cf. p. 553.
168. Prof. K. H. Miskotte of the theological faculty of the University of Leiden writes: "If one were seriously to believe that the basis for the exclusive choice of men rested on the order of creation with an absolute distribution of tasks, then one would also have to reject a female monarch, female judges, etc., indeed, even woman suffrage. "De vrouw in het ambt, "*Kerk en Theologie* 1 (1950): 177.
169. Rahner, *Theological Investigations,* vol. 3, pp. 242 ff.
170. *Summa Theologiae* III, q. 30, a. 1; Leo XIII, Octobri mense: Denz.-Schönm. 3321.
171. A good overview can be found in E. Doronzo, "De sacerdotali ministerio B. V. Mariae," in *Maria et Ecclesia* (Rome, 1959), vol. 2, pp. 149–67, and C. Koser, "De Sacerdotio B.M.V.," ibid., pp. 169–206. The standard work is still the two-volume work by Laurentin.
172. Laurentin, vol. 2, pp. 37–38.
173. Cf. Doronzo, passim.
174. Laurentin, vol. 2, 38–39.
175. Rondet, p. 924.
176. *Summa Theologiae* II-II, q. 153, a. 2.
177. Rondet, p. 929.
178. Ibid., p. 926.
179. Laurentin, vol. 1, pp. 93–94.
180. Evdokimov, pp. 273 ff.
181. *Lexikon für Theologie und Kirche,* 2d ed., IV, p. 200.
182. S. G. M. Trooster, "De leek in huwelijk en gezinsleven (I), VI Man en vrouw," *Katholiek Archief* 11 (1956): pp. 1245–46.
183. Cf. Karl Rahner, "Bemerkungen über das Naturgesetz und seine Erkennbarkeit," *Orientierung* 19 (1955): 239–43.
184. John McHugh, "Num solus panis triticeus sit materia valida SS. Eucharistiae?" *Verbum Domini* 39 (1961): 229–39.

Chapter VI

1. Leenhardt and Blanke, *Die Stellung der Frau* (see chap. II, n. 73, above), pp. 3–4.

2. Krebs, "Priestertum der Frau" (see chap. I, n. 5, above), p. 199.

3. Cf. *Katholieke Illustratie*, 17 June 1961.

4. Barth, *CD* III/4, p. 156.

5. Therefore the solution suggested by Charlotte von Kirschbaum does not appear adequate to me: "The matter does not concern the supplementing of the profession of pastors with a number of female members. . . . The woman should be a servant of the word within the congregation, not over it. In her person she will create not greater distance but greater bonds between office and congregation." *Der Dienst der Frau* (see chap. I, n. 17, above), p. 28.

6. Cf. Thurn, "Animus und Anima" (see chap. 5, n. 123, above), pp. 50 ff.

7. Augustinus, Sermo 244: *PL* 38, c. 1149.

Translators' Afterword

1. *Reform und Anerkennung kirchlicher Ämter,* Ein Memorandum der Arbeitsgemeinschaft ökumenischer Universitätsinstitute (Munich-Mainz, 1973), p. 13. An English translation of the joint memorandum is scheduled for the *Journal of Ecumenical Studies,* vol. 10, no. 3 (Spring, 1973). The memorandum included a recommendation for the ordination of women.

Index

Index